ABSOLUT

Martin Buckley began his writing career as a journalist in
Bombay, and has written widely in the British press. He
spent ten years with the BBC, where his work ranged
from reports on *From Our Own Correspondent* to a
documentary about Tantra. His previous book, *Grains
of Sand*, told the story of a circumnavigation of the world
– via the deserts.

ALSO BY MARTIN BUCKLEY

Grains of Sand

Martin Buckley

ABSOLUTE ALTITUDE

A Hitch-hiker's Guide to the Sky

𝒱

VINTAGE

Published by Vintage 2004

2 4 6 8 10 9 7 5 3 1

First published in Great Britain in 2003 by
Hutchinson

Vintage
Random House, 20 Vauxhall Bridge Road,
London SW1V 2SA

Random House Australia (Pty) Limited
20 Alfred Street, Milsons Point, Sydney
New South Wales 2061, Australia

Random House New Zealand Limited
18 Poland Road, Glenfield,
Auckland 10, New Zealand

Random House (Pty) Limited
Endulini, 5A Jubilee Road, Parktown 2193,
South Africa

The Random House Group Limited Reg. No. 954009
www.randomhouse.co.uk

A CIP catalogue record for this book
is available from the British Library

ISBN 0 099 27352 7

Printed and bound in Great Britain by
Bookmarque Ltd, Croydon, Surrey

To Penny.
And to my mother,
sine qua non

CONTENTS

ACKNOWLEDGEMENTS

It has not been possible to name individually all the pilots who, usually just for the love of flying, took me up in their beloved aeroplanes. I'd like to thank them here.

Many others helped make possible the journey described in *Absolute Altitude*. Peter Morrow and Dominic Cardy unknowingly started me off. Nigel Sellwood, one of the Linvic instructors, taught me the valuable lesson not to be over-cautious with my joystick.

Clive Langmead led me to MAF, where Bernard Terlouw showed generosity above and beyond . . .

Jane Tait put me on the trail of Richard Pearse. Peter Layne and John King initiated me into the aviation world of New Zealand. The always enthusiastic Judith Watson opened doors to Air New Zealand, Mount Cook Airlines and others. My thanks also go to Rob Bates, Garth Downey, Max Clear and Bill Bonanno.

Several people in journalism helped fund the research and writing of the book: Stephen Pritchard and Desmond Balmer commissioned a column about my journey for the *Observer* newspaper, Sarah Spankie, Dave Calderwood and Nick Wall commissioned articles for *Condé Nast Traveller* and *Flyer*.

Tessa Boase, Jules Tapper and John King kindly read the book in manuscript, pointing out a flock of flying blunders and other infelicities. Responsibility for remaining errors is, of course, mine.

I am very grateful to my publisher Paul Sidey for his unfailing support, patience and good humour.

Finally, a special thank-you to John Robertson.

PREFACE

This book records journeys through over fifteen nations—but the country I explore is the sky, and its inhabitants are pilots. It's a romantic and slightly dangerous destination, which seduces most who travel there. One trip is rarely enough: it leaves you with an irresistible longing to return.

Two centuries ago one of aviation's visionaries called the sky an 'uninterrupted navigable ocean that comes to the threshold of every man's door'. But how many drifters have used aircraft the way stowaways and deckhands once used ships? That was the starting point of this book: an attempt to bum my way around the world by plane. I wanted to know how accessible aviation could be. If I, in my early forties, could go from scratch to holding a pilot's licence in just a few weeks, then surely, anyone could learn to fly. But *hitch-hike*? How far would I be able to get?

Absolute Altitude is also a brief history of manned flight, the story of how a glorified kite evolved into the perfect fusion of form and technology we know today. Our ancestors always dreamed of imitating the birds. The ancient Chinese, the Romans, Arabs, medieval Europeans—they were all far more interested in flight than we generally assume. Flight as fantasy, as erotic symbol, as fairground spectacular, and even, sometimes, as fact. Before recorded history, aspiring bird-men were fluttering to injury or death from trees and crags, later shifting to castles and cathedrals. In great fairs, acrobats 'flew' down invisible tightropes with feathered wings upon their backs. When the 19th century ushered in a revolutionary age of new technologies, Victorian inventors pursued the goal of a flying machine with manic intensity and, at last, the prospect of success. Our own age has been deeply marked by aviation, from the destruction of Guernica and Hiroshima, to the advent of airliners like the Douglas DC-3 and Boeing 707 which established flight as mass transit, to the Boeing 767s that ploughed into New York's Twin Towers.

The history of aviation is a supreme example of human ingenuity and achievement. I cannot claim to have added to the sum of historic knowledge, but I do believe I've challenged some pervasive myths. Did Leonardo invent the aeroplane? No. Did the Wright brothers invent it? Contrary to popular belief, they did not. The first aeroplane in history was invented in the 18th century by an Englishman called —but I mustn't get ahead of myself.

Flying is a fraternity—almost a cult. Becoming a member opened cockpits to me, getting me dozens of lifts in everything from airliners to microlights. A pioneering spirit still exists in aviation, among UN pilots bumping Cessnas into dusty dirt strips, acrobats barnstorming their way round summer airshows, and amateur inventors building aeroplanes from scratch and somehow—despite the nervous nannying of the safety bodies—taking to the air. The world-wide community of aviators still has its mavericks, its clowns, its hopeless obsessives. Above all, this book is about them.

Pilots of small commercial planes sometimes let me fly beside them as First Officer, I the possessor of a Private Licence with a hundred hours' flying experience, and maybe a dozen unsuspecting passengers sitting behind us. The uninitiated might feel that any professional pilot allowing this was a psycho, but it's an established part of aviation to hand a fellow pilot the controls (and monitor carefully)—this is how we learn, how we transmit knowledge, how we foster a sense of trust and fraternity. I was even on occasion lent shirts and nice golden epaulettes, so that we could fly across international borders passing me off as a *bona fide* commercial pilot. As unknown functionaries saluted me—'Good Morning, Captain!'—I knew briefly the erotic thrall of the uniform.

Crews of big jets, too, welcomed me into their cockpits, and while they never let me take the controls, as a pilot I was encouraged to join them, absorb something of their lore, stay with them for take-offs and landings. I have a vivid memory of a jumbo cockpit in mid-Pacific— the Business Class passengers prone and somnolent under their blankets, but the crew alert and cool in their white short-sleeves, the steady levels of the instruments, the vast, viscous ocean oozing past the armoured glass windscreens.

All that was before 11 September 2001. I had finished the journey described in this book just a few days earlier. It was the merest coincidence that I turned on the television that late summer afternoon —I wanted to make a copy of the movie, *Now Voyager*, for my mother. And there was that fantastic, silencing image from across the Atlantic, one of the towers of the World Trade Center belching smoke, the shaken voices of reporters, the incredible speculation that this might have been deliberate. Then, to clinch the question, a second passenger jet plunging into a second tower; one tower falling, a juddering cascade of grey rubble and smoke; then the other.

Geopolitics and individual lives were changed that day. Nor will aviation ever be the same. The airliner had already lost its glamour, devolved into a sort of modern omnibus, associated more with thrombosis support stockings than romance. The '70s vogue for hijacking airliners, usually with no loss of life, and usually to Cuba, was almost forgotten. But on a brilliant late summer day in 2001, airliners became terror weapons. The cockpit doors are locked now, reinforced, bolted. Air marshals travel incognito. The changes will be felt not by passengers—who'll be encouraged to keep thinking of flight as a banally safe affair—but by flyers, who share a holy sense of flying's dangerous magic, and who will now be even further circumscribed by red tape.

Aeroplanes have made the world smaller. They have eroded cultural diversity, and accelerated the spread of white, Christian, Western values. They have united far-flung families in a way unhoped-for even half a century ago; they have increased noise and atmospheric pollution; they have permitted armed forces to drop poison gas on their enemies, and sometimes on their own citizens.

Above all, aircraft have actualized the ancient dream of human flight. Yet only a handful of human beings have taken advantage of our unprecedented opportunities to take to the sky like birds. When I was learning to fly, I was struck by the contrast with sailing. Anyone can buy a yacht, and without licence or training, be whisked by the winds around the world. But flying tends to seem remote, the realm of the professional or the rich. Could this explain why, over the last twenty years, the number of private pilots has almost halved?

This, I am convinced, is about to change. Small, simple and safe aircraft like hang gliders and paragliders are finally with us, introducing an age of affordable hobby flying. Factories are starting to make them cheaply, in increasing numbers. Anyone with a couple of thousand pounds to spend can learn to fly, buy these modern wings, and realize man's most ancient dream. Perhaps—I hope—this book will encourage a few of its readers to do so.

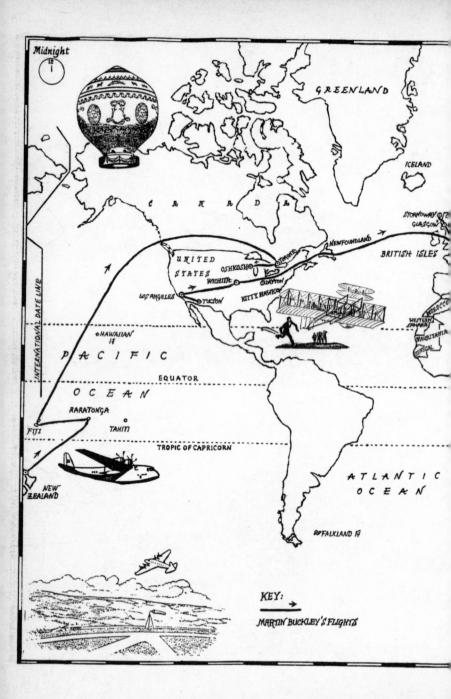

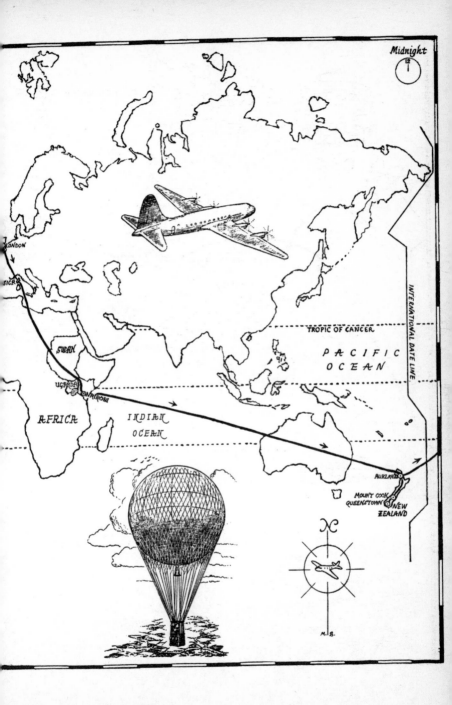

Midnight

LONDON

SICILY

SUDAN

UGANDA

NAIROBI

AFRICA

INDIAN
OCEAN

TROPIC OF CANCER

PACIFIC
OCEAN

INTERNATIONAL DATE LINE

AUKLAND

MOUNT COOK
QUEENSTOWN   NEW
ZEALAND

N

M.S.

PART I

CHAPTER I

Bird-Happy

Bird-happy adj. *(coll.)* 1 *Light-hearted* 2 *Slightly mad.*
Universal English Dictionary

Six months ago, on a bright, crisp morning like this one, the sky unblemished and fathomless, I was squeezed tight in the cockpit of a twin-seat jet trainer; my fist gripping the joystick, 230 knots indicated—the first time I'd flown a plane at such speed. I was orange-suited in flame-resistant Nomex, crouching on my parachute, my head bound in fibreglass, the canopy a dome of Plexiglas over me. The vintage fighter's stubby outflung Duralumin wings sustained it in flight. A roar from the twin jets, a steady electric crackle from the headset. The surface of Hauraki Gulf surging by, our onrush making stolid Auckland-bound merchant ships dart at us like speedboats.

I made a right turn—dipped the stick to the right, tipping the wing, careful to stay nose-high to ward off the pilot's nightmare of an unintended spiral dive. White wave-tops shuddered past; the razor edge of the Magister's right wing seemed to slice through the wake of a merchantman. Roll left, level once more. The coastline ahead growing rapidly. The sky over Auckland on a bright, June, winter's day.

'I'll take her.' Ken Walker, the plane's owner, ahead of me in the tandem cockpit.

Reluctantly I surrendered the joystick. 'You have control.'

He catapulted us off Hauraki Gulf on to a stretch of the North Island coastline designated for low flight. And we *were* low, so low that I looked down and saw in fleeting frozen detail upturned faces, open mouths.

It's a paradox, perhaps, that flight is not at its most exhilarating when you are soaring through the heavens, but when you're close enough to the ground to see it and sense it and know, because every

3

instinct screams it, that a mysterious alchemy has transmuted you from man (legs, ground) to bird (wings, *air*).

We hurtled towards a ridge of hills. Someone's microlight went past like a scrap of wind-borne rag. Ken tipped the nose up and in a heart's beat—the time it took for me to retighten my grip on the steel handles welded to the canopy frame—the Magister had shown her tail feathers to the deck and leapt 1800 feet, and again assumed level trajectory. The earth settled into a remoter grid of green and yellow squares.

This was flying.

The French-built Fouga Magister was the world's first small jet trainer, a flying machine so sensitive, so minutely calibrated to the liquid laws of aerodynamics, that it would be adopted by the aerobatic teams of France and a dozen other nations. First rolled out in 1954, the butterfly-tailed plane would become a classic, some 900 or so built during a production run of over two decades. Celebrated for its balletic grace, the Magister spilled blood, too, in the other rôle for which it had been designed—ground attack—notably for the Israelis during the 1967 Six Day War.

The mountains of the Coromandel Range swelled ahead of us. We held our altitude, scraped across peaks of exposed honey-hued rock and continued east over the dense-packed forests of the Coromandel Peninsula. The Pacific yawned before us as we flew over the silver fretwork delta of the River Tairua and reached the seaside town of Pauanui. Ken was planning some peacockery over his beach house here. I looked down, and tried to imagine his girlfriend looking up and smiling at the roar of the engines, stepping out into the sunshine knowing that the sleek jet was about to perform a tribute to her.

Ken's voice crackled faintly over the RT. 'Y'ready, Martin?'

'I'm ready.'

'This is the most fun you'll ever have without taking your clothes off. Hold on tight.'

Our speed climbed to 280 knots into a 45-degree vertical roll, followed by a Cuban 8—a horizontal figure of eight with two inverted half-rolls in the middle of the 'eight'—and then a loop, and then another vertical roll. I whooped for joy, as the sky above us was replaced by sea, and we languidly revolved, like insects suspended in some cerulean amber. Outrageous beauty, not eclipsed but intensified by the g-forces squeezing your body, compressing your chest and viscera.

Ken broke out of the roll into a curving dive. The Magister swooped towards the cliffs south of Pauanui. We made a low turn in a cleft in the hills, and climbed back over the town. Ken flicked the Fouga half inverted and finished his display with a low fly-by over the beach—so low that we carved a groove in the yolky sand with our wing-tip.

I swear it.

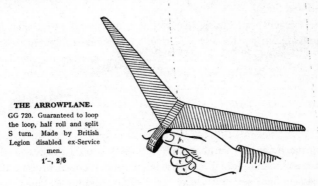

THE ARROWPLANE.
GG 720. Guaranteed to loop the loop, half roll and split S turn. Made by British Legion disabled ex-Service men.
1′-, 2/6

I have dreamed of flying since childhood—and so have you. Didn't we all spend our earliest childhood nights flying, reliving the weightless suspension of the womb? So many children are convinced they can fly that they quite often try to do so, breaking arms and ankles. My dreams were so vivid and familiar (they always began with me gliding with mesmeric languor out of my room, along the landing and down the stair carpet that my mother says was patterned but I remember as womb-red) that I was certain of their literal reality. At night, while others slept, I flew.

We lived in a cul-de-sac of steep-gabled cottages off a country lane. On sunny days the local kids would play in the surrounding fields. I remember a few of us lying on the mounds of glossy blade-edged grass that lined the stream and looking straight into an azure sky bellied with summer cumulus, marvelling at the clouds' tireless, playful mutations into human profiles, or boots, or swords.

And then there were the planes.

We were close to Farnborough, the historic homeland of English aviation. As a short-trousered boy of five I stood in a corner of the village school playground and watched as the sky was darkened by the solid triangle of an Avro Vulcan, Britain's strategic nuclear bomber. (Our neighbour Mrs Williamson blamed the Vulcan for her miscarriage: one day she was walking up the lane and it arrived like the Apocalypse, just above the treetops, turning day to night and making the very ground tremble, scaring her half to death.)

During the annual Farnborough Airshow—a public display and a professional market for air force hardware—I could look up from our back lawn and see the Battle of Britain Memorial Flight pass overhead, Hurricane, Spitfire and Lancaster, synchronised with the unguent patrician tones of Raymond Baxter's live BBC1 commentary. It was rare on any sunny day for five minutes to go by without the rumble of an aeroplane, and we would shade our eyes and wait to capture the silver flash like a fish as it passed, seemingly still yet straight and fast, between the chimney and the woods, and we would try to read its shape against the sky—Vampire, Meteor, Hunter—those evocative names. Now, perversely, I am reassured when the summer silence of the countryside, the distant lowing of cows, the hum of bees, wind in the grass, is disturbed by the faint rumble of an aero engine. *This*, the rumble says, *is how it should be.*

I experienced livid, full-colour flying dreams into my late teens. Then they stopped, perhaps because, as the shrinks tell us, dreams of flight are associated with erotic longing. I suspect that the improvement in my love life grounded my dreams.

I seized every opportunity to fly—in gliders, small Cessnas, open biplanes. I even had some flying lessons, but never made the sustained effort to get a licence. It took a level of technical aptitude I wasn't sure I had, and a depth of pocket I knew I didn't have. Then, a few years back, an American acquaintance asked me which single invention separated modern man from our ancestors.

'Penicillin,' I suggested. 'Photography?'

'No, *flight*! For centuries they dreamed about it, our ancestors, from Icarus to Leonardo. But we can actually *do* it—we can do this miraculous thing. We can fly! And we *should*!'

'It's a moral obligation?'

'That's *exactly* what it is! We owe it to their *memory* to learn to fly!'

An extreme position, but Peter Morrow was an extreme pilot—the owner, I discovered, of three aeroplanes, which lived with him in the turquoise, white and emerald Caribbean. Peter, the evangelist, sensing my sympathy for the true faith, struck: he intended to hire a plane for some practice the following week. Would I care to go up with him?

It was a brilliant summer day in the Cotswolds. The flying club was a broad acreage of cracked white, grass-tufted concrete that had once witnessed the rumbling of a hundred Lancaster bombers. As I wandered among the parked aircraft I was seized anew by their nautical properties. The Cessnas and Beechcraft were tied down, to prevent the wind from catching under their wings and carrying them off like kites, with fraying, coarse, orange or blue nylon ropes run through rings cemented into the ground; the planes had red banners draped from them, actually sleeves that protected propellers and slender exterior steel organs, and these chivalric pennants flapped and flopped in the summer breeze. I marvelled at the delicacy of the machines, for seen up close they manifestly had little inherent strength. Again like boats, they were ribbed and tautly skinned, and I recognised that just as a small boat so improbably shields its crew from the hostile ocean, and even more improbably holds a chosen course, the aeroplane's ability to navigate the invisible vapour of the air relies on precise observations made by its designers of the element it has to master, translated into the stressed curves of its fabric. What was more, the plane Peter had directed me to was not an aluminium Cessna but a Motorfalke, a classic motor glider with a wooden frame and doped fabric skin—like a Gypsy Moth biplane, or the earliest aircraft, made over a century ago.

Peter went into the club office and handed over some tenners. No credit cards, no initialling forms in five places: it was easier to rent a plane than a car. We strapped ourselves side by side in the tiny two-seater and he did the engine checks, tapping the glass instruments with a fingertip and muttering ritually.

We accelerated down the prairie expanse of the runway, and in a few hundred feet—at fifty knots—we were airborne, unstuck from our dark earthbound shadow like a soul departing the gross body. We climbed away from the bosomy Cotswolds and levelled at 5000 feet. Almost at once Peter demonstrated the pedals and joystick, and gave me control. I tipped the nose and wings, the plane banked and soared. We scampered among summer clouds of teased candyfloss. One tiny cloud was the shape of a doughnut and I asked if we could fly through it.

'It's against the rules,' said Peter. 'We have to keep away from clouds, so that other planes can see us.'

'Oh,' I said.

I must have looked like a crestfallen child, because Peter twisted in his seat to scan the horizon and said, 'OK—do it.'

I nosed the little aircraft towards the halo of vapour that seemed, as clouds can do, immaterial, whimsical, existing solely to delight. We became wrapped in whipped-white, tendrilled, ectoplasmic mist; aerial acrobats, we danced through the ring and beyond it into a circle of cobalt blue. It was freedom beyond anything I had ever known and I began to laugh, a high-pitched, euphoric giggle. 'Peter, I feel like an angel!'

He looked at me askance. 'Taking people flying I've had some weird reactions, but no one ever thought they were an angel before.'

Yet the mystery to me is how anyone can experience flight in a small plane and *not* be euphoric. Professional pilots will tell you flying is a technical affair, precise to the point of dullness—but they are sticking to the party line to tranquillize the nervous public: I know two pilots who earn an unadrenal, commercial living, but spend their private time boy-racing round the skies in aerobatic Pitts Specials. If flying takes concentration, it gives back magic.

That afternoon with Peter, a dream was reborn: to learn to fly.

A few months later I was in Kenya, researching a book about deserts. A contact at UNESCO's Nairobi desertification programme,

Franklin Cardy, had invited me home for dinner and introduced me to his son, Dominic, who was an amateur pilot. Dominic suggested we go flying over the Rift Valley and I quickly agreed. The problem was, neither of us had enough money to hire a plane.

The following afternoon we went out to Wilson Airport, Nairobi's general aviation aerodrome, and hung around the Aero Club doing plane talk until someone offered us a joyride.

It was late afternoon when we flew due west out of Wilson, over a landscape of equatorial green. All too soon, the setting sun was staining the towering cumulus clouds red—we would have to return to the drome. We dropped low and traced the vast Longonot crater's dense-forested rim. It was a display of what a small plane can do, of that dimension of aviation that is so wholly unrelated to *transport*: the incontestable magic that a century ago threw the world into flying fever. We wheeled, like the hawks that ride the warm exhalations from the crater's lip, while the sky flamed around us.

Dominic had told me that in Africa the aviation scene was small and friendly, that he'd often been offered free flights. What was more, the holder of a pilot's licence could sometimes take the right seat on one-man commercial flights, since insurance companies and even national customs took a sanguine view of anyone with a pilot's licence. As we crossed the Wilson apron at dusk, I turned to him. 'Do you think someone could hitch-hike by plane—get lifts from one aerodrome to the next? How far do you think they'd get?'

A vision quivered through me: maybe I could concoct such a journey, and tell the story of the pilots and planes I encountered along the way—the kind of flying that really interests me, that is, Cessnas before Boeings. Bush flying, aid flying, air ambulances, barn-stormers. It was no more than the germ of an idea, but it stayed in me, and grew. Its beauty lay in the fact that to undertake such a journey, I *had* to learn to fly.

CHAPTER II

Taking Off

I ARRIVED AT TORONTO AIRPORT on a glittering late-summer after-noon and Captain Neil Kelly was waiting to collect me. He'd flown a 747 from Tel Aviv that morning and cut the crisp, gold-braided, Ray-Ban'd figure of an airline captain. I was overawed to have this aristocrat of the Arrivals Lounge seizing my suitcase and leading me through the mob.

It took two hours to reach the town of Lindsay, driving north through flattish countryside where the maples were already turning red. Lindsay Airpark was a rural drome with a couple of dozen small planes tethered in the shadow of a retired but still watchful McDonnell CF-101 Voodoo fighter.

I had decided to get my flying licence this year. No more odd lessons here and there, no more resolutions made and broken: I needed total immersion—a crash course. North America is general aviation's Mecca; there are American commuters who fly to work and small towns have busy, publicly subsidised airports. This healthy bustle is due in part to the low cost of aviation fuel, in part to America's vast skies, which are a positive incitement to fly. But Jeremiahs in England warned me that the marzipan-blue skies of Florida were no preparation for a midsummer squall over Middlesex a mile from Heathrow airspace. I considered Canada, where the flying syllabus is closer to the British, as is the weather (though the autumn, when I planned to learn, is supposedly dry and bright). The matter was clinched when I met Neil Kelly, who combined his Air Canada captaincy with the ownership of Linvic Flying School and told me about Canada's unique 'Recreational Licence', which allows you to acquire a licence to fly a single-engine plane, with one passenger, in a minimum of *twenty-five hours*. This seemed an amazing, even alarming, prospect.

'You can come over and qualify for your "Rec" in two or three weeks,' Neil suggested. 'Then your wife could come out and join you and you could take her on a flying holiday. Build up your experience, take your PPL exams and return to Britain a licensed pilot.'

I was hooked—though it all sounded suspiciously easy.

'Where exactly is Linvic?' I asked.

'Lindsay, northern Ontario.'

'Is there anything interesting within easy flying distance?'

'Oh, Toronto, the Great Lakes, Niagara Falls . . .'

It would turn out that I'd underestimated what was involved in making the leap from novice to Private Pilot. Many who sign on for an intensive course have a number of flying hours behind them and some grasp of the theory. I had a few hours of formal instruction under my belt—most of them years earlier—and no knowledge at all of the theory. Learning to fly was not going to prove easy. But I vowed that every day that was even marginally clement I'd get into the air, if only for a few minutes.

And barely three hours after climbing off the airbus at Toronto airport, I was flying a plane.

I'll never forget it: an ancient Cessna 152, Golf Oscar Echo Foxtrot (Geoff, I called it), a neat little dual-control trainer. I have seen the 152 included, improbably, in a book of 'The World's Greatest Aircraft', on the grounds that more pilots have learned their craft in this spindly two-seat aluminium trainer than in any other plane. First flown in 1957 as the 150, the last 152 was built in 1984, so your local flying school's fleet is likely to be at least twenty-five years old. But Geoff was an unusually smart little plane, with bright-red livery and seats which gave it, like a January robin, an air of jauntiness and pluck.

Instructors like to build your confidence fast and usually have you take off first time (it's landing that requires the skill). We lined up. Brakes on, I applied full throttle (not a pedal but a dash-mounted plunger), built up the revs, then let go: the plane shimmied down the runway.

'Pull back—gently.'

At fifty-five knots, you ease back the control column. The plane becomes airborne with the delicacy of a completed kiss. And at once a new perspective: a vast retreating disc of field and lake and red-roofed barns—so different from anything you've seen from a passenger jet. The jet zooms to 30,000 feet, while a small plane hovers a few hundred feet up. The jet defies the landscape, while a small plane is intimate with it.

My attention was quickly torn from this rapture of the steep, when it was pointed out that I wasn't paying to enjoy the view, but to learn to fly. Pay attention: you climb by raising the nose and turn by dipping the wings with a touch of rudder. Got that? Simple, really.

But if my experiences of flight had hitherto been of lightness and joy, they were abruptly revealed at Lindsay to have been illusory. An aeroplane, I now learned, was an engine of death so fickle and treacherous that every encounter demanded the focus of a Zen warrior preparing for the ultimate battle. Tradition taught that this brush with eternity was most likely to be survived if a series of stringent safety checks were observed. As a sage might have put it, a wise horseman examines not only his horse's hooves, but its bowel movements. First there was the Walk Around: like pioneer aviators, pilots still begin every flight with a physical inspection of the plane, waggling its ailerons, elevators and rudder, checking the engine-oil level, even poking a length of wood into the fuel tanks to verify the fuel levels (gauges can be unreliable). Then the cabin checks, which include making sure there are no loose objects aboard to knock you on the head during a manœuvre. And then engine checks, putting the metal through maximum revs while you carefully monitor its response. To the uninitiated all this checking smacks of uncertainty about the plane's airworthiness, but this is the aviator's Highway Code: when a car breaks down, the driver coasts onto the hard shoulder, but aeroplanes are less forgiving—and therefore simply *are not allowed* to go wrong. None of this could be learned by rote; I, the pilot, needed to know the internal state of my mount. I needed to understand how a plane flew, how its limbs retained their springiness, how its engine functioned and responded to temperature and (especially) atmospheric vapour, how to ensure the good order and accuracy of the compass and gyroscopic and vacuum-based instruments. Check. Check. Check again.

The checks are read from a list on a small clipboard. My first lessons with Linvic's senior instructor, Tim Coombs, would go something like this:

Me: 'Cabin Checks: Avionics *off*, switches *off*, throttle er, *closed*—that's in, is it?'

Tim: 'Out.'

'Out. Mixture lean, that's . . .'

'Out.'

'Out. Flaps down, fuel gauges check, Master *off*. Now. Is that the Cabin Checks finished?'

'Have you left anything out?'

'Have I?'

'Do *you* think you have?'

'No.'

'Then go on to your Start Checks.'

'OK. Passenger briefing, seat belts—we'll assume we've done that. Fuel valve is on "both", carb heat cold—that's out, is it?'

'In.'

'The, er, lettering's rubbed off the knob. Throttle ¼-inch *in*, mixture rich that's *in*, beacon, where's the beacon?'

'Here.'

'Push it down?'

'Correct.'

'Beacon *on,* touch of primer and lock, master switch *on*, brakes on, yell clear. (*Open window.*) CLEAR PROP!'

Having made sure there's no one standing out of view before you spin the prop, you turn a key and a 110-horsepower engine, a burly monstrous Continental, kicks into life with an angry roar, whipping the air behind you into a tornado. But the brakes are on and the machine trembles with frustrated energy.

Me: 'Right, After-Start Checks: Avionics *on*. Oil pressure is good; flaps check: up, down, good; radio on and check—*Lindsay Unicom, this is, er, Golf Oscar, er, Echo Foxtrot requesting a radio check.*'

The radio: 'Echo Foxtrot you are four by four Lindsay.'

Me: 'OK, brake test, roll forward a bit and brake, yup, they're working—sorry I'm boring you.'

Tim: 'No, I'm yawning 'cause I had a late night.'

'The wages of sin?'

'Oh, I believe there's a phrase that involves kettles and black pots?'

'If I'm up late it's because I'm studying all this stuff, mate.'

'*This* stuff? *Really*?'

'Very funny. Taxi and test instruments . . . We seem to be turning, I mean they seem to be swinging, compass is moving a bit too.'

'"Compass is free and swinging?"'

'That's what I meant.'

'Look, instruments Tests means you check *all* the instruments: "Left turn, needle to the left, ball to the right; attitude indicator steady, altimeter steady, compass is free and swinging".'

'Thanks. And I'd turn into the wind if I could see the windsock.'

'It's right there, buddy.'

'Oh—yeah. So, into wind. And, er, Run Up Checks. Idle at 1000 revs and: Prop Blast Check, that's oil pressure green. Is there—no, nobody behind us, so throttle to 1700 and Suction Check, it's in the green; Alternator Check—which one's that? I can't remember that one.'

'Accessories on, flaps down, you're looking to see if the needle flickers.'

'It did flicker. Magnetos, er, fine—'

'What are you looking for in the magnetos?'

'Er, a maximum 100 rpm drop in each, with a difference of not more than 50 rpm between the two.'

'That's correct, sir.'

'Phew. Carb heat to hot, that's *out*. Lean the mixture— '

'That's too fast. What we're doing here is turning this red lever and leaning out the mixture till what?'

'Till we see a slight rise in rpm?'

'Correct, then what?'

'Lower the revs?'

'Throttle back to stop, to check that the engine's running smoothly. This means that if we suddenly reduce revs in flight the engine won't cut out on us. Now?'

'Back to 1000 revs.'

'If you don't get that plunger back in fast enough the engine's gonna die on you, so that's why we keep our hand on the button.'

'Hand on plunger, OK. Idle slow and—'

'Keep it right down, I wanna hear what it sounds like at slow revs, does it sound like it's gonna die on you or it's gonna run?'

'Sounds fine.'

'OK—push it in smartish.'

'Smartish. Back to 1000 revs, carb heat cold. OK, swing round and on to the apron—somebody coming in over there—'

'Just *relax* on those brakes, buddy—*relax on the brakes*. OK, he's visibly turning wide to avoid us. Now just roll ahead, take your feet off the brake now and just use the rudder. When you're rolling you're using the rudder to control the direction, you *gotta* resist the temptation to step on those brakes 'cause one day you're gonna step on 'em too hard or in the wrong conditions and turn this baby right over.'

Most of this witch-doctoring or science is aimed at warding off the spectre of engine failure. Aircraft engines are built and maintained to standards that, if applied to car engines, would make car ownership affordable only for the rich. The manufacturers are so obsessive about reliability and therefore so conservative that, having established the basic designs in the 1940s, they have merely refined them ever since. Today's engines, almost all of which are manufactured in the US, are simple and—providing their maintenance schedules are observed— almost incapable of going wrong. (They're also expensive and gas-guzzling, but that's another matter.) I was told that in Linvic's sixteen years of operation and currently owning thirteen aircraft, it had only ever experienced *one* engine failure; and that, happily, was on a twin-engined plane.

Once Tim and I had determined that all the systems were indeed working, the test ritual concluded with our eyes raised to the skies and the question, 'Are we alone?' If there were no fluttering Cessnas in our immediate vicinity, we could clear ourselves for take-off.

LINDSAY ON	CNF4	ELEV 882

REF	N44 21 53 W78 47 02 1.1WNW 11°W UTC-5(4) Elev 882′ A5000 F-21 LO6 HI5 CAP
OPR	Lindsay Airpark Ltd. 705-324-8921 Cert ltd hrs
PF	B-1,2 C-3,4,5,6
CUST	AOE-X 888-226-7277 14-22Z‡ Mon-Fri exc hols
FLT PLN **FSS**	NOTAM FILE CYPQ/CZYZ W1 800-INFO FSS
SERVICES FUEL OIL S	 80, 100LL Nov-Apr 14-22Z‡, May-Oct 13-23Z‡ All 3
RWY DATA RCR	Rwy 13/31 3500x75 asphalt Rwy 02/20 2642x75 turf Thld 02 displ 360′. Opr No win maint rwy 02/20.
LIGHTING	13-(TE LO), 31-(TE LO) ARCAL-122.8 type J; rotating bcn inop after 0459Z‡.
COMM ATF ARR DEP	 unicom ltd hrs O/T tfc 122.8 5NM 3900 ASL Toronto Centre 134.25 Toronto Centre 134.25
NAV VOR/DME	SIMCOE YSO 117.35 Ch 120(Y) N44 14 19 W79 10 18 (931′) 076° 18.4NM to A/D
PRO	Rgt hand circuits rwys 13 & 20. Trng activity btwn Toronto/Buttonville Municipal & Oshawa aprts. See Planning, Ontario, Hazards to acft ops, Claremont trng area.

Tim: 'Now there's no one on the base leg and no one in the last portion of the downwind, so we're free to enter the runway and take off. Now, call Lindsay traffic, which means you're addressing everyone in the area. Golf Oscar Echo Foxtrot.'

Me: 'Lindsay traffic, Goff Exford-eurgh.'

'Golf Oxford Ex—you got me doing it. Golf Oscar Echo Foxtrot.'

'Lindsay traffic, Golf. Oscar. Echo. Foxtrot is taking position on three, er, three-one.'

'You're clear for take-off.'

'Right. Taxi on to the runway. Few revs here, turn us round—oops, too much power . . . Right, I'm ready for take-off.'

'Just pause here for a sec. You just want to double-check that your heading indicator is set?'

'Heading is set.'

'OK, release your brakes.'

'They are released!'

'*Full* power!'

'Sorry—*full* power.'

'Squeezing your rudders and watch your airspeed.'

'I'm trying to keep straight.'

'Fifty-five knots rotation speed, ease back. *And* up we go, ease that pressure, little bit of rudder, try to keep us on course. A little bit of right rudder. Eyes are outside.'

'Eyes are outside.'

'Climb attitude.'

'Climb attitude.'

'Have a look at your runway, we're right off the end of the runway. Keep that nose high. OK, speed's up to seventy-five.'

'Seventy-five.'

'So we're too low.'

'Sorry—nose up.'

'Best rate of climb is?'

'S-er, sev—?'

'Sixty-seven.'

'Yeah. Sixty-seven. Climbing at . . . 500 feet a minute.'

'That's better. And we're going to depart the circuit and climb to 4000 feet indicated, which is?'

'Which is around 3100 above ground level because the airfield's 880 feet above sea level.'

'Correct.'

'Coming up to 1800 feet.'

'Clear behind, clear to the right, give me a gentle turn. If you could give me 30 degrees of bank please, er, check for traffic here, nose up . . . *nose higher.*'

'Nose higher?'

'Yessir. Why are we turning on the spot at an angle of 40 degrees?'

'Sorry, I was keeping my eyes open for traffic. There we are—just under 30 degrees.'

'A wee bit more right rudder. More right rudder there. Just watch the—*relax the bank angle*, or it'll want to over-bank on you.'

'Sorry.'

'That's better . . . OK, we'll level off at Balsam Lake.'

'That's the little one, is it?'

'The *big* one. With the island in it.'

'OK. So, I'm levelled out, assuming cruise attitude, bring my power back to cruise power, nose, trim, OK we're flying straight and level at about, what, just under 4000 a.g.l.'

'We've gone five miles from the airport so we can call clear of the area.'

'Fine. Lindsay traffic, Golf. Oscar. Echo. Foxtrot is clear of the area five miles to the north.'

'OK. Today's lesson is Slow Flight. You're gonna put the plane into slow flight, which is what?'

'Er, setting up the plane for the lowest speed above stall speed commensurate with maximum endurance?'

'Cor-rect. So how you gonna do it?'

CHAPTER III

Dissect the Bat

Dædalus: in Greek mythology, the craftsman and inventor who built the Minotaur's labyrinth in Crete. When King Minos refused to let him leave, Dædalus made wax and feather wings for himself and his son Icarus, and they flew away. But while Dædalus reached Sicily in safety, Icarus strove to fly too high, where the sun melted his wings, and he fell to his death.
Dictionary of World Mythology, Odhams Press

'Dissect the bat . . . and on this model construct the machine.'
Leonardo da Vinci, 'Of Artificial Flight', *Notebooks*

ICARUS: BLOND, SMOOTH-SKINNED, impetuous Grecian youth. Blond? Artists have tended to imagine him so (as did the illustration in the children's book I still recall vividly after four decades), perhaps inevitably, for his association with the sun—chasing the rays or contrails of Helios the sun god's golden chariot. Straining to be off and into the sky, against his Platonically bald and bearded father's caution and cautious half-embracing arms, against earth itself and its dull harness of gravity. Gravity is a quality of elderly newscasters, not youth.

Man has always envied the birds and ascribed to them the numinous qualities of heaven. Flying metaphors are woven into the very language—our dreams and ambitions *take flight*, our enterprises *take off*, we entertain *flights of fancy*; even the intensely functional stairs between two floors are called a *flight*, and the room at the top of the house is *a loft*—aloft. The construction of forts at high elevations may be dictated by strategy, but we are also drawn to heights for reasons of the soul. When Edmund Hillary attained the summit of Everest, his feat had for the subjects of Queen Elizabeth II, in the year of her coronation, a metaphysical meaning beyond a mere sporting achievement. Close by Everest is the fabulous Mount Meru, navel of the earth, abode of the Hindu gods. The Greek and Roman gods also inhabited the heavens—as do the Christian Trinity and angels and all the virtuous souls. Jesus's departure from the earth was in the form of a visible *ascension* and today His worshippers are *uplifted*, offered a foretaste of the joy the soul will know in heaven.

The death of Icarus is usually taken to imply that any attempt to fly is an act of hubris. In Brueghel's sarcastic sixteenth-century portrait an unperturbed shepherd stands with his back to the sea, and only on close inspection do you make out Icarus's wiggly legs, poking comically from the water. Yet the fable does not condemn enterprise and curiosity: Dædalus does, after all, *succeed*: his invention carries him home to Sicily. Icarus's mistake was to ignore his father's warnings against flying too high—see what happens, children, when you disobey Daddy—but again, this is no mere cautionary tale. The hubris lies in Icarus's presumption that he could penetrate the realm of the gods. Dædalus applied his ingenuity in the service of good and it allowed him to escape from an unjust king; Icarus, however, had made no contribution to the invention, he saw it merely as a vehicle for his ego. Technology divorced from a human context, we are warned, will destroy its users.

Greek mythology abounded in winged creatures—Cupid and Pegasus, the phoenix, the harpies, the Furies and Hermes (later the Roman Mercury), god of (among others) travellers, cheats and thieves, who darted round the world in his winged helmet and sandals. Almost every time and culture has imagined flying creatures, from faeries and pixies, sylphs and will-o'-the-wisps, to dragons, griffins, incubi, banshees, vampires. Even twentieth-century America produced an aerial god: Superman, an omnipotent alien with reassuring, small-town Christian values. Four years ago in an African village in Niger, I was warned about the spirits of animals which flew around at night, disturbing the dreams of those who angered them during the day.

In 1648 the English Bishop, John Wilkins of Chester, wrote in his *Mathematical Magick* of the four ways 'whereby this flying in the air hath been or may be attempted'. Naturally he nominated first the flights of 'Spirits or Angels'. Judaism, Christianity and Islam agree on the existence of angels, most elaborately in the case of Christianity, with its cherubs, cherubim and seraphim, the latter taking their place at the apex of the ninefold angelic order, so ethereally blissful they can only be represented symbolically—as a perfect circle of wings.

Having one's own wings is not essential for flight: certain gods use winged accoutrements, like Mercury's footwear or Thor's helmet. And even ordinary mortals have sometimes achieved flight, with the aid of levitational elixirs, carpets and machines drawn either by birds or mythical creatures. In very rare cases, flying machines have been self-propelled, the earliest examples in imaginative writing of aircraft.

In the Indian epic *Ramayana*, written roughly 400 BC, the hero-god King Rama makes a triumphal journey across India by 'aërial chariot'. An even earlier self-propelling chariot is found in the Chinese tales of Ki-Kung-Shi, dating from the eighteenth century BC. The flying warriors of Chinese mythology are alive and kicking today in spiritual-martial arts films like *Crouching Tiger, Hidden Dragon*, their half-acrobatic, half-flying combats so dreamlike, so seductive.

One chilly desert morning I found myself on the tarmac of the small aerodrome of Nazca, in Peru. Dawn is the best moment to witness the Nazca lines—when the shallow ridges are shadowed by the low sun and the air is dry and translucent.

I climbed into a battered but still apparently serviceable (flight requires of us an act of faith) four-seat Cessna and Carlos, the pilot, fired up the engine. Climbing over the pampas, we soon saw them: thousands of straight lines scored into the desert, radiating towards loci of power in the Andes; then the animal forms, including the iconic humming bird, with its wings outstretched. We dropped out of the dawn-pink sky to buzz the drawings. As we banked tightly they flew around us—monkey, dog, 'owlman', spider.

Most anthropologists now believe that these lines, engraved in the stony desert crust 1500 years ago, played a role in hallucinogenic rituals. Andean museum collections groan with the paraphernalia of shamanistic drug use and it was—is—common for shamans in psychedelic trances to identify with some symbolic creature. They believe their spirits take to the sky and soar. Each of the creatures on the Nazcan crust is etched in a single line. Perhaps they were paths,

walked by the shamans during their possession by the animal—
spiritual, not alien, runways from which man's soul took flight.

A few months after that Nazcan flight, I found myself in the
Amazon, sitting in a wooden cabin with a velvet night sky overhead
and the jungle raucous with insects. A shaman and I had been into the
jungle that day and found the *ayahuasca* vine and back at his village
house had boiled it into a thick, bilious stew. There were four of us
sitting on the oil-lamp-lit porch, two of them women smoking
tobacco pipes. Daniel Rodriguez, the shaman, passed around the
potion in a plastic Inca Cola bottle and while we sipped it he hummed
a tune, an invocation to the spirits of *ayahuasca*.

After perhaps half an hour the visions began. I was airborne, my
wings outstretched, flying over endless fantastic cityscapes, their
geometric boulevards, Gothic towers and frothing parks delirious
shades of crimson, lime-green and turquoise.

Our first imitations of birds weren't aeroplanes, but tools and toys.
Arrows and boomerangs go back thousands of years, and both employ
aerodynamics. Arrows usually incorporate feathers, of course, which
played a rôle in many an early attempt at flight. When in 1507 Abbot
John Damian leapt in a feathered costume from the ramparts of
Stirling Castle and failed to fly, he blamed himself for using feathers
from a chicken—an earthbound bird. As for the boomerang, it
evolved in two varieties. The non-return type was used as a weapon
in north-east Africa, India and North America; the return variety, an
instrument of real aerodynamic sophistication, evolved among
Australian Aboriginals, who used it both to hunt birds and as a toy.

The 1965 movie *Those Magnificent Men in their Flying Machines* opened
with a slapstick montage of fur-clad cavemen futilely flapping their arms,
but bird-men probably do go back into prehistory. Icarus's tale is a
strong candidate to be the folk memory, wrapped in mythopoeic garb,
of some genuine doomed flight of forty centuries ago.

There's evidence that the Chinese knew of parachutes 4000 years
ago. Emperor Shun (2258–08 BC) was said to have escaped from a
burning granary (which his father had him climb, in order to murder
him) by using two large reed hats as parachutes. Millennia later, circa
AD 1306, Indian fakirs are said to have given parachute displays at the
coronation of Emperor Fo-Kien, and around 1650 the French

ambassador to the court of the King of Siam reported seeing an Indian juggler descend from a tall bamboo tree using two parasols.

A millenium earlier, the Roman author Suetonius wrote of an actor at a feast given by Nero leaping, dressed as a bird, to his death. Did he jump, or was he pushed?

Shakespeare named his flying spirit Ariel, and another of his characters has a connection with aviation: King Lear's father, King Bladud, was famous for having believed he could fly.

> By Neckromanticke Artes, to fly he sought:
> From a Tower he sought to scale the Sky,
> He brake his necke, because he soared too high.

Neckromanticke: it is not surprising that the desire to fly was tarred with the brush of witchcraft. But despite such opposition, the irrepressible desire to fly led to a great number of leaps from high places, for which we now have the verb: 'tower-jumping'.

Tower-jumpers usually followed the Dædalus method of attaching wings directly to the body (a method perfected only in the 1970s, with hang-gliding). Circa AD 1000, a man called al-Djawhari jumped from a minaret in Arabia wearing wooden wings, and died. Around AD 1010, the English monk Oliver of Malmesbury leapt off a tower of Malmesbury Abbey, with rigid wings strapped to his hands and feet.

> He flew more than a furlong; but the wind being too high, came fluttering down, to the maiming of all his limbs; yet so conceited was his Art, that he attributed the cause of his fall to the want of a Tail, as Birds have. (Milton's *History of Britain*, 1670)

In the same century a certain Saracen of Constantinople sought to impress the Sultan. He put on a long cloak with stiffeners in it and leapt off a tower at the hippodrome, where the Sultan was attending a race:

> The weight of his body having more power to drag him down than the wings to sustain him, he broke his bones and his evil plight was such that he did not long survive. (Nicetas Choniates, *Historia*)

23

Another graphic account of a failed bird-man can be found in a 17th century French chronicle. Circa 1550, we are told, an Italian wearing wings leaped from a tower and dropped 'like a pig'.

But flapping bird costumes may occasionally have performed as primitive parachutes. Was Abbot Damian simply lucky, or aided by air resistance, when, leaping from the ramparts of Stirling Castle in 1507, he merely 'fell to the ground and brak his thee bane'?

Some tower-jumpers were visionaries, convinced they had birdlike powers; others were under the influence of narcotics or alcohol. Often they were clerics or aristocrats, men of education and influence, who could act on the impulse to fly by constructing an apparatus and launching it from a turret or tower. There were a total of perhaps fifty recorded cases of tower-jumping, a long history of short and often terminal descents.

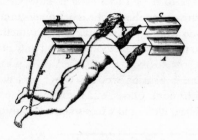

Besnier's flying machine 1678. Besnier in fact made his attempted glide fully-clothed

The first man to take a systematic, scientific approach to aviation was the Renaissance painter and polymath Leonardo da Vinci. Born in Italy in 1452, Leonardo became a happy and curious child, who loved nature and hated the ill-treatment of animals. He particularly loved birds, on many occasions buying the caged birds in the market place to liberate them far from town. He grew up to become history's favourite genius, a master of science and art. But flight obsessed him throughout his life. His writings on bird physiology and speculations about human flight fill 160 pages of his *Notebooks* and show awe-inspiring inventiveness based on scrupulous observation.

Bat man: design for human wing by Leonardo da Vinci

There are many birds which move their wings as swiftly when they raise them as when they let them fall, such as magpies . . . There are others which move their wings more swiftly when they raise them, as with rooks and similar birds . . . The speed of birds is checked by the opening and spreading out of the tail . . . When birds in descending are near to the ground . . . they lower the tail, which is spread wide open, and take short strokes with the wings . . . and consequently the head becomes higher than the tail and the speed is checked to such an extent that the bird alights on the ground without any shock.

When a modern aeroplane is landing it does precisely what Leonardo observes in birds, raising its nose ('the head becomes higher than the tail') to increase the surface area facing forward so that the increased air resistance slows it down.

Leonardo commends the structural simplicity of the bat's wing over the vast complexity of a feathered wing:

> . . . Remember that your bird [aeroplane] should have no other model than the bat . . . the bat is aided by its membrane which binds the whole together and is not penetrated by the air. . . Dissect the bat, study it carefully and on this model construct the machine.

He goes on to delineate what we now describe as aerodynamics and to discuss the relative strength of birds and men:

> . . . Observe how the beating of the wings against the air suffices to bear up the weight of the eagle and how the air moving over

the sea, beaten back by the bellying sails, causes the heavily laden ship to glide onwards! So that . . . man when he has great wings attached to him, by exerting his strength against the resistance of the air and conquering it, is enabled to subdue it and raise himself upon it.

You will say perhaps that the sinews and muscles of a bird are incomparably more powerful than those of a man . . . But the reply to this is that such reserves of strength give it a reserve of power . . . to escape from its pursuer or follow its prey . . . birds need but little force in order to sustain themselves and balance themselves on their wings . . .

Leonardo was occupied chiefly with devising a machine with flapping wings—an ornithopter (Greek *ornis, ornithos,* bird; *pter,* wing). Dissecting birds had led him to understand the massive weight of their bone structures and musculature, but in his insistence that man had similar reserves of unexploited strength, he utterly misjudged human muscle power.

Leonardo did recognise that birds had two forms of flight—wing power and soaring (gliding)—and he designed one device which some historians argue was a kite, but others insist was a manned glider. Recent TV-funded reconstructions have achieved brief flights, albeit aided by significant new features, like a tail to increase stability. And of course, the designers had the benefit of hindsight, the knowledge of modern hang-glider construction and control.

Leonardo apparently did make some experiments with models, but appears never to have undertaken full-scale research and development. The engineering in his final ornithopter designs is of staggering sophistication, and if he had been able to devote the required funds and years to developing a manned glider, the history of aviation might have been kick-started centuries earlier. Even if his work on flight had been known about sooner, it would have inspired others. But after his death in 1519, his manuscripts had to wait 300 years for Napoleon to loot them from Italy, and they were not widely disseminated until the mid-nineteenth century.

Leonardo's name is also linked with two other flying devices. Observing that 'An object offers as much resistance to the air as the air does to the object', he sketched a pyramid-shaped parachute with which a man 'would be able to let himself fall from any great height without danger to himself'. It is not certain that Leonardo invented the parachute, since another, probably earlier, drawing by a Siennese engineer shows a conical parachute. And there is no evidence that Leonardo ever personally attempted a parachute jump, though he almost certainly built models, as with his helicopter. Some sort of helicopter-principle toys had existed before Leonardo, but nothing of the sophistication of his spring-powered helix which, if turned at great speed, was 'able to form a screw in the air and climb high'. When Leonardo died, however, to all intents and purposes his insights into flight died with him.

Two centuries passed. There are inconclusive hints that Leonardo had also made small floating devices, and people had recognized the lifting potential of hot air at least as early as the 15th century. But the first recorded instance of a balloon flight came in 1709, in Lisbon, when the Jesuit priest Laurenço de Gusmão launched a miniature hot air balloon. Clearly de Gusmão had already been experimenting, for this was a high-profile demonstration before no less a personage than the King of Portugal. Unfortunately, de Gusmão's device set light to drapings on the chamber's walls and the inventor disappeared—amidst rumours of interest from the officers of the Inquisition—from the history of aviation.

As the eighteenth century advanced, the idea of human flight exercised increasing fascination. Over fifty works published in England and France imagined flights as far afield as the moon and Mars, powered by everything from geese in harness to magnetism. The extent of the fascination can be gauged from a satiric letter published in the *Guardian* in 1713, pointing out that these 'new *highways*' would be likely to provoke

> innumerable immoralities . . . You could have a couple of lovers make a midnight assignation on top of the Monument and see the cupola of St Paul's covered with both sexes like the outside of a pigeon-house. Nothing would be more frequent than to see a beau flying in at a garret window, or a gallant giving chase to his mistress, like a hawk after a lark.

Jonathan Swift imagined in *Gulliver's Travels* (1726) a 'flying island . . . vast, opaque . . . exactly circular, its diameter 7837 yards, or about four miles and a half . . .', whose ruler could punish errant territories by bombing them.

In 1742 the Baron de Bacqueville adopted the Icarus method of strapping wings to his arms (and legs), and leapt from the balcony of his mansion on the corner of the Rue des Saints Pères in Paris, overlooking the Seine. He had announced his intention to fly across the river to the Tuilleries. Instead, he crashed into a washerwoman's barge moored under his balcony and was lucky to escape with nothing worse than a broken leg. The baron's folly was one of the last episodes of tower-jumping. The age of science had arrived.

The Montgolfier brothers (Joseph, 1740–1810, and Jacques, 1745–99) were papermakers from near Lyons in France. They stand among the authentic geniuses of aviation, because they grasped the possibilities of a technology and pursued it to its logical conclusion. On 19 September, 1783 they were ready to exhibit before the King and Queen a balloon from which a sheep, a cock and a rooster dangled in a wicker cage. On 21 November a *Montgolfière* with a two-man crew drifted across Paris. It was a sensation: 'balloonomania' swept the world, inspiring countless caricatures in newspapers and the depiction of balloons on everything from dresses to dinner plates.

In 1784 the Frenchmen Launoy and Bienvenu demonstrated the principle of the helicopter to the French *Académie des Sciences*. They built a model helicopter, with eight feathers arranged as two sets of 'rotor blades' at either end of a shaft and rotated by a cord twisted round it. Similar toys had been around for hundreds of years—it is even possible that Leonardo was given one as a child. But they became immensely popular after the end of the eighteenth century, and would inspire the next century's most important theorists of flight.

Elsewhere, experiments had begun with parachutes. In 1779 one of the Montgolfier brothers had launched a sheep on a parasol-like parachute from a tower in Avignon, and in 1783 Europe's first recorded parachute flights were made by Sébastien Lenormand, leaping first from a tree and then from the tower of Montpellier Observatory.

It seemed that a new era of manned flight was dawning. But by

1789 the King and Queen of France, who had witnessed the historic flight at Versailles, had lost their heads, and ballooning impinged little upon the public consciousness—despite English fears of a Napoleonic balloon invasion. With the exception of flights by a few pioneering meteorologists, the balloon would be relegated to a fairground attraction for the first half of the nineteenth century. The key to manned flight would be discovered through another recreational diversion: the kite.

No one knows exactly how or when the kite first appeared, though it may have emerged during the fifteenth century from the Arab world. The Romans had kites of some kind and it is possible that they gave them to the Arabs—unless the Arabs had them first, having encountered Chinese kites via the Silk Route (the Arabs *apparently* introduced into Europe a Chinese dragon-kite illuminated by lamps). All very uncertain, and a headache for historians.

Marco Polo, who was supposed to have travelled the Silk Route to China circa 1300, talked of man-carrying kites being used for that great Chinese preoccupation, prediction. Businessmen were reluctant to board a merchant ship until it had been ascertained that the journey would be prosperous—so the winds had to be tested. A drunkard or fool was seized by the ship's company and tied to a large kite, which was attached by eight ropes to the main tethering rope,

A kite is a flat surface, or plane, inclined into the wind: an aero-plane

which the crew held fast. The kite was held into the wind until it rose, with its terrified passenger screaming. The kite was then flown in the familiar manner—tugged on if it began to lean, the rope slowly extended as the kite went higher and higher. Once it was seen to fly well, the businessmen would feel the confidence to board. If the kite was reluctant to fly, or swerved back to earth with a sickening crunch of bamboo and bone, the merchants looked for another ship.

Kites never disappeared from view in China. By the seventeenth century both the Chinese and Japanese were strapping soldiers to kites for reconnaissance. Europeans were far slower to see the kite's potential to lift a man. But at the end of the eighteenth century an English country gentleman would at last use the principle of the kite—a plane, inclined into the wind—to invent the aero-plane.

CHAPTER IV

Crash, Burn, Die

IT WAS A GOOD JOB I got on well with my instructor, Tim Coombs, since we were together most of the day. I had been installed in his home—that is, the home of his mother, Virginia, who ran a B&B on the far edge of Lindsay. It was a large but modest two-storey wood-built house, with a converted brick basement where Tim lived with his wife and two young children.

Tim was a six-and-a-half-foot, big-boned, blond clown who outside an aeroplane cockpit and church found it hard to keep a straight face for more than a few seconds. He would tease, gibber, whoop, throw his screaming children in the air and weave his car—a vast and ugly 1980s V6 Buick—down the wrong side of the road, roaring hymns at the top of his voice. All the adult members of the Coombs household were soldiers of the Salvation Army.

On my first Sunday, Tim invited me to church. I put on the only tie I had with me. The church was an angular modern building with exposed-brick walls and dense fitted carpets. Ruddy-faced Christians in crisp uniforms held hands and sang, with an air of believing that being good in voice before God was itself a surety of salvation.

Tim's personal Bible flamed with long passages highlighted pink, yellow and green, which he knew by heart and would often quote, *very loudly*. Frenetically cross-referenced, these texts provided him not only with a philosophy but with a ready-reference on every aspect of the human condition. A few days after that visit, a conversation about sexual morality provoked Tim to condemn me, half-humorously, as the spawn of Satan. But it was my first and last invitation to church.

Lindsay was a near parody of a small town, with pristine streets of clapboard houses, pin-neat churches and picket fences, where neighbourliness was a second religion. For the ironic Britishers at the airport, it was not Lindsay but *Lindsayworld,* a doppelgänger universe where everyone is always friendly and the sun always shines. No one locks a house or car in Lindsay, for there is no crime. Nor is there death or illness. Despite its immense retired population, I never saw a cemetery in Lindsay, even from the air—though the town did boast an astounding number of Dental Repair laboratories.

Lindsay proclaimed itself the 'Gateway to the Kawarthas'—a lake-splattered tract in north-western Ontario. Kawartha is where Torontoans take holidays in Nature—healthful hiking, or lolling in a boat with a beer can, waiting for the fish to bite; they call it 'cottaging' (a word with a very different meaning in London's Soho). There are nineteenth-century stone lodges on lake shores, some so remote they can only be reached by boat or floatplane; there are upmarket B&Bs, elegant clapboard Victorian buildings, usually brand new, chosen from select building catalogues.

I was sceptical about the self-image of a town that designates itself the gateway to somewhere else. Bypassed by modern highways, a medium-size farming town has little choice but to reinvent itself, as 'historic' (if there's some history left standing), or as a retirement centre and 'gateway'. Attempts to historify Lindsay's main street with wrought iron were undermined by the town's decision to allow strip development and malls. The old family stores had withered into charity shops, while townsfolk drove to chain store sheds staffed by bored teenagers. American planners call this outer ring/empty centre syndrome 'the doughnut effect'. This has particular resonance in Canada, given its national dish.

Canadians are the world's most devoted doughnut (or donut) eaters. On frosty mornings Lindsay's two branches of Timothy Horton's—a sort of doughnut McDonald's—were centres of pilgrimage, their windows steamed up as puffa-jacketed Lindsayers chewed on wads of factory-frozen and reheated cinnamon, or blueberry, or 'traditional'-flavoured dough.

On Friday nights, Lindsay's teens gathered to be raucous (in a muted, Canadian way) in front of the CEN LURY CINEMA, a fleapit with a loose 'T' on its hoarding. Others headed for the Grand, once a noble Victorian railway hotel (the railroad no longer comes to Lindsay), now a brash maze of nylon-upholstered snugs with big-screen TV. Beer was by the jug, chef's special was Deep-Fried Wings and Friday night was WWA Wrestling Night. The lads from Linvic would try to chat up the local talent by claiming to be British Airways pilots. You could read the question on the girls' sceptical faces: 'Then what the hell are you doing *here*?'

Lindsay was kind enough to me. Canadians don't gush at strangers, nor do they have—in spite of the Queen's head on their coins and the word 'Royal' attached to institutions like the Mounted Police—the Australian love–hate or the New Zealand love–love relationship with the Old Country. Lindsay was a sleepy, conservative, neighbourly little town. I had been in Canada three weeks when Pierre Trudeau died. Trudeau had been the only Canadian politician ever to make an impact in the international arena, doing so with a movie star charisma equalled only by John F. Kennedy. His socialism and internationalism left a lasting mark on Canada, which set it apart from its brasher southern neighbour. One morning I stood in a Lindsay bank queue as people around me silently watched the televised funeral, tears on their cheeks.

Gradually, I grew accustomed to life at the airport. I ate breakfast—and did most of my studying—at a window table in the café. Cheerful waitresses provided me with half-hourly coffee hits and served all-day breakfasts to the pilots who weren't in the air, their cigarette smoke forming a greasy knot under the ceiling tiles. I turned down an offer from Denise, Linvic's office secretary, of free moose ('My husband keeps shootin' 'em and I have a freezer full and I don't want to buy another freezer!'). And I practised crash landings over Neil Kelly's sprawling house, which sat in its own grounds, conveniently equipped with a private airstrip.

I was the only full-time pilot at Lindsay not to be studying commercial flight. The others were a motley crowd of British, Irish, French and Canadians, aged from twenty-five to thirty-five, most of them working as instructors, all dreaming of the cockpit of a 747. Some days it felt like a scene from the Battle of Britain, half a dozen young pilots sprawling lazily on the lawns, smoking and joking in the late-summer sunshine, waiting for the next jeepload of denim-dungaree'd farmers to turn up and hand over twenty-five bucks for a joyride. One time, a man had had his car stolen (a rare case of Lindsay crime) and thought he knew the culprit. He wanted to circle the suspect's house in the hope of spotting the car. Then there was the guy who'd lost his remote-control model aeroplane, and hired a real plane and pilot to conduct an airborne search. For over an hour they circled above the maple woods, peering for the yellow wings like would-be rescuers of lost Amazonian explorers, but the little aeroplane was never found. Most puzzling were the people who did not communicate a specific purpose, but enigmatically instructed the pilot to circle some house or lake or outcrop.

Conversation in the mess (well, the café) often revolved around aviation's unspoken freemasonic secret: the fact that it's dangerous. There's a rich vein of gallows humour among pilots, and Ian Ross, an expat British instructor, was particularly morbid. 'Landing is your most complex manœuvre, involving subtle control of the plane's motion in three dimensions,' he told me. He was holding a plastic model of our Cessna. 'Remember, if you get it wrong' —he belly-flopped the toy on to the carpet— 'you crash, burn and die in a bright plume of orange flame. And we don't really want that, now, do we?'

Then there was Paul, the mechanic, who would finish a crucial repair, wipe his hands on his overalls and respond to the automatic query as to whether the plane was now airworthy with, 'Well, *you* can take that junk-heap flying, friend, but I'm keeping both *my* feet on the ground!'

Not all the trainee pilots were young. Alastair was closer to me in age than all the breezily self-confident youngsters. He had none of the cockiness of the younger guys, who *knew* they were just a few flying hours from the smug techno-supremacy of an airliner cockpit; Alastair was modest, realistic, dogged. 'I don't even want to fly a fuckin' 747, Martin, anyway I'm probably too old and ugly to be accepted. I just want to be a working pilot. I'd love to fly bush planes, up in the north of Canada. No glamour, but good honest flying. Good enough for me.'

Alastair had seen a bit of life. Born in Northern Ireland, he had spent a decade building up a successful car-spray business in Eire, then sold it to finance his dream of becoming a pilot. He had started out as a taxi driver in Belfast. 'I was a young feller in those days, I'd no family

34

and I was just wanting to earn a few bob. Well, the British squaddies on a Friday night, they'd go to certain pubs and discos, you know, an' of course come the early hours they're ringing for a cab to take 'em home. And it happened that I got told to pick some up—you know, control would get on the radio and tell me such-and-such a pick-up, drop off at so and so. I didn't even know they were fucking soldiers, sure, though after a while you get to know the pick-ups. But to be honest I really thought nothing of it, I didn't give a fuck about politics! Keep your bloody head down and get on with it. Well, this went on for a while—I suppose I must have picked up squaddies five or six times.

'One night I get a call to go somewhere or other and I do the pick-up, it's a single man. We get where he's going and it's a quiet, dark street, I'm suspecting nothin'—and the next thing I know he's got a gun, a fuckin' great monster of a thing, it's stickin' in my neck! I shit a brick, I can tell you, Martin. All but pissed myself. He says, "We hear you've been associating with the British Army." I said—you know, fuckin' stuttering, I mean, there's been so many fuckin' taxi drivers on both sides of the divide topped, I thought my time had come—I said, "It's just a job, I don't really notice who's in the back to be sure." He said, "Don't give me any of that fucking bullshit you little toss-pot. You've been very lucky. If we get any more reports that you've been collaborating with the British Army it won't be a talking-to you get next time. Do you understand?" You know, with his pistol stickin' in the side of my head. I started nodding, I said, "You can be 100 per cent certain I'll never ever go anywhere near a British soldier again."

'And that was that—he was out the door and into the darkness, gone. Well, I fuckin' reached out the window and pulled the "taxi" sign off the roof—you know, we had these illuminated signs on magnets—and I threw the bastard down on the floor by the passenger's seat, I drove back to the office like a fuckin' bat out of hell, I went in and I threw the keys on the desk and I said, "That's it, I'll never drive another fucking son-of-a-bitch taxi as long as I live!" Those bastards, sending me like an innocent fuckin' lamb to the slaughter to pick up squaddies!'

Alastair was now being instructed in flying twins, and he invited me to go up in the back seat. There really was something about cutting around the Ontarian skies with the Cessna 310's twin engines pushing out 570 horsepower, giving us a top speed of over 200 mph. It was sexy, but it was a rich man's sport and if a working lad wanted that life he had to train to be a pilot and work for rich men. Alastair could justify the gallons guzzled by the twin Continentals every hour, because he was fast-tracking his way to a career in aviation. Eating into the heap he'd taken ten years to build; knowingly taking a risk.

I was in the cabin when he made his first twin-engine landing. The ground comes up at you a lot faster when you're doing a hundred knots. Alastair wiped the sweat from his forehead and turned to give me a loopy grin. 'Forget those bloody old 152 crates, Martin, this is a real fuckin' aeroplane.'

The Flight Training Manual, fourth edition, published by the Minister of Public Works and Government Services Canada, is an admirable document. Part One, Chapter One, Sub-section One is entitled: 'The Third Law of Motion'.

> Heavier-than-air flight can be explained by various scientific laws and theorems. Of these, Newton's Third Law of Motion is possibly the fundamental one. 'For every action there is an equal and opposite reaction.' A propeller accelerates a mass of air backward and thereby receives an equal thrust forward. This forward force, called *thrust*, pulls the aircraft ahead.

So far, we could almost be talking about a boat. But it continues:

> As the aircraft is thrust forward by the propeller on take-off, the wing meeting the oncoming air begins to generate *lift*. As the forward speed of the aircraft increases, this lift increases proportionately. When the lift force is equal to the weight of the aircraft, the aircraft begins to fly.

I can't see that all this has a lot to do with the great seventeenth-century physicist, who seems to me to be mentioned mostly to intimidate, to remind the student of his lowly place in the order of things: 'At the top of the pyramid is Newton; you are at the bottom, in a gang dragging a large block of granite.' Be that as it may, the Third Law of Motion does act as a sort of proclamation of things to come, a warning shot. What the Manual really means is this:

> Between now and your pilot's licence, you will have to grasp load factors and airflows—to learn *how* a wing achieves lift—to understand how the atmosphere functions, to be able to calculate how a plane's weight and balance critically alter as its fuel burns off in the course of a flight, and to make complex navigational decisions in the face of varying winds, magnetic variations and compass deviations. It is no joke, matey.

No one at Linvic had mentioned that the course I had signed up for was purely *practical*—it did not include lessons in flying theory. Canadian aviation law states that a private pilot must have a minimum of 64 per cent in the 3½-hour theory exam; to this end, I was sold five fat textbooks and told to inwardly digest. To these were added half a dozen cramming guides and anthologies of test questions. The knowledge pilots must possess includes aerodynamics, meteorology, navigation, radio operation, air law, even engine maintenance—as though anyone taking a driving test first had to qualify as a car mechanic. A lifelong mathematical dyslexic, I discovered to my horror the black forest of calculations demanded of a pilot—weight, fuel consumption, moment envelopes, density altitude, wind correction angles, crosswind components, true track and true heading, closing angles and reciprocal tracks, ETAs and ETEs, IASs and CASs and TASs, TC + L/+R WCA = TH—all of these arcana to be calculated on a slide rule with a million minute figures engraved into it like Buddhist *slokas* on a grain of rice.

And while navigation and weight loadings were difficult, it was meteorology that gave me the fiercest headaches, as I sought to come to terms with that great seething cauldron over our heads, 78 per cent nitrogen, 21 per cent oxygen and 1 per cent argon, with its troposphere and tropopause and stratosphere, its air density (weight of air per cubic foot) and mean sea level pressure (29.92 inches of mercury), its highs and anti-cyclones, its dry vs. saturated adiabatic lapse rates, its convection, condensation and saturation, its orographic and convective turbulence, its fronts, masses and layers—and the ridiculous cuneiform encryptions with which meteorologists seek to confuse everyone else about an already, God knows, unstable and inscrutable system. Here is an example of the kind of handy hint the MET boys put out to help you have a nice day's recreational flying:

```
CYTZ TAF 200438Z 200505 05015KT 5SM BR
SCT008 BKN100
TEMPO 0510 2SM BR OVC005 FM1100Z
06010G10KT
3/4SM—RA BR VV003 TEMPO 1420 1/2SM RA FG
VV001
FM2100Z 01015G14KT 2SM—RA BR OVCOO9
```

Crystal clear, eh?

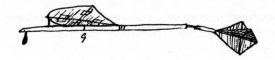

CHAPTER V

Eureka

A new era in society will commence from the moment that aerial navigation is familiarly realized . . . we shall soon be able to transport ourselves and families, and their goods and chattels, more securely by air than by water, and with a velocity of from 20 to 100 miles per hour.

Sir George Cayley, *Nicholson's Journal of Natural Philosophy*, 1809

FLYING HAS BECOME so ordinary, almost to the point of banality, that the average person spends as much time speculating about the origins of the aeroplane as those of the phone, the TV, or the light bulb. But history is still largely taught according to the Great Men theory, and we keep in a corner of our brains a small store of names like Bell, Baird, Edison. So let us ask the question: 'Who invented the aeroplane?'

Rather than a nice, clear answer, the question prompts a question in return. Do we mean the person who

(a) first envisaged the possibility of a machine that could imitate the birds? Or,
(b) built the first device capable of defying gravity? Or,
(c) built the first working model of a modern aeroplane? Or,
(d) built the first aeroplane that carried an adult human being? Or,
(e) first perfected a practical, flyable aircraft?

Or, to consider the matter from a less individualistic, more post-modern angle:

(f) Was the invention of the aeroplane a continuous process, in part the product of unknown imaginations, advancing through

39

paper and feather toys, stories and myths, the windmill, the kite, the glider, the propeller, the aileron . . .?

One thing, however, is certain: the modern aeroplane, which exploits the principle of lift and takes the now standard form of a fuselage, two wings and a T-shaped tail, was invented in 1799, in Scarborough.

The seaside resort of Scarborough in north-east England, famous in Victorian times as a spa, has all but forgotten—if it ever knew—its part in aviation history. It looks backward only to recall its irretrievably lost time in the sun. Given the frenzied tourist exploitation of Kitty Hawk, where the Wright Brothers first flew, it seems incomprehensible that the elders of Scarborough have not even raised a statue to alert citizens or visitors to the town's central rôle in the development of manned flight. Here on this salty promontory, overlooking the small and near redundant fleet of fishing trawlers, the novelty shops, the ice cream and tattoo parlours, was born the vision that blossomed into the Jumbo Jet, the air hostess, Heathrow, Easyjet, 'September Eleven'. Only a blue wall plaque, on a house quaintly named Paradise near the churchyard in the old town, informs passers-by:

BOROUGH OF SCARBOROUGH

SIR
GEORGE
CAYLEY

'The Father of Aeronautics'
BORN AT SCARBOROUGH
27TH. December 1773
DIED AT
BROMPTON HALL
15TH. DECEMBER
1857

Cayley's invention may have come about like this:
  One day, young George is riding briskly in the open family carriage from Scarborough to the family seat at Brompton, opposite his parents Thomas and Isabella. It is an unusually warm summer day and

George extends his hand into the breeze. He has noticed before how a hand dangled over the side of a rowing boat and angled into the water is forced up or down by the water's resistance. Now, he observes that the air (which he will later describe as an 'uninterrupted navigable ocean that comes to the threshold of every man's door') is forcing his hand upwards. He makes a connection: it is thus that a bird's wings, driven forward by its flapping efforts, meeting the air's resistance, but being angled into the flow, achieve lift. Eureka!

This is fanciful; Cayley's breakthrough probably came about as a result of his playing with kites as a boy and later, as a scientifically educated young man, questioning the physics. But we are obliged to imagine the circumstances, because Cayley left us no account of the nature of his revelation. I believe there *was* an Archimedean moment, for what else would have moved Cayley, at the age of twenty-six, to take a silver disc and etch upon it an esoteric diagram and a date? No one at the time—no one in the world—could have understood its significance. Now, we recognise that the disc memorialised Cayley's penetration into the mystery of flight. It was passed through his family until 1935 and is now held at the Science Museum in London. One side shows a diagram representing the forces of lift, drag and thrust— the resolution of the problem of flight, which Cayley defined as making 'a surface support a given weight by the application of power to the resistance of air'. This was the theory, which he surely arrived at after pondering his original observations at length. The obverse of the coin depicts, in three dimensions, the theory pushed to its logical conclusion: an entirely recognisable modern aeroplane, a manned compartment with a wing above it, a stabilising T-section tail to the aft and a paddle—the antecedent of a propeller—for propulsion. Cayley had grasped the principle of the 'inclined plane', as he called it, and its potential to become an aerial vehicle.

From roughly the middle of the eighteenth century a group of modest, politically liberal, religiously nonconformist men in the Midlands and north of England took steps in the observation of gases and the development of mechanics that would, via the Industrial Revolution, change the face of this planet. Cayley was a quintessential example of the educated country gentlemen-polymath. He came from an old and wealthy family, with roots in Ancient Rome, who had arrived on British shores with William the Conqueror. George Cayley succeeded to the baronetcy in 1792, at the age of eighteen. At a time when education, especially scientific education, was for most people non-existent, Cayley had been sent to York and Nottingham to study chemistry and electricity with tutors of renowned and open intellect. He developed into a brilliant man, tolerant in terms of human relationships and politics (he was a Whig, or liberal, an advocate of land reform and sympathetic to the American colonists) as well as 'natural philosophy'.

Cayley's mild manners were legendary and apparently they came in useful: in 1795 he had married a woman who was said to have been born with brains and beauty, and to have known how to make best use of both. Sarah Walker had been spoilt by her father, people said, she had a short temper and a wicked tongue. Sir George, it was quipped, had been born in Paradise, but lived in Purgatory.

The year that he married, he made a toy helicopter of the type demonstrated to the *Académie des Sciences* in 1784. Two corks were put on either end of a shaft and each cork had four feathers stuck in it. A string was wrapped round the shaft, tensioned by a bow. When the string was released, the shaft rotated, turning the upper rotors, causing the toy to dart upwards. Cayley would later make a metal version of this 'screw propeller', which rose eighty feet into the air. He casually observed that by replacing the surface area with large man-made rotors and adding an engine, the resulting machine might be the best type of vehicle for 'the mere purpose of ascent'. *Mere ascent?* Cayley wanted more—he wanted to imitate the birds.

In 1799, he had engraved his silver disc; most books claim that he went on to invent the glider in 1804, but there are numerous hints that he had been adapting kites long before that date. In an unpublished essay of 1804 he wrote, 'I have kept the subject to myself for eight or nine years', and other sources suggest that he had been experimenting since his teens. The image on his silver disc of 1799 must have resulted from practical experimentation, making it almost certain that Cayley invented and flew a recognisable modern aircraft before the end of the eighteenth century. By 1804 his kite-derived glider, with a pole as fuselage and a cruciform tail for stability, was flying well: the first-ever aeroplane. Cayley's success with small gliders spurred him on to a stream of experiments. He made intense studies of the wing structures of common birds, and constructed a 'whirling arm' which allowed him to test the aerodynamic properties of miniature wings. Then he built a very large model glider, with a wing surface of 300 square feet. He wrote in *Nicholson's Journal of Natural Philosophy* in 1809,

> It was beautiful to see this noble white bird sail majestically from the top of a hill to any given point of the plane below with perfect steadiness and safety, according to the set of the rudder, merely by its own weight descending in an angle of about 8 degrees with the horizon.
> . . . it would sail downwards in any direction according to the set of the rudder. Its weight was 56 lbs, and it was loaded with 94 lbs . . . Even in this state, when any person ran forward in it with his full speed, taking advantage of a gentle breeze in front, it would bear up so strongly as scarcely to allow him to touch the ground and would frequently lift him up and convey him several yards together.

It is virtually forgotten today that circa 1805, the principle of the kite had been developed into an aeroplane capable of flying with a man's weight beneath it. This pioneering achievement—more substantial than Leonardo's, far more original than the Wrights'—is absent from almost every history of aviation. Posterity has denied Cayley the recognition he deserves.

Cayley believed that with a source of power, his glider should be capable of ascent. He had something in mind, but the glider 'was accidentally broken before there was an opportunity of trying the effect of the propelling apparatus'. Cayley saw that a small 'prime mover', or engine, would be essential to give a plane the ability to climb. He was to devote many of the next years of his life to designing and building engines, but it would be a hundred years before lightweight internal combustion engines would make powered flight feasible.

Cayley's aviation achievements were published in small-circulation specialist journals, with little impact. He made three unsuccessful attempts to found a Royal Aeronautical Society, but the organisation would not be formed until eight years after his death. In 1849, however, he returned to the preoccupations of his youth, beginning work on a series of large gliders designed to carry an adult human being. He was seventy-five.

Why did Cayley return to plane-building as an old man? The reason may be the first ever wave of public interest in aeroplanes, sparked in 1843 when a design for a powered monoplane was patented and publicised all around the world. William Henson's Aerial, or Aerial Steam Carriage had a narrow, hull-like fuselage, twin 'pusher' (aft-facing) propellers, bore a patriotic white ensign on a pole and trailed plumes of dark smoke from its twin steam engines. It looks to modern eyes like one of the riper products of the Victorian imagination; it was never built and it stood no chance of flying if it had been (largely because of its weight); but Henson's design was a breakthrough.

Little is known about Henson, other than that he worked with his father in the lace industry in Chard, Somerset. Evidently he had an inventive mind—he registered several patents, not only for lace machinery but for steam engines and safety razors, but it is his aeroplane design that marks him out as a genius. Henson had been born into a time of great leaps in transportation—the first public railway in Stockton and Darlington (1825), Stephenson's Rocket (1829), the first steamships to cross the Atlantic (1838). Henson decided to apply his mind to *aerial* transport. The Aerial Carriage drew heavily on Cayley's work, but was an original vision of the way forward—the world's first detailed, thought-through design for a powered aircraft, incorporating most of the ideas which would later be found in the first successful aeroplanes. The Jules Verne-like artists' impressions of it in flight were matched by mechanical drawings that were masterpieces of their kind.

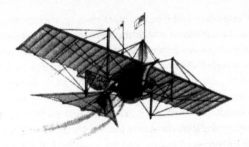

Boldly going, 1843-style: Henson's Aerial Steam Carriage

Henson had a collaborator, John Stringfellow, a fellow engineer in the lace industry and engine specialist. The two men had high hopes, setting up the 'Aerial Transit Company' to build and operate aerial carriages. It was their attorney, D. E. Colombine, who generated the storm of publicity which led to magazines such as the *Illustrated London News* and *L'Illustration* reproducing artists' impressions of the Carriage steaming over London and Paris, the Pyramids and India.

Sir George Cayley was impressed by Henson's audacity, but his public reaction was drily cautious: 'In these days of mechanical wonders, some were supposed to give full credence to the practicality of the undertaking and others to reject it as a visionary hoax on public credulity.' He estimated that the leverage on the Aerial's giant wings would snap them in half, and thought Henson had given far too little thought to the *practicalities* of flight—navigating the turbulent currents of the sky. Three years later he received a letter from Henson, appealing to him as 'Father of Aerial Navigation' for assistance. Henson claimed to be 'sanguine' about the result of his endeavours, but cash-strapped. Cayley's reply was a polite snub:

> I had thought you had abandoned the subject, which tho' true in principle, you had rushed upon with far too great confidence as to its practice . . . I have not any weight of capital to apply to such matters. . . I [do not] think that any *money*, excepting by exhibition of a novelty, can be made by it. A hundred necks have to be broken before all the sources of accident can be ascertained and guarded against.

After their company failed to generate enough money to construct a full-sized aircraft, Henson and Stringfellow set about building a model with a twenty-foot wingspan. It was completed in 1847, seven years after Henson had started work on his original design. To his horror and frustration, the plane would only achieve a 'powered glide'—it could not sustain itself in flight.

Henson had had enough. In 1848 he emigrated to America, where he died forty years later. He never lost his interest in aviation, but did not fulfil his promise. Henson has been sneered at for his failure to keep working at aeroplane design, dismissed in aviation histories as 'temperamental'. We like our heroes to struggle against adversity—including our own blind prejudices. And it is, of course, easier to stick to your guns if, like Cayley, you've inherited a fortune. History has been unfair to William Henson, a man of genius who, fed up with poverty and public ridicule, chose like so many others to try his luck in the more optimistic climes of the New World.

The more practical-minded Stringfellow remained convinced that they had been close to success. He continued on a smaller model with a ten-foot wingspan, in 1848 testing it inside a disused lace factory at Chard. There are contradictory reports about the performance of his machine. It was said to have flown steadily for forty feet, until caught by a safety net—which would make it the world's first *powered* aircraft. It was later demonstrated twice in London before large crowds, and the bright red-painted model allegedly performed well on one of these occasions (but not, alas, the evening the man from *The Times* was there). Now it was Stringfellow's turn to become discouraged, 'finding nothing but pecuniary loss and little honour' in plane-making. He had a living to make and a family to support.

Why did Stringfellow's demonstrations fail to have any impact? Perhaps the expectations of the public and the press—raised, in all fairness, by Henson's grandiose schemes—contrasted too greatly with the reality of Stringfellow's model. The public were not interested in the practical realities of developing a new technology from modest beginnings—they wanted a magnificent achievement, some Empire-girdling titan to stir their patriotic pride. Stringfellow's little red model plane very obviously was not that.

Reinvigorated, perhaps, by Henson's headline grabbing, Sir George

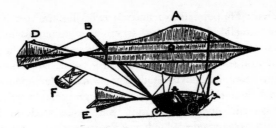

The world's first manned aircraft, 1852

Cayley had again started work on gliders, after a gap of forty years. Now semi-retired, liberated from trips to London and most of his business cares, he could oversee the construction of large-scale machines. In 1849 he launched a glider carrying, in a canoe-like cradle slung under the wing, a ten-year-old boy. In 1852 he at last launched a glider with an adult pilot. These flights stand beside his achievements a half-century earlier as defining moments in the history of aviation.

The glider was very like a modern microlight, its fuselage a dinghy-like pod. Just as today's gliders are launched by tows, Cayley's was launched by a cantering horse. By now Cayley was seventy-eight years old, and the job of handling his aeroplane fell to a coachman. This servant was by no means grateful for this opportunity to make history. After the glider came to earth with a crash, he is supposed to have struggled to his feet and said, 'Please, Sir George, I wish to give notice. I was hired to drive and not to fly.'

In 1921 Cayley's granddaughter, Mrs Dora Thompson, recalled having seen, when she was nine, a manned glider fly perhaps 500 yards over the dale behind Brompton Hall. No one knows how many gliders were built during these last years of Cayley's life, or how often they flew. But fly they did. I know this, because in 2002 I met, at Brompton, the nearest thing to a living witness.

He was a man of maybe sixty years, out walking his dog. I ventured to ask if he'd heard of George Cayley.

'O' *course* I 'ave,' he replied, with a dollop of good Yorkshire scorn.

Well, did he have any idea where Sir George's glider was launched?

'Better than that: I know *fer shewer* where it was. My father was the butler at the house and so was his father and *he* remembered it vividly.

It was *thuur.*' He pointed to a steep-browed hill, the sort that might attract a paraglider pilot today. It was easy to envisage Cayley's plane—a winged dinghy, steered with a tiller—taking to the air from that grassy ridge.

During a long life, Cayley studied economics and unemployment, advocated land reform, worked for the propagation of scientific knowledge and popular education and co-founded the London Polytechnic. He served as Member of Parliament for Scarborough. In his workshop at the High Hall he invented, among other things, the spoked (bicycle) wheel and the caterpillar track, forerunner of the twentieth-century tank and JCB. When a servant lost a hand in an accident, Cayley devised a mechanical replacement. He designed engines and experimented with heat systems, optics, electricity. He speculated that if a distant star gave out as much light as our sun, then a comparison of their respective light intensities would make it possible to calculate the star's distance. He invented streamlining (the sleek wing sections he designed, inspired by his study of trout and dolphins, are identical to some modern wing sections) and predicted commercial flight, propeller power and jet engines. Who knows what direction history might have taken had Cayley focused all his inventive skills on aeronautics during the first decades of the nineteenth century, when he had many years of vigour ahead of him? Still, this scientist-gentleman, alone and far from any centre of industrial manufacture, virtually invented the science of aerodynamics, then devised, built and successfully launched a manned aeroplane.

Cayley died in 1857, a few days before his eighty-fourth birthday. Throughout his life he had retained a reputation for fairness and for speaking his mind fearlessly. He had fathered ten children and maintained a warm bond with the volatile Sarah. His attempts at manned flight were considered by most people to be the aberrations of a wealthy eccentric, best forgotten, and *The Times*'s obituary of Sir George Cayley made no mention of his invention of the aeroplane. His son was embarrassed by the old man's experiments; the gliders became chicken coops, and were allowed to rot.

Why is Cayley so little-known *today*? In contrast to the orgies of publicity surrounding the centenary of the Wright brothers' achievements, the centenary of an even more important date in aviation history—1799, the year the aeroplane was invented—slithered past unnoticed.

It took the noted French aviation historian, Charles Dolfus, to write in 1955:

> The aeroplane is a British invention: it was conceived in all its essentials by George Cayley, the great English engineer . . . The name of Cayley is little known even in his own country, and very few people are aware of the work of this admirable man, the greatest genius of aviation.

CHAPTER VI

Zen and the Art of Aviation

I HAD SOON REALISED that sticking to my determination to fly every day would be impossible with just one instructor. Tim had many calls on his time, including captaining the school's Cessna twin on air charters, which took him to the US for days at a time. I was probably a tad *too* gung-ho: by my tenth day in Canada, I had notched up twenty flying hours, with five different instructors. The practical flying syllabus consists of twenty-five lessons. My insistence on flying every day meant that I kept meeting weather conditions that did not suit the next prescribed lesson, obliging me to do them out of sequence. By day ten I had done twelve lessons, in the following order: 1, 2, 3, 8, 4, 25, 19, 18, 12, 5, 7 and 9.

Tim took me to one side and warned me that I was throwing my money away. 'You're flying every hour God sends and not getting through the syllabus properly. The lessons are supposed to build on each other, they have to be done in the right order. You can't keep jumping backwards and forwards.'

'But I've only got three weeks to pass my Rec!'

'How do you know the weather's going to play ball? Three weeks is an impossible deadline!'

'It's a bit late to tell me that now I'm here! I was sold on the sunny autumn.'

'I'm telling you for your own good, buddy.'

'Well, thanks.'

'And how do you know you'll pass the theory exam?'

'Tim, my wife's coming out here to fly with me; I *have* to pass the theory.'

'Did you know that if you *fail* it, Transport Canada makes you wait a month to retake?'

It took me a moment to absorb that. 'Actually, nobody told me that, no . . .'

I was starting to understand why another Englishman who'd come to study intensively for a Private Pilot's Licence the previous year had gone home after six weeks empty-handed.

I started work at nine every morning and studied into the early hours. It was something like cramming for university finals, yet—because 99 per cent of the information was wholly new to me—far worse. My brain boiled. For occasional relief, I would steal down to Tim's lair to scrounge a cup of tea from his wife Sarah and maybe share some toast and peanut butter with the kids, Victoria and Benjamin.

Every evening Tim had two inviolable dates with the TV. The first was with a preacher called Benny Hinn, a bouffant-haired showman who specialised in stadium evangelism, where nervous invalids tottered on to a vast stage and—amidst the clatter of falling crutches, egged on by a Colosseum of screaming Christians—raised arms and tearful eyes to heaven. Hinn would prod his cordless microphone in the faces of the healed, artfully ensuring that they never uttered more than a pious soundbite. Tim was touched by the high emotions of these spectacles. When Hinn blessed the TV viewers, his plump palm and heavy gold bracelet filling the screen, Tim would lower his head and raise his own hand to the TV, partaking of Hinn's televisual blessing. For failing to be similarly moved, I was branded 'a godless heathen'.

And then there was *Star Trek*, shown in some permutation every night of the week. The secular religiosity of this sci-fi soap opera seemed to me at odds with Tim's belief in the literality of the Good Book. His faith was so secure that my sardonic criticisms of Hinn could be brushed aside—but having *Star Trek* mocked really got to him.

Late one afternoon, as I was strolling along the apron, I saw Neil Kelly staring meditatively into the west, where the sun was sinking over the end of the runway. Tentatively I mentioned that I'd heard the school might be up for sale.

He ran his eyes along the row of tethered aircraft. 'Yeah, I don't think I need a flying school to play with any more. This started as a hobby sixteen years ago, y'know, and now I've got thirteen aircraft. It's been fun. Satisfying, too—introducing hundreds of people to flying. But now I guess I'd like to worry less about helping other folks to fly and fly some more myself . . . Have you been inside here?'

He led me to the big hangar on the far side of the airport's mascot, the McDonnell Voodoo, and slid back the heavy doors. There were about five planes jammed in there, including a 152 with its wings off. Along the far wall was a pile of metal tubes, a propeller, a windscreen and various bundles tied up with string.

'That's a Citabria,' said Neil, 'a neat little two-seater, fully aerobatic, a terrific plane. It used to belong to my wife, but she flies much less now, and after the plane's last full overhaul we somehow never put it back together again. I'd love to see that plane flying again. It's finding the time . . .'

He locked the hangar. The sun was below the horizon now. A 152 was landing from the last training flight of the day, its nose-mounted landing light, near invisible by day, shining a sharp beam ahead of it.

Neil looked at his watch. 'He's cutting it fine,' he said. 'Two minutes later and it would have been a night flight.'

'Naughty,' I said.

'It's not *naughty*,' Neil said tersely, 'it's bloody dangerous. You cannot judge distances. People have died that way.'

We watched the 152 taxi through the gloom.

'Any buyers, yet?' I asked.

He gave a sigh. 'Three people interested. I guess you know some of them. I'm not expecting to make a huge killing. What I don't want is someone to take over and just sell off all the planes. I want it to be someone who'll keep it all going.'

There were two internal candidates, it turned out: Tim and another senior instructor, Adam Bradley. Adam was in his fifties, a lean, husky-voiced chain smoker with a face like a walnut. He did a constitutional trot around the 3500-foot runway at 7 a.m. every morning, in all weathers. His natural manner was a cautious obliquity, when a frown would crease his face vertically. When he spoke, it was a jab of no-bullshit staccato and his laugh was a wicked crow's cough that cracked his face horizontally.

Despite his Old Testament name, Adam had no time for 'Bible

bashers', and he and Tim never seemed to talk. As I began to grasp Linvic's internal politics, I noticed that Tim mostly kept himself aloof from café culture, venturing there only for the occasional bacon sandwich or hot chocolate, while Adam had a clique with whom he was often deep in conclave. Thus were the battle lines drawn. For a week it seemed that no one spoke unless it was *à deux* and *sotto voce*. Unnamed schools from other towns were rumoured to be interested in a takeover—*are our jobs safe*? Half the school seemed to have sided with one party or the other. Business plans and bank managers consumed Tim's daylight hours, and Ian Ross became my instructor.

I was not, to say the least, the most intuitive of pilots; first among my weaknesses was an excessive tendency to *think* about—rather than *feel*—the plane. This was perhaps understandable in someone whose last efforts at mastering a new form of physical co-ordination had been the automobile at seventeen. The difficulty was exacerbated by the fact that I was spending twelve hours a day reading textbooks. I desperately needed—and *longed*—to develop a more intuitive sense of the plane.

When I started flying with Ian, I asked if we could forget the syllabus for a couple of hours and just fly. His approach was more *laissez faire* than Tim's. 'It's your money,' he said, with a shrug.

We went up and just—flew. For the first time I was able to gaze down on the rich transformations in the Ontarian forests, where millions of maples were turning from green to their colour on the national flag.

The day after the sightseeing, we went up for a proper lesson. When I made some grave error, Ian would merely shrug and say, 'Don't worry, we all make mistakes,' gently returning the plane to safe and level flight, 'want to try again?' I did not fly well—making a hash of things I was supposed to have learned in previous lessons.

At the end of the hour, I was despondent. 'That was crap,' I said.

'You need to relax.'

'How can I *relax* when there's so much to do and I'm doing it all *wrong*?'

'Look. You're studying too much, too fast and it's making you tense. You *do* know how to do this stuff; what you have to do is just relax, and *let* yourself do it.'

Zen and the Art of Aviation.

CHAPTER VII

High Victorian

THE VICTORIAN AGE saw an abrupt increase of interest in manned flight. Henson's Aerial Steam Carriage had stirred imaginations around the world—though the first successful powered aircraft would be more like kites than aerial locomotives.

In the early 1850s Felix du Temple, a French naval officer and engineer, built a small clockwork aeroplane which achieved a breakthrough: it *ascended under its own power*, making it the world's first powered aircraft. Du Temple's next model was driven by a miniature steam engine and again it flew. Convinced that he had a template for a manned aircraft, du Temple patented the design of a full-sized aeroplane in 1857. But his ambition to build it would take two decades to fulfil.

Meanwhile, another French seaman was building an aircraft—a glider. The retired sea captain J. M. le Bris is one of aviation history's most attractively eccentric figures. During his ocean voyages he had much admired the superbly soaring albatross—even capturing one, to study its wings—and had resolved to build an artificial albatross in which he, too, might soar. By 1857 the glider was complete and le Bris was ready to test-fly it. He had himself towed along a road and the wooden albatross briefly lifted into the air. Over-confident now, le Bris decided to attempt a soar from the edge of a quarry. But the albatross veered into the ground and was smashed up. Le Bris was lucky to get away with only a broken leg.

Back in England, the society which the late Sir George Cayley had proposed so energetically, the Aeronautical Society of Great Britain, at last came to fruition in 1866. A few far-sighted intellectuals, many of them Cayley's acquaintances, were seeing the possibilities of human flight (though much of the scientific community still dismissed them as cranks). The Society invited a man who was acquiring a reputation as an aeronautics researcher, F. H. Wenham, to deliver its inaugural lecture. Wenham's approach was impeccably scientific—he invented the wind tunnel to pursue his researches—and his lecture was a milestone in explaining the principle of lift. Wenham was particularly interested in Cayley's suggestion for multiple layers of wings, and his research would lead to the biplanes with which powered flight was ultimately obtained. (In 1894 the Australian Lawrence Hargrave would invent the box kite, which would also have an important influence on early biplane design. Hargrave did not patent his design, but offered it to the wider world. Like Wenham, Cayley and many others, he has been elbowed out of the limelight by the near-exclusive attention paid to the Wright brothers.)

In 1868 the Society mounted the world's first aeronautical exhibition, at the immense Crystal Palace exhibition hall in London. It was a hit. Among the fabulous (and unflyable) machines on display was a model locomotive sprouting birds' wings, and a set of personal strap-on wings that looked straight out of Dædalus's workshop and would have brought certain death to anyone who tried them out. The most popular exhibit was a triplane, which whizzed over the spectators' heads. It was built by John Stringfellow, who had not, after all, deserted aviation. But despite being based on Wenham's cutting-edge research, the triplane was unable to fly unaided—it was suspended from a fine wire.

Over the Channel, the plucky *capitaine* le Bris was at work on his second artificial albatross. A photograph of it exists, showing a boat-shaped hull, pendulous wings and what seems at first glance an unfeasibly large undercarriage—in fact, the launch trolley. During trials in 1868, Le Bris was persuaded by friends not to pilot the albatross himself. Tests went ahead with a load of ballast in the pilot's place and the machine crashed irreparably. By now, the patience of Le Bris's investors was exhausted and he had to give up his gliding dreams. Four years later the captain, who had become a special constable, was murdered by 'ruffians whose enmity he had incurred'.

It was time for Alphonse Pénaud to enter the stage. In 1870 Pénaud sparked off a craze with his *planophore*, a rubber-band-powered model

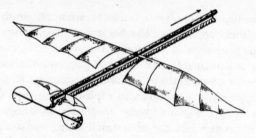

The original wind-up aeroplane. Pénaud's planophore

plane that was very stable and could be built by anyone—and was, by the thousands, as its successors still are. This humble toy did a great deal to persuade the general public that manned, powered flight was feasible. Patent offices around the world began to be besieged with designs for flying machines. Most of them were crackpot, but the race to build the first practical aeroplane was finally on.

Meanwhile, Felix du Temple was about to re-enter the stage. Almost twenty years had passed since he had flown his clockwork model. Now a senior naval officer, he had at last achieved his dream of a full-size plane—the first manned, powered aircraft yet attempted. Some time in 1874 the machine swept down a ramp, piloted not by du Temple himself, but a young sailor (early aeroplane designers showed a marked disinclination to pilot their own inventions). It left the ground, but only under the momentum of its descent and only for an instant. Du Temple, now aged fifty-one, would never build another plane.

Alphonse Pénaud believed he could do better. Pénaud is one of the most interesting characters in the long ascent of aviation, a sensitive and creative man. His father was another seafaring man, an admiral, but a hip disease had confined Alphonse to a wheelchair. He devoted himself to flight and proved to have an original and tenacious engineering mind. As well as the *planophore*, he designed model helicopters and ornithopters and harboured ambitions to build a full-sized plane.

In 1876 he patented a full-scale aeroplane with many forward-looking ideas, including a glass cockpit and a retractable under-carriage. But far from being recognised as a brilliant innovator, Pénaud was mocked, while his health continued to deteriorate. In

1880, at the age of thirty, he committed suicide. His death deprived aviation of a brilliant inventor, but left it with the enduring legacy of a Romantic hero.

In 1884 a Russian, Alexander Mozhaiski, built a plane directly modelled on Henson's Aerial Carriage—it was even powered by a smoke-belching English steam engine. It had two squarish wings and *three* propellers—a forward 'puller' and two aft-facing 'pushers'. Mozhaiski launched the enormous contraption down a wooden ski ramp, but like du Temple's plane, it 'flew' for barely a second or two. Attempts have been made to claim Mozhaiski's or du Temple's lurches into the air as flight. But both depended on the momentum of a slope to get even fleetingly airborne; if this was flying, then a skier leaving a ramp is flying.

One of the oddest episodes in Victorian aviation occurred in 1890, when the Frenchman Clément Ader tested his *Eole*. It was another Jules Vernesque machine, with a propeller exactly resembling four giant feathers and superb fifteen-metre bat wings that swooped from a streamlined cabin in which, in a contemporary engraving, the bearded M. Ader looks out with the superior air of someone having his shoes shined. On 9 October 1890, Ader fired up his steam engine and, he later asserted (there were no witnesses), leapt fifty metres; but this claim to have made the first powered flight, energetically espoused by some in France, seems shaky—especially given Ader's subsequent tendency, with reference to his later machines, not quite to tell the truth.

The closest Victorian England ever came to actualising Henson's Aerial Steam Carriage was the controversial four-ton behemoth built by Sir Hiram Maxim in 1894. Maxim was the millionaire inventor of the rapid-fire machine-gun, which did so much to quell the enemies of the British Empire and led to the legendary Vickers gun. Maxim spent a fortune—£20,000, it was said—on a 'flying machine' constructed on a scale that would not be seen again for years and which, with its vast, sail-like wings, was also rather beautiful. It had a wingspan of 104 feet, a wing area of 4000 square feet and a proposed crew of four. The twin propellers had diameters of almost eighteen feet each, driven by highly advanced, super high pressure steam engines generating the then astounding output of 180 horsepower each. Maxim was justifiably proud of these wonders and assured the Press they would have no trouble getting his machine off the ground.

One summer morning it went hurtling down a broad-gauge railway track specially built in the grounds of Baldwyns Park, in Kent. At just over 42 mph, it lifted briefly into the air, but a propeller fouled a guard rail and Maxim hastily shut down the engines. And that was that. Maxim claimed that he had not *intended* it to fly, merely to demonstrate that it was *possible* for a machine to get off the ground. This sounds perverse, to say the least, and critics have been dubious of Maxim's explanations for not testing the machine further. In any case, he had not incorporated any systems for his 'crewmen' to attempt to control the plane; if it had flown, it would certainly have veered rapidly back to earth, with unpleasant consequences for everyone on board.

To take to the air without learning *how* to fly, and without any means of control, strikes us as absurd. A boat cannot be sailed without mastering complex systems of ropes and pulleys and knowing the winds and tides; Cayley had warned in the 1840s that 'the atmosphere near the earth, even in moderately calm weather, is subject to eddies'. The difference between flying a small model on a calm day and an aeroplane with hundreds of square feet of wing, is immense. Yet most nineteenth-century designers were too obsessed with trying to get off the ground to ask, 'What then?' Amazingly few experimenters showed any inclination to walk before they could run (as it were), to build steadily larger models, facing the problems as they met them and devising ways of controlling an aerofoil that was likely to prove capricious—as anyone who has ever fought with the jib of a sailing boat in a stiff breeze, or even a sun umbrella on a windy day, will recognise. Between 1850 and 1910 there were something like forty occasions when would-be pilots got themselves catapulted into the sky in a variety of 'flying machines' with no idea at all of how they were going to control them. Control was a vital intellectual step in aviation, but it remained a mysterious, near total, blind spot.

In 1908, Maxim would claim that he had invented the aeroplane. No one would agree with him, his name joining Ader's on a long list of almost-flews. Everyone wanted to be the first to have done it. But to qualify as an aeroplane, it was argued, a machine had to be able to *remain* airborne and go wherever its pilot intended. Slowly, a consensus evolved that credit for the first flight would go to the first person to achieve a *sustained* and *controlled* flight, as opposed to a brief, quivering moment of weightlessness.

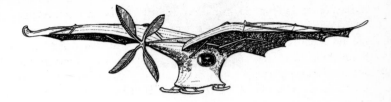

Feather-brained? Clément Ader's Eole

When the nineteenth century started, there was one man in the world, a prophet in the wilderness, who saw the possibility of heavier-than-air manned flight. As the century drew to a close, few designers had matched George Cayley's steady, empirical approach—and no one else had achieved manned flight. The bug had spread widely, with thousands dreaming of being the first to invent a flying machine and of the wealth that would follow. From Scotland to Germany, from America to New Zealand, 'flying machines' were being earnestly constructed. But the secrets of flight would prove far more elusive than anyone expected. Among the weird and sometimes risible designs patented, the few of true genius were ignored and forgotten. There was little recognition that a real breakthrough would take years of patient, systematic research. Few of the enthusiasts labouring in their workshops with beech and bamboo, cloth and glue, had the material or intellectual resources to meet the challenges of fluid dynamics, or to undertake the required research and development; and governments were too sceptical about aviation to invest public funds.

By the late 1800s, some experimenters were doubting that any of these heavy, engined machines could ever fly; perhaps, they mused, they should return to Cayley for inspiration—try to build a glider. Half a century after Cayley's successful experiments, the cutting edge of aeronautics turned back towards gliding.

CHAPTER VIII

Solo

'You never forget your first solo.'
Pilot's lore

'*W*HAT!' I SAID.

Ian had undone his harness. Now he was climbing out of the right seat, picking up his clipboard, gathering the wires of his headset.

He looked up. 'Go ahead and do a circuit. On your own.'

'You're not *serious*!'

He smiled, inclining his head slightly. 'I'm perfectly serious. I think you're ready to solo.' A pause. 'Happy?'

'If you think I'm ready, I suppose I must be.'

He smiled again, making eye contact, a slight furrow between his eyes. Then he nodded decisively and closed the door. And winked and gave a thumbs up—in terms of symbolic encouragement, Ian was doing everything he possibly could.

Which left *me*. Suddenly I felt as though I were on stage, the sunlit cockpit seemed full of unnaturally white, bright light. The scratched aluminium and plastic dash, the slightly crazed, insect-dotted windscreen, all seen with visionary clarity.

Here, now, me. This machine. The runway, the sky. I have to do all those things I've learned, the litany of control surface checks, wind and engine checks, instrument checks, radio checks, check to see the runway and the sky are clear; taxi on to the runway; then it's a matter of co-ordination, of doing—no, of letting my body do—those things in which I, we (my body and I, the two of us, the team) have been learning. Co-ordination. *Feel* the plane.

Pulse racing, I went through the checks in a state that oscillated between a dreamy haziness and absolute focus. The focus, adrenalin-fuelled, derived from the certain knowledge that on these specific actions my life depended. The haziness applied to the next moment; it was the prospect of the whole flight ahead, the series of actions to be performed correctly if this operation—a take-off, a single circuit of the aerodrome, a landing—was, to have existence, to end, to have been. It already existed in a way it was merely what had happened so many times before, five times in the previous hour alone, circuits in the brilliant sky—only there was always someone else along, then, someone who could make it right.

Full revs. Brakes on. The little plane quivers. I hold it a moment longer than I need to. They're watching, I'm putting it off. Why?

I can't put it off.

Release brakes. Ooh. Little wobble. Keep her straight. Nice, nice. Revs building. Watching, keeping her straight. God, fifty-five knots already, rotation speed. And—

Ease back. We're off, into the air, pass through ground effect, feel your speed building, OK, starting to climb. Steady. Quick look over your shoulder: runway's straight, not angled, good. Quick look over the nose: no traffic. Back to the instrument panel: looking for 500 feet . . . 500—and start a slow left-hand turn, 15 degree angle of bank, touch of left rudder—oh, you *remembered* the rudder, did you, and smoothly done for once.

Remember too, through the veils of your trance, that there *is* a world beyond this cockpit.

Compass? Is good. Visual check? Those lakes to the south, glittering spots of mercury. And climbing. Quick look right: no traffic on long inbound. Approaching 1000 feet. Level off, power down to 2300 rpm, airspeed back to ninety-five knots and immediately into left-hand turn, watch your damned *height*!

Compass check, visual check. Height, good. And radio: 'Lindsay traffic this is Golf, Oscar, Echo, Foxtrot turning left downwind for three-one full stop, Lindsay.'

How officious I sound!

At which point I disappeared. This is the time, the downwind leg, when it's possible briefly to pause. I was so concentrated, so tensely and abnormally there, not only remembering but anticipating the things I often overlooked, and this was becoming a perfect circuit and—

I wasn't there.

I came round too late, not in any dangerous sense, but too late to do the pre-landing checks—primer locked, master on, mags on both, carb heat hot, mixture rich, fuel is on, gauges and temperature good, pressure good, seat-belt tension check, doors and windows closed, brakes pressure check—damn it, it *was* a ritual and I had other things to do, but now everything is sharp again and *here*—

Look out to the left, the field is just about over my shoulder now, so reduce power to 1500 revs, touch of left rudder and turn—dropping 10 degrees of flap in the turn—onto 040 degrees, visual check: yes, the lakes to the north and: radio, 'Lindsay traffic this is Golf, Oscar, Echo, Foxtrot on base for three-one' and: flaps another 10 degrees. Watch revs, speed, both good—losing height at good rate. Visuals all good—there go the jade-green mall roofs, I'm in the right place, there's the field over to the left and . . . *turn to three-one*, radio, 'LindsaytrafficGolfOscarEcho-FoxtrotonfinalsforfullstopthreeoneLindsay,' full flaps, engine 1500 rpm, raise the nose for an airspeed of sixty knots.

We are now a small plane approaching the end of a runway, a speck in the sky, white from above, black from below, a point on a notional rectangle above a rural aerodrome, flying into the wind at a descent angle of roughly 3 degrees, a descent rate of 500 feet-per-minute. Falling.

Planes have to land, it's an unfortunate fact. They love to take off, but landings they hate. As Wilbur Wright said to the woman who was worried about her son going up in an aeroplane: 'It's all right, ma'am, there's been no recorded case of a plane failing to return to earth.'

That radio mast disappears underneath me at about the right height. Check it: yes.

Descending.

And the row of trees.

Dropping—too much? Yes.

See the road ahead? Yes, put on a few revs for a little extra height, the plunger sits in the cup of your hand, you ease it in a fraction, good, you're crossing the road, crossing the perimeter fence, here comes the runway, rising towards you, the fields green triangles in your peripheral vision, concentrate on them, *they're* the 3-D reference that lets you sense your height, ease the revs back, watch that speed, nose up nose up, let your revs bleed off and—

Touch down and rolling, roll, keep straight and a touch of brakes—not too much, you don't want them to pivot you forward—then firmer on the brakes. Radio: 'Lindsay traffic, this is Golf Oscar Echo Foxtrot backtracking on three-one Lindsay.'

Cocky bastard!

You taxi back to the apron, grinning ear to ear. Solo! Climb out and someone gets you with a bucket of water, you don't even see it coming. So there you are, wet through, grinning, having your hand shaken by a row of similarly grinning people. Late-afternoon sunlight.

How bright the moment seems.

That night, I went out and had my first beer in three weeks.

CHAPTER IX

The Wright Stuff

If there be a domineering, tyrant thought, it is the conception that the problem of flight may be solved by man. Once this idea has invaded the brain, it possesses it exclusively.

Louis–Pierre Mouillard

ONE NIGHT at the Coombs place everyone in the house was playing a demented game of Scrabble in which I, the supposed wordsmith, was lagging humiliatingly behind. The nine of us had eaten dinner together and the table was littered with empty dessert bowls and orangeade glasses. The game was played with gleeful indifference to the rules, as a springboard for the wildest jokes we could produce—without violating the decorum of a Salvationist home.

Wilbur and Orville Wright lived in a large timber house not dissimilar to the Coombs's and not so far away, either—in Dayton, Ohio, a city south of Ontario on the shores of Lake Erie. The sons of a bishop, they belonged to a religious household that was both disciplined and gleeful. Friends and relatives alive in the 1970s remembered siblings, uncles, grandchildren, each of them endowed with an outlandish nickname, constantly toing and froing, a house of large meals, songs around the piano and manic after-dinner games. This was the base from which Orville and Wilbur Wright mastered, unfunded by the military–industrial complex, the technology that would change the world.

It was only when I began to study my elementary aerodynamics that I realised how many contradictory forces are harmonised in an aeroplane and how crucial the Wrights' breakthroughs had been. I became curious about the bicycle manufacturers who famously combined earnest Christianity with inventive genius; what surprised me, when I did some research, was to discover how faint much of the praise lavished on them had been.

The American Press has always liked to make and break idols: Charles Lindbergh was the pre-eminent example, aviator-superstar turned Nazi sympathiser, but I was surprised to learn that the Wrights' media career followed a similar curve. At first venerated as shy, Gary Cooperish small-town heroes, they were soon caricatured as greedy businessmen who ruthlessly used the courts to suppress their competitors. The Establishment had it in for them, too: what right did two back-street bike makers have to go around flying aeroplanes, when their social and intellectual betters had tried and failed? Widespread allegations that the Wrights had stolen all their ideas threatened to deny them the recognition they did deserve. Time, TV and patriotism have restored them to the realm of apple-pie Americana—the brothers famous for doing their test-flights in a starched collar and tie and never on a Sunday, inventing the aeroplane with self-effacing aplomb. The truth is harder to pin down.

The name came from England; their lineage has been traced back as far as John Wright of Kelvedon Hall in Essex, whose descendant Samuel Wright migrated to Massachusetts in 1636. One of his descendants, Bishop Milton Wright, bought a house at 7 Hawthorn Street, Dayton, in 1871. He and his wife Susan already had two children, Reuchlin and Lorin, and three more would be born in Hawthorn Street: Wilbur (1867), Orville (1871) and Katherine (1874).

The atmosphere at number 7 was not religiose. Bishop Wright of the Church of the United Brethren in Christ was bookish, anticlerical and liberal, and both brothers later acknowledged their good fortune in being raised in a literate household. Wilbur had an impressive intellect and good literary style (he would spend his spare time reading ancient Greek), but both brothers were familiar with that canon of modern and classical works then considered, in an anglophile, Jamesian way, essential to any educated person, including Plutarch's *Lives*, Boswell's *Life of Johnson*, Gibbon's *Decline and Fall*, the novels of Scott and Hawthorne, Chambers, Britannica. They also read a famous work of animal physiology, E. J. Marey's *Animal Mechanism*, which led them to conclude early on that ornithopters were a cul-de-sac. The Wrights were not hicks, but nor were they Dostoevskian bohemians. Victorian mores prescribed smartness and the Wrights were proud members of an ascendant provincial bourgeoisie. Orville was a sartorialist, posing in one portrait with his tweaked-up trouser cuffs revealing pointedly immaculate fine-weave tartan socks. Their sister Katherine once chased away photographers who tried to photograph the brothers in their shirtsleeves.

Wilbur wrote in later life that he and Orville 'lived together, played together, worked together and, in fact, thought together.' But it was not always on the cards that they would be close as adults. Orville had a twinkling eye and a mercurial nature, was easily bored and somewhat rebellious. Wilbur was a success at school—intellectually bright, an excellent athlete—and hoped to attend Yale Divinity School and enter the ministry. He had hawkish, saturnine looks, but the taciturnity that would become legendary later in his life may in part be explained by an accident that befell him at the age of eighteen.

On an icy March day in 1885, he was playing a game of 'shinny' on ice skates on a frozen lake. Caught up in the excitement, he did not see the bat swinging: it hit him full in the mouth, smashing his gums and lips, and breaking teeth. It was months before the full extent of the trauma was clear. It left him with persistent pain, which flared particularly each time the doctors tried to prepare his mouth for false teeth. He experienced severe heart palpitations, which led him to believe his heart might fail. The psychological aftermath of the accident was probably worse than the physical. He was convinced that fate had shattered any promise he had shown, bringing his life to an early halt. He abandoned his ambitions, retreated into himself and lost weight, staying in his room reading. The depression would last four years. During this time his mother became ill with terminal tuberculosis and Wilbur, who had been nursed by her for two years, found their roles reversed. Every morning he would carry his emaciated mother downstairs and, at night, carry her upstairs again. His father later wrote that the last two years of his wife's life were a gift from her son; if he had not risen above his own pain and despair, she would have died soon after her confinement to bed. As it was, Susan Wright died in July 1889, aged fifty-eight.

This little-discussed episode in Wilbur's life was surely a key event, perhaps the turning point. The brothers' lack of interest in women has been much commented on, but at least in Wilbur's case it might bear some relation to the smashing of his mouth—and his self-confidence—at eighteen. Perhaps his fixity of purpose and fierce defence of his aeroplane patents can be traced back to the accident and his mother's death: everything had been taken away from him and out of the ruins he achieved, by sheer determination, something that made the whole world gawp.

Orville had left school during Wilbur's illness and, uninterested in further education, applied himself to his hobby of printing, using presses he had built himself. Both brothers were good with machinery. When Orville was just six, his father had bought him a model helicopter (probably identical to the one that had intrigued George Cayley a century earlier and perhaps even Leonardo da Vinci in the 1500s). In no time, Orville and his brothers had taken it to pieces, discovered how it worked and made working copies. Orville built up a successful printing business and Wilbur showed his mechanical flair in building printing presses at a fraction of the cost of commercial ones. By 1890, the year after their mother's death, Orville's business was printing newspapers and had several staff—including Wilbur.

The Victorian Age was pre-eminently one of manufacture. The very *idea* of America involved the subjugation of nature (and hostile races) with machinery—the wagon, the saw, the railroad, the Winchester repeater rifle. The Wrights' workshop was one among many hives of industry in the eastern United States. The West was still slightly Wild (the last major battle of the Indian Wars, Wounded Knee, when US troops killed almost 200 Sioux Indians including women and children, occurred in December 1890), but the East was stable and, with its immense prairies and raw material wealth, turning the United States into the powerhouse that would replace Britain as the workshop of the world.

The 1890s would see the last great transport revolution before the internal combustion engine: the 'safety' bicycle. In 1892 Orville bought one of the new machines for the considerable sum of $160 and soon became involved in cycle racing. The brothers quickly got to grips with the designs and by December 1892 they were running the Wright Cycle Company.

The Victorians had girded the vast United States with railroads and mastered the seas in steamships; now, urban streets were swarming with bicycles. But the air remained provocatively untrammelled. The occasional bird-man fluttering to his death from the Eiffel Tower merely strengthened officialdom's conviction that manned flight was a suicidal pipe dream. Incredible as it now seems, no nation was engaged in R&D to try and conquer the air. But aviation had its enthusiasts, its amateur model builders and its millionaire Maxims, and gliding was about to re-emerge from the shadows.

The Prussian engineer Otto Lilienthal was born in 1848, the year before Cayley's first full-sized glider lifted a boy into the air. He was fascinated by the theory of flight, and in 1889 published an important book applying a study of birds' wings to the design of aeroplanes. Unlike the builders of bulky machines catapulted into the sky without a thought for *how* they'd be flown, Lilienthal wanted to build the most lightweight, manœuvrable apparatus possible—a set of human wings: 'The manner in which we have to meet the irregularities of the wind, when soaring in the air, can only be learned by being in the air itself . . .'

He built his first successful glider in 1891 and went on to make over 2000 flights in progressively improved designs, soaring up to sixty-five

Lilienthal's hang-glider

feet above the ground. His gliders were elegant, ribbed, birdlike structures, superbly engineered to obtain the greatest strength for the lightest weight. They were, however, provisional designs—Lilienthal never managed to stay in the air for more than fifteen seconds. But he was an obvious candidate to be the first person to achieve powered flight. There were two other candidates: an American and an Englishman.

Samuel Pierpont Langley was one of the pillars of public science in the US, the Secretary of the Smithsonian Institution, America's pre-eminent scientific body. In 1886 he had first successfully flown a model aeroplane he called the 'Aerodrome' (from the Greek *dromos*, running course), powered by a small steam engine. Langley's Aerodromes were the best model aeroplanes yet built; one eventually flew as far as 4200 feet, in the presence of no less a personage than the inventor of the telephone (and aviation enthusiast) Alexander Graham Bell. Langley, a scientist of considerable influence, was convinced that all he had to do was build a *full-scale* version of the Aerodrome. The fact that such a highly respected scientist took aviation seriously gave the fledgling science credibility. By 1898, during the Spanish–American War, the US War Department, with the personal backing of President McKinley, provided Langley with the enormous sum of $50,000 to develop his models into a manned military spotter.

The English member of this triumverate was a young man called Percy Sinclair Pilcher, whose achievements over a few short years made him the most important Briton in aeronautics of his generation. Pilcher built his own glider in Glasgow, where he lectured in engineering at the university. In 1895 he visited Lilienthal and glided with him. Back in Britain, he built several gliders, the most successful of which, the 'Hawk', bore an astonishingly close resemblance to a modern-day microlight. Like Lilienthal's gliders, Pilcher's achieved manoeuvrability by being lightweight and depended for control on the pilot, who hung underneath the wing and threw his weight around. Pilcher did some work for Sir Hiram Maxim and had his own sights set on powered flight: the internal combustion engine had recently come on the scene and he calculated that a 4-horsepower motor weighing a maximum of 40 lbs would be sufficient to lift the Hawk. Since no such machine was commercially available, he built one. Pilcher's plans, held at the Royal Aeronautical Society in London, show that he was well on his way to designing a flyable, powered plane.

30 September 1899 was a rainy day at Market Harborough in the English Midlands, where Pilcher had gone to demonstrate his yet unengined Hawk. During a flight, the plane's tail assembly became water-sodden and suddenly collapsed. It crashed to the ground, severely injuring Pilcher, who died two days later. He was thirty years old.

Otto Lilienthal was already dead. Two years earlier, on 9 August 1896, a gust of wind had halted his glider in mid-air; it stalled and crashed to the ground, breaking Lilienthal's spine. It had been one of his maxims that 'sacrifices must be made' and these are said to have been his last words; either way, they are carved upon his gravestone.

The two likeliest candidates to have beaten the Wrights to the goal of powered flight were dead.

It was probably Lilienthal who ignited the Wrights' interest in aviation, and when his death was reported, they discussed it in anguished detail. They felt that certain fundamental laws—instinctive for birds—were still obscure to human beings. The question began to obsess Wilbur. Perhaps the abstract beauty of flight became, for the frustrated divinity student, a substitute for metaphysics. He liked to stroll around a small wild area outside Dayton known as the Pinnacles, where vast numbers of birds soared. He would observe them closely through binoculars, trying to work out how *exactly* they achieved their miraculous glides.

The bike business was booming, but seasonal, leaving long periods for other distractions. In May 1899 Wilbur wrote a letter to the Smithsonian Institution, requesting a list of works on aviation in print in English.

I have been interested in the problem of mechanical and human flight ever since as a boy I constructed a number of bats of various sizes after the style of Cayley's and Pénaud's . . . The experiments and investigations of a large number of independent workers . . . will result in the accumulation of information and knowledge and skill which will finally lead to accomplished flight . . . I wish . . . [to] add my mite to help on the future worker who will attain final success . . .'

He ordered a mountain of books and papers, and he and Orville began ploughing through them. They felt that lack of *control* over the flying wing was the chief obstacle. They had greatly admired Percy Pilcher's gliders, and his death—so soon after Lilienthal's—weighed heavily on them. They agreed that they were not in the business of becoming aviation's next martyrs.

In the summer of 1899, a few weeks before Pilcher's death, Wilbur

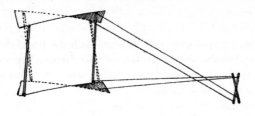

Is it a bird, is it a plane? 'Wing-warping'

told Orville he had solved the problem of control: it went back to his observations of buzzards soaring. Birds twisted their wing-tips to regain their balance when partly overturned by a gust of wind: it followed that aeroplanes needed wing-tips that could be similarly twisted, or warped. Today, all aircraft have small wing sections that move independently of the main wing—Wilbur had invented the aileron. In fact, he had reinvented it: several others had grasped the principles of leverage to turn a plane, and the Englishman Matthew Boulton had even patented the idea in 1868—a fact that would have damaged the Wrights' claims of exclusivity, had not the lack of a working aeroplane to make use of Boulton's innovation led to its being completely forgotten. A New Zealander, Richard Pearse, patented a design for an aileron just three months after the Wrights. The concept was not new, but the Wrights would be the first to apply it to a working aircraft.

That aircraft was a biplane glider based on the designs of Lilienthal and the French-born American engineer, Octave Chanute. It had a five-foot wingspan and wires that could be tugged to warp the wings. The wing-warping worked, and the Wrights decided to construct a full-size glider.

In May 1900 Wilbur made contact with Chanute, who was an important conduit for all things aeronautical. Chanute was convinced that manned flight was just a matter of time—after all, the 'safety' bicycle 'took some eighty years for its development from the original despised velocipede'. Chanute would be a critically useful contact for the Wrights, though what started as a warm friendship would end in bitter recriminations. But that was still a decade away. Making the first contact, Wilbur made clear that he was in the Lilienthal rather than the Maxim camp:

> For some years I have been afflicted with the belief that flight is possible to man. My disease has increased in severity and I feel it will soon cost me an increased amount of money if not my life . . .
>
> . . . The flight of the buzzard and similar sailors is a convincing demonstration of the value of skill . . . It is possible to fly without motors, but not without skill.
>
> . . . the fact that in five years [Lilienthal] spent only about five hours, altogether, in actual flight is sufficient to show that his method was inadequate.
>
> . . . My observation of buzzards is that they regain their lateral balance, when partly overturned by a gust of wind, by a torsion of the tips of the wings . . .
>
> . . . my object is to learn to what extent similar plans have been tested and found to be failures and also to obtain such suggestions as your great knowledge and experience might enable you to give me.
>
> . . . I believe no financial profit will accrue to the inventor of the first flying machine and . . . [such inventors can] only hope to link their names with the honour of its discovery. The problem is too great for one man alone and unaided to solve its secret.

This last paragraph is, with hindsight, deeply ironic. Not one man, but two men, *would* perfect the first practical aeroplane. And they would not be content with a drop of collective honour.

The area around Kitty Hawk in North Carolina has strong and constant winds—ideal conditions for gliding. It was also, in 1900, very remote. Wilbur's journey to Kitty Hawk was an epic example of nineteenth-century public transport. Encumbered by tools, a trunk and the crated components of the disassembled glider, he travelled by steam locomotive and ferry steamer to Elizabeth City. Here he was just thirty-five miles from Kitty Hawk, but separated from it by the broad expanse of the Albermarle Sound. It was three days before he met Israel Perry, the owner of a flat-bottomed schooner called the *Curlicue*. A charter was agreed and Wilbur's luggage and lumber were transferred to a leaking skiff rowed by Perry and his deckhand, with all three men bailing constantly. The schooner had a rotten rudder post, split sails and a cabin—which the fastidious Wilbur refused even to enter—infested with vermin. The mildest of airs pushed them ponderously down the Pasquotank river and through Dismal Swamp, and by the time they bobbed on to the open waters of the Albermarle Sound it was almost dark. Suddenly the tail end of a hurricane that had killed 6000 people in Galveston, Texas swept across the Sound. The *Curlicue* lurched violently on the chop and sprang a leak. Bailing began in earnest. As the winds rose to gale force, the foresail ripped apart and Wilbur and Perry's deckhand struggled forward to secure it. Next, the mainsail blew out. With only the jib remaining, Perry managed to run across a sandbar to a sheltered cove and drop anchor to ride out the storm. Wilbur, about to risk his neck at gliding, had narrowly escaped death by drowning.

Kitty Hawk's small population of fisher folk lived lives of extreme simplicity, striving heroically to grow beans, corn and turnips in the sandy soil. Wilbur stayed at the house of the postmaster. He wrote to his father, 'I have my machine nearly finished . . . I have not taken up the problem [of flight] with the expectation of financial profit . . . [or of] achieving the solution at the present time or possibly any time. I look upon it as a pleasure trip . . .'

On 28 September Orville arrived at Kitty Hawk by the more conventional means of the mailboat, and the two set up a camp on the sands. They quickly discovered that there was much more to gliding in practice than in theory. The glider needed dangerously high winds to lift off and was difficult to control. The wing-warping, at least, worked well.

There was one other aspect of their design which was—though they didn't yet know it—a tremendous success, and would save their lives time and again. When an aeroplane climbs at such an angle that the smooth flow of air over its wings is broken, it 'stalls'. The wing abruptly loses its lifting power, often causing the plane to dive. It was a stall that had killed Otto Lilienthal. Inadvertently the Wrights had incorporated into their design a device that made it 'stall-proof'. A 'stabiliser' placed in front of the wing performed the role of a modern plane's elevator, controlling the up-and-down motion. The anti-stall effect was something which took the Wrights several years to understand. But it allowed them to survive stalls miraculously and to experiment in far greater safety than their predecessors.

They left Kitty Hawk after three weeks, having spent all of three minutes in the air. Back home that Christmas, the family was consulted. Should they carry on, ploughing in yet more time and money? They believed they did have a real chance of mastering controlled flight. With success, they'd been thinking, their financial losses might be turned into sizeable gains—surely the manufacturer of a practical powered aircraft would be courted by every army on earth. And so the Wrights abandoned the utopianistic notion of a brotherhood of aviators working unselfishly towards a common goal. According to their detractors, they sold their souls to the devil.

In 1902 they built the largest glider ever constructed, based on Lilienthal's research. It proved unpredictable and difficult to control, and the Wrights realised with some shock that Lilienthal's celebrated calculations were unreliable. The only way forward would be to design their own wings. They turned to F. H. Wenham's invention, the wind tunnel, and set about testing every conceivable wing form—rounded, oblong, elliptical, flat, square, or curved like the sections of birds' wings, in biplane and monoplane configurations—two hundred in all. The results were painstakingly tabulated and translated into formulae that permitted calculations of wind velocity, wing area, drag, lift etc. They were now equipped with a unique set of data.

The next Wright glider was very different, its biplane wings narrower, slimmer and longer (like a modern glider's). It was characterised at first by a tendency for one wing to drop and plunge into the sand—they called it 'well digging'. They had thought that wing-warping made a rudder unnecessary, but they now restored the rudder and found turning much easier and safer.

In the last weeks of October 1902 they made almost 1000 flights, of up to twenty-six seconds and 600 feet. Elated, they applied for patents on their innovations. (For this purpose, various drawings had to be transferred from the brown wrapping paper on which they'd been made and calculations from scraps of wallpaper.) The brothers had achieved controllable flight. But the greater prize remained: *powered* flight.

They planned to fit a motor to their glider and perhaps modify a marine propeller; but, like Percy Pilcher, they found that no lightweight engine existed, and had to design their own. Charlie Taylor, their machinist and assistant, recalled, 'One of us would sketch out the part we were talking about on a piece of scratch paper and I'd spike the sketch over my bench. It took me six weeks to make that engine . . .'

Next came the propeller. The Wrights discovered that while marine screws had been in use for over half a century, no theory or systematic research existed. They decided to devise mathematical formulae to help them to design and build the most efficient airscrew possible. For weeks, they were consumed by mind-numbing calculations. The propeller their formulae told them to make worked exactly as predicted, giving them far more thrust than competitors with much bigger engines. This was the Wrights' boldest theoretical work, demonstrating that even without the benefit of formal engineering training, they were brilliant aeronautical engineers.

As the Wrights finalised the design of their powered machine, they knew they had some heavyweight competition: Dr Langley of the Smithsonian Institution, who had been labouring in conditions of high secrecy on his military-funded Aerodrome (in fact, the Smithsonian Institution had by now added $23,000 to the military's $50,000). Langley *should* have represented a serious challenge; but this prominent man of science had flaws which would prevent him from achieving his goal. His approach was arrogant and in some ways bizarrely unscientific—particularly in his insistence that wings had to be flat, contradicting the discoveries of Cayley, Wenham and Lilienthal. Langley did construct a quarter-scale model of his full-size Aerodrome, and it flew. But he suffered from the customary blind spot over *control*. Lilienthal and Pilcher had used their body weight to control their gliders, but Langley gave the matter little consideration. Nor was he much concerned about the personal safety of his twenty-two-year-old personal assistant Charles Manly, who had the unenviable task of riding this overgrown toy plane: there were neither skis nor wheels beneath the fuselage, and if the Aerodrome did fly, it would only do so until the fuel ran out—and then crash.

Langley decided to launch his machine from a huge houseboat on the Potomac river, where it was lashed to a catapult of intersecting cross-members resembling nothing so much as a medieval bell tower.

Long before the great occasion came, word of the secret project had leaked out. On the morning of 7 October 1903, the eyes and camera lenses of hundreds of onlookers and eager newsmen were directed at the outstretched 'sails' of the flying machine. Dr Langley was so confident that success was a mere formality that he did not see fit to attend the launch himself.

Dr Langley makes a splash: the launch of the Aerodrome

Charles Manly, sporting a cap, automobile goggles and white ducks with a barometer sewn into them—for indicating altitude—climbed into the cockpit. The massive Aerodrome was evicted from its launch pad and, in the words of one reporter, 'simply slid into the water like a handful of mortar'. Laughter, pandemonium. From his office at the Smithsonian, a flustered Langley issued a statement insisting that the Aerodrome had snagged itself on the launch mechanism and would be sure to work next time. The plane was fished out of the Potomac, rebuilt and scheduled for relaunch on 8 December.

Isolated in Kitty Hawk, the Wrights beavered away, nervously expecting to hear that Langley had pipped them to the post. But on the occasion of its second launch the Aerodrome delighted an equally large audience by dismembering itself almost before it was off its ramp and flailing into the Potomac, where the unfortunate Manly almost drowned. Langley's failure was complete; it was also a humiliation for his employer, the prestigious Smithsonian. One newspaper suggested that Langley should take up submarine research. The débâcle conditioned opinion formers in the US and around the world against the very possibility of manned flight and the *New York Times* concluded that it would take 'from one to ten million years' for the aeroplane to evolve. In fact, it took just over a week. On 17 December, exactly nine days after the Aerodrome's second swim, the Wright brothers succeeded where Langley had failed. But almost nobody noticed.

'After a while they shook hands,' a witness remembered, 'and we couldn't help notice how they held on to each other's hand, sort o' like they hated to let go; like two folks parting who weren't sure they'd ever see each other again.'

On the morning of 17 December 1903 winds were gusting twenty-four to thirty miles an hour (perilous conditions even for today's small planes), while the brothers knew that their recent modifications to the 'Flyer' (as they had now christened the plane) would have altered its behaviour in the air. Contrary to their self-imposed rule, they had not tested the new set-up unmanned before flying it. Winter was coming on fast and it might be their last chance before the spring.

They had dressed in suits, starched collar and tie. Five walrus-moustached fishermen were present as witnesses, as Orville set up his camera on its tripod. It was his turn to fly first—they always took it in turns. He climbed on to the wing and lay face down. Wilbur urged the sceptical onlookers 'not to look sad, but to laugh and hollo and clap our hands and try to cheer Orville up when he started'.

Three days earlier, they had hopped into the air for three and a half seconds, covering sixty feet. But even a stone, spun at the correct angle at the surface of a pond, can be made to fly. Wilbur had calculated that at a high enough speed, the most unaerodynamic of aircraft might be persuaded to 'leap' around 250 feet. To be beyond all contestation *in controlled flight*, a machine would have to achieve a sustained, powered flight of at least a quarter of a mile.

Just after 10.30 a.m. Orville yelled that he was ready. The restraining wire was released and the Flyer leapt 120 feet before plunging into the sand—sixty feet further than the previous attempt, but not controlled flight.

At 11.20 Wilbur tried: 175 feet.

At 11.40 Orville tried again: just over 200 feet.

At twelve o'clock Wilbur made the fourth flight. This time, he reached the 175 feet mark with the plane bucking violently in the strong winds—and he was still aloft. He reached 300 feet and the flight became steadier. At 400 feet he was flying smoothly, at the 'safe' altitude of fifteen feet they tried never to exceed—500, 600, 700 feet. When a sudden gust brought the oversensitive machine back to earth, he stopped the stopwatch and cut the engine.

Fifty-nine seconds and a surface distance of 852 feet.

The Wright brothers had ushered in the age of manned flight. And they were going to be home in time for Christmas.

The Wrights issued a press release, but most newspapers were convinced after the Langley fiasco that this must be a hoax and the few accounts published were full of inaccuracies. On 2 January 1904 the *Scientific American* reported:

> . . . the successful flight of a motor-driven aeroplane built by the brothers Orville and Wilbur Wright—an event of supreme importance in the history of aeronautics inasmuch as it is the first case of an aeroplane, carrying its own engine and an operator, making a trip over several miles of distance . . .

Even a prestigious scientific journal had somehow turned 852 feet into several miles.

The brothers now had to choose whether to publicize their achievement—which meant their idea might be imitated, indeed improved on, by others—or concentrate on developing the Flyer into a stable, controllable, marketable product. They chose the latter course and worked as discreetly as they could.

Bizarrely, the first eyewitness account of a Wright brothers flight appeared in 1904 in an apiarist journal called *Gleanings in Bee Culture*, by its editor, Amos I. Root, who saw a Flyer execute a circle under perfect control.

Late in life, Orville Wright would wring his hands over the use of aeroplanes in warfare, but he and Wilbur had always foreseen military sales as their prime revenue earner. They now spent much of their energy proposing the Flyer as a military spotter to the US Army and then—since they quickly felt snubbed by America—to the European Great Powers. But they found the British and French equally sceptical and reluctant to part with cash.

In Europe, aviation continued its slower progress. Many details of the Wrights' work were spread by Octave Chanute. They considered this to be a kind of inadvertent industrial espionage, and the bad feeling generated would lead eventually to their falling out with their oldest supporter, just months before his death. Inevitably, history has contrasted Chanute's desire to disseminate information among the brotherhood of aviators with the Wrights' obsession with protecting their patents. But no one in Europe equalled the Wrights' finely tuned, systematic approach, and no one grasped the significance of wing-warping. Nevertheless, in the five years since the Flyer's first fifty-nine-second flight, European aviation had made considerable advances. A variety of planes had achieved flights of up to a minute and a half, and the few people who were aware of the Wrights' claims were inclined to dismiss them. The time had come for a major public demonstration.

Europe—and in particular France—was the world centre of aviation in 1908. In May, Wilbur took a crated Flyer to Le Mans for a display attended by a Who's Who of the French aviation fraternity. He faced a wall of scepticism and derision.

On the afternoon of 8 August he took off—and provided a display of precision flying that annihilated his critics. 'We are beaten,' said France's most successful aviator, Léon Delagrange, 'we just don't exist.' Wilbur wrote to Orville, 'You never saw anything like the complete reversal of position that took place . . . You would have almost died of laughter if you could have seen them.'

'Il vole!' screamed the headlines. The public response was hysterical, catapulting Europe and the world into an 'aviation fever' that far exceeded later responses to the Sputnik or the Moon Walk. Wilbur was fêted by the crowned heads of Europe—his backwards-worn cap became a fashion icon. Throughout it all, he remained modest and taciturn, resolutely his own man. The Wrights had won the race to build a plane that stayed aloft and under control. They had secured their place in history—or so, for a few heady months, it seemed.

Now that the Wrights have been canonised by popular mythology, it is hard to comprehend the four years of bitterness that would lead to Wilbur's premature death. The real question is, *why* did the Wrights become so ruthless? They appear to have felt themselves forced into litigation. As soon as their success with wing-warping became public knowledge, several of their aviation acquaintances began to build and sell machines that not only used the Wrights' systems, but used them rather better, resulting in cheaper and faster aircraft. Just a year after Wilbur astonished the world at Le Mans, a score of competitors' planes were making his achievements look tame. After nine years of research and development, the Wrights had expected fame and fortune. Le Mans had brought them brief fame, but they were in danger of losing out on the fortune.

The Wrights argued that for *any* plane to be controllable, it must use the principles of control *they* had worked out; so they demanded a piece of the action on *every plane built*. Foreign aviators arriving from around the world for US airshows had injunctions slapped on them and, to avoid legal problems, they coughed up tens of thousands of dollars. The Wrights' opponents replied with vicious personal attacks. Desperate to get out of commerce and be free to concentrate on innovation, the Wrights found themselves embroiled in patent wars.

Eventually the courts found in their favour, but their restrictive lawsuits were cited by many, including Henry Ford, as having suffocated the development of aviation for years. As the glamour wore off the Wright brothers, many—even their old friend Octave Chanute—accused them of simple greed. And they did become very rich, completing a vast, purpose-built mansion in 1912. Wilbur died that year, aged forty-five, of typhoid brought on, Orville maintained, by the stress of dealing with lawsuits—in particular the courts' delays in granting them the monopoly on aircraft manufacture they were demanding.

A century on, there are those who insist that the Wrights did not achieve what they claimed, or that others beat them to it. In a scandal it is still trying to live down, the mighty Smithsonian engaged in a fraudulent reconstruction of the Langley Aerodrome with Glenn Curtiss, one of the people the Wrights were suing for breach of patent! The Smithsonian then spent thirty-four years asserting that the Aerodrome was the first aeroplane capable of sustained free flight. Orville's astutely political response was to send the original 1903 Flyer to England, generating immense publicity and embarrassment for the Smithsonian. The Flyer was exhibited at the Science Museum in South Kensington until 1942, when the Smithsonian made a full and grovelling recantation. The Flyer had to wait until the end of World War II to go on display in Washington, in December 1948. Orville had died eleven months earlier.

He was seventy-seven when he died. He had lived to see Guernica, the Battle of Britain, Hiroshima, to take the controls of a Lockheed Super Constellation airliner, and to witness the start of the space age—for a supersonic jet reached the edge of the earth's atmosphere in 1947. For much of the last forty years of his life he was a crusty and eccentric millionaire, fighting the American Establishment and a legion of others for recognition of what he and Wilbur had achieved. Isolated with his sister in their mansion, he looked back nostalgically on happier days at 7 Hawthorn Street. But in 1926, aged fifty-one, Katherine had the gall to get married. Convinced that she had violated a sacred pact of celibacy they had shared with Wilbur, Orville estranged himself from his sister.

The story of the Wright brothers records how two open-hearted young men were turned, by circumstances, into bitter middle-aged ones. Others *did* set out to exploit their inventions and deny their achievements. But their legacy is ambiguous. The Wrights did not, as mythology has it, invent the aeroplane—they built on the work of Cayley, Wenham, Pénaud, Lilienthal, Chanute, et al. They were not the first to invent the aileron, though they were—just—the first to apply it. But they did make crucial breakthroughs in the co-ordinated use of elevators, rudders and propellers that enabled them to win the race to build a self-sustaining, controllable aeroplane. The Wrights were brilliant and tenacious aeronautical engineers; they were also

Wright Flyer (climbing, left to right)

businessmen. Aircraft inventors had been patenting their designs for decades and the Victorian age unembarrassedly equated enterprise with profit. But the image of Saint Wilbur and Saint Orville would be easier to swallow had they stuck to their assertion that aviation was for all men; had they not done a volte-face on their claim not to want to make money out of aeroplanes; had they not tried so hard to sell aeroplanes to the world's armies; had they not, after working out the principles of controlled flight, insisted on profiting from their discovery to the extent of threatening every pilot in the world with litigation, and stifling the development of aviation while lining their own pockets. Be all that as it may, in August 1908, when Wilbur made his first public flight, the age of the aeroplane was born.

If I were writing exclusively a history of aviation, I'd want to devote further chapters to all the ways in which the aeroplane had yet to evolve—and I'll touch on some of them—but there may be readers eager for me to get on with the advertised aerial hitch-hike. Before I do, I want to spend one chapter describing how pilots penetrated the final mysteries of flight—and how I at last became confident of my own ability to fly.

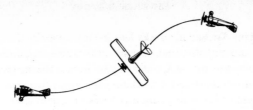

CHAPTER X

Extreme Attitudes

T HEY ARE THE PART of flying you hate at first, but learn to love and finally, to crave. They call them 'extreme attitudes'.

It was Tim who took me for my first spin. He drily explained what he was going to do—then did it, talking his way through the terrible manœuvre. '. . . OK, so we start with a power-off stall, pull the power back to stop, raise the nose to around about forty-five knots and you hear that stall horn going? Pull the control column *all the way* back and put your foot *all the way down*. Hold these inputs, and *into the spin.*'

Imagine a diver, poised at the edge of the top board, suddenly fainting—his twisting, forward tumble. This was the sense I had of the plane's motion. The patch of sky that had filled the Cessna's narrow windscreen made an abrupt exit over my right shoulder, to be replaced by a gyrating field. Like a drunk clutching the rim of a washbasin, I grabbed the dashboard—an instinctive but entirely pointless act, since the dashboard was itself revolving. I merely earned myself a raised eyebrow from Tim—I was supposed to be paying attention.

'Aaaand, once round, *opposite* rudder to stop the spin, *lower* the nose to break the stall, *full power* and ease out . . . OK.' Stable again, the Cessna began to climb back to its previous height. 'Ready for another one?'

No, I thought, *no*: I've been learning to fly for twelve days, I am just getting some confidence, and I'm suddenly expected to dangle upside down in a death machine. 'No,' I said.

'*Really?*'

I felt nauseous—either from disequilibrium, or fear. 'If you insist,' I muttered.

'It's in the curriculum,' Tim said, 'sooner or later if you want to qualify as a pilot you're gonna have to—'

'Oh, Tim, for goodness sake let's get on with it!'

Unlike cars, planes tend to crash from being flown too slowly. I have mentioned stalls, when the air passing over the wings is suddenly insufficient to generate lift, and the plane stops flying. A stall might occur when a pilot is so intent on giving passengers a bird's-eye view of, say, his new swimming pool, that he takes his eye off the speedo. A well-designed plane stalls benignly—recoverably—but some models will drop one wing like a trapdoor, or even turn upside down. One of the most skilful pre-World War I British pilots was Gustav Hamel (born of Norwegian stock), who talked about 'what is known as "stalled"—that momentary pause before the aeroplane turns over on its nose and falls . . .'. Some notable planes had unpleasantly abrupt stall characteristics (for example, the World War II Mustang), while others, like the Spitfire, stalled in a way that gave its pilots immense confidence. The Spitfire's test pilot, Jeffrey Quill, did a period of active service in 1940 to analyse the plane's combat performance. He wrote,

> . . . in fighter engagements inadvertent stalls are very frequent and the fact that the Spitfire gives good warning and maintains good lateral stability . . . is a very great advantage. The Messerschmitt pilots appear to be frightened of stalling . . .

Conservatively designed trainers like those used by flying clubs can be stalled at 3000 feet and be flying again at 2900. Try the same manœuvre at 300 feet, however, and you may find that your propeller is ploughing a field—which, as Tim drolly put it, 'exceeds its design specification'.

The great fear is of a stall that is not 'caught' and develops into either a spin or a spiral dive. Canadian novices spend much time plunging earthwards in the terminal tumbles you see in World War I movies, learning how to recover from the consequences of an inadvertent spin or spiral. The British have removed such man-œuvres, which place the pilot within seconds of death, from the flying syllabus. In their judgement accidental spins are rare, and it's actually more dangerous to have novices practising spins. According to one Canadian instructor, that makes the Brits 'a bunch of woossies'.

Spin practice starts with a climb to at least 3000 feet above ground level. A 360 degree turn to ensure that the surrounding airspace, through which you will soon be plunging like a lift with broken cables, is free of traffic. Then—there's no putting it off—nose up, full rudder—uurgh! An incipient spin soon develops into full-blown 'autorotation', and the plane will, left to its own devices, spin itself straight into the ground. The actual motion is a fairly tight corkscrew, or helix.

During a training spin the plane's nose will not be pointed straight down, but at an angle of 45 or 60 degrees, so that the friction between the air and the plane's surfaces produces a sort of gyroscopic waddle, slowing the plane somewhat. During its first rotation the plane will lose around 400 feet, during the second 500 and so on. A pilot who unintentionally entered a spin at, say, 1000 feet, could theoretically—in most planes—recover. But only a display aerobatic pilot would much fancy trying it at that altitude.

Even more to be feared is the unintentional spiral dive, which has caused many fatal accidents—and continues to cause them. It can be entered inadvertently during a steep turn, if you drop your nose too far. At low altitudes this is the real nightmare, because it is a *rapid* descent.

During practice, spirals are entered, like spins, by putting the plane in a stall; the wings are rolled into a steep bank and the nose is sharply dropped. When I think about spirals, I think about a piece of archive film I saw of a Spitfire in flight: one moment the plane's silhouette—with those pointed, elliptical wing-tips—filled the frame; the next moment the plane dropped its nose and right wing, then vanished in a sabre slash out of the corner of the frame.

Unlike the busy flutter of a spin, a spiral dive sees the plane carving through the air at its aerodynamic best. I was learning in a Cessna 152 with no special strengthening for aerobatic manœuvres and a Vne (Velocity never to be exceeded) of 150 knots. I would enter a spiral dive from slow flight at sixty knots; at sixty-five, the instructor would say, 'Recover', and I would break out by eighty or eighty-five knots. When I began actually to *enjoy* doing spirals and once held one a little longer than I should—long enough for the instructor to start and say with the beginnings of alarm, 'Pull out!'—I saw the speedo needle leap to 120. The rate-of-descent needle showed 2000 feet a minute, which just goes to show how misleading instruments can be: the descent rate in a spiral dive is closer to *12,000* feet a minute. In other words, if I had not broken out of the dive, I would have hit the ground approximately twelve seconds later. At such speeds, however, the wing loading—the pressure imposed by the resistance of the air—increases sharply. At perhaps 250 knots and before I hit the ground, my wings would have been torn off. (Even an extended period exceeding top speed can do invisible damage to wing structures, which is why some people prefer to avoid elderly flying school crates.)

'Extreme attitudes' must be endured, then learned, to the point that you can prove you can do them. But why did I soon find them, for all the fear they had aroused in me, so addictive? The obvious answer is adrenalin. And also because the dream of flight is not to drive an aerial charabanc from A to B without disturbing the passengers' plastic coffee cups; it is the ancient ambition to imitate the swift, the bat, the dragonfly. These natural denizens of the sky do not fly straight and level between suburban car parks. Human beings have tried to domesticate flight, almost to the point of clipping its wings.

The first great spurt in aeroplane design came—*plus ça change*—in wartime. In World War I aeroplanes were the cutting edge of military hardware and thousands of young men were involved in mortal combat in the sky. Yet so little research had been done into aeronautics that, at the outbreak of war, no one really knew how planes flew, or what they were capable of. Stalls—which usually occurred when a pilot changed direction too rapidly—were the predominant cause of accidental deaths. But at least there was a technique to recover from a stall; if it developed into a spin, death was all but inevitable. Yet what came to be known as 'aerobatics' had started almost immediately after the Wrights' first demonstration of controlled flight at Le Mans in 1908.

1909 saw the glamorous and spectacular Reims 'Grand Champagne Air Week', with all the trappings of a Derby race meeting or Henley Regatta, attended by Europe's leisured classes. In front of a vast crowd, Eugène Lefebre pushed a Wright Flyer to its limits, demonstrating figures of eight, steep dives, and turns where his wing-tip skimmed the grass and made photographers dive for cover. Aviation, this new sport of the wealthy, at once thrilled the masses. The following twelve months saw more than thirty air meets worldwide, with flying circuses formed to cash in on the new craze.

While aviation was seen in Europe as an exciting new sport, in America it soon became an arena for gladiatorial combats. As the sums American promoters offered for exhibition flights far exceeded the money that could be made from manufacturing and selling aircraft, both the Wright brothers and their bitter rival Glenn Curtiss quickly set up exhibition teams. Audiences wanted the spectacle of aeronauts visibly risking their lives, challenging each other to ever greater feats of daring. Flyers were driven by a mixture of potential wealth, competitiveness and adrenalin (one of the most reckless was Charles K. Hamilton, who suffered from tuberculosis and believed that, with few years left to live, he had little to lose). Unscrupulous promoters sometimes booked pilots into venues totally unsuitable for landing aircraft, and there were cases of audiences attacking planes or pilots when an advertised show was cancelled. As one of the Wrights' pilots, Ralph Johnstone, philosophically observed, 'The people who go to see us want thrills. And, if we fall, do they go away weeping? Not by a long shot. They're too busy watching the next man and wondering if he will repeat the performance.'

The greatest American stunter was Lincoln Beachey, a showman who had started his career barnstorming in balloons. Beachey became famous for flying aircraft under telegraph wires and tree branches—always dressed in an immaculate suit with a starched collar and diamond tiepin. At the climax of his act, he would climb to 5000 feet and dive vertically, pulling out of his 'death dip' so close to the ground that the spectators leapt to their feet in horror. When you consider that this was done in 1910, just two years after the Wrights' cautious demonstrations of turns, it is difficult to know whether to be horrified or impressed.

The death toll among stunt flyers mounted rapidly. The philosophical Ralph Johnstone died at a display in November 1910 when, during a steep bank following a vertical dive, the airframe on his Flyer collapsed. The band played on as spectators rushed on to the field and clawed for souvenirs: fragments of wood, scraps of fabric, Johnstone's gloves, his blood-sodden cap. The devout Wrights were appalled by the audience's blood lust, and after a string of spectacular deaths, they pulled out of exhibition flying. By the end of 1911 more than a hundred pilots and passengers had died in accidents. Aviation's age of innocence was over.

Lincoln Beachey survived until 1915, by which time he was the king of aerial stunters. Nicknamed the 'Master Birdman', he had performed before 17 million people in 126 cities and was earning a staggering $4000 a week. On 14 March 1915 he was persuaded to make a display before an audience of 50,000 in the prototype of a fast new monoplane that had been built to his own specifications. Monoplanes offer much less resistance to the air than braced and cross-strutted biplanes—and Beachey's monoplane proved even faster than he expected: its 'Velocity never exceed' was 103 mph, but in a dive Beachey found himself ripping through the sky over San Francisco Bay at 200 mph. There was a terrible crack as the wings folded backwards, and seconds later the plane plunged into the water and vanished. The 50,000 San Franciscan spectators apparently bared their heads in respect, a gesture Beachey might have taken a jaded view of. He had once said, 'They call me Master Birdman, but they pay to see me die.'

Today, air show organisers insist that it's all good clean fun. Is there a touch of hypocrisy in this? Modern aerobatic pilots, military and commercial, perform (for their own adrenalin-fuelled reasons) stunts that put them within split seconds of disaster—and don't air show spectators still secretly yearn to witness an accident? An ancient, instinctive part of us knows we are witnessing something *that should not be*. Surely these daredevils are committing hubris, like Icarus? Surely, sooner or later, they will provoke the gods into retribution? And that ancient part of us, the same part that loves all competitive sports—all sublimated, ritualised violence—would love to see the fall. TV channels would not screen programmes with titles like *The World's Worst Air Accidents*, replaying crashes in ghoulish slow motion, if there were no popular appetite for blood.

Perhaps a certain grim sense of balance is restored when the spectators become the victims. The first such was in 1913, when a woman stuck her head above the top of a marquee just as Lincoln Beachey accidentally hit it. When something really catastrophic happens, like the 1988 collision of three Italian display jets at a NATO air show in Germany, which sprayed the crowds with plumes of flaming aviation fuel, killing seventy and injuring 400, it is impossible not to be affected by the horror. But aren't the audiences at these hair-raising spectacles aware of the risks? Since the crash of a prototype de Havilland at the 1952 Farnborough Air Show when thirty people died, no spectator has been killed at a British air show—but pilots continue to die at the rate of 1.5 a year. A British magazine recently observed with breathtaking pomposity that 'the Air Show season was marred by three deaths . . . Fortunately neither incident caused injury to the public, though both had a significant effect on those present.' No word about the 'significant effect' on the pilots!

The greatest aerobatic innovator before World War I was the Frenchman Adolphe Pégoud, who was employed by Louis Blériot (the first man to fly across the English Channel) to test-fly his monoplanes. The programme required the fearless Pégoud to push the Blériots to their limits, including exploring the possibilities of inverted (upside-down) flight. Pégoud said of this manœuvre: 'I simply start coming down, stop the engine and push the steering pillar right forward until the machine has turned over on its back.' His modesty is disarming. He elaborated this astonishing advance in aerial manœuvrability into a variety of S-dives, half-rolls, tail-slides and spirals, and was soon earning £2000 a day in exhibitions.

Pégoud was not the only pilot pushing the envelope. The first tail slide (climbing, then allowing the plane to 'fly' backwards) had been attempted by the Englishman Will Rhodes Moorhouse in 1912. The Frenchman Maurice Chevillard invented what he called '*un* looping *hélicoidal*'—a very steeply banked climbing turn—which would soon become famous as the German Ace Max Immelman's pounce and escape: the Immelman Turn.

Until the start of hostilities in 1914, only a few far-sighted individuals (none of them in air ministries) believed that the aeroplane would revolutionize warfare. Flyers were pushing planes to their limits either to test them, or to thrill audiences. When in 1913 a military pilot killed himself trying to imitate Pégoud, the French war ministry embargoed 'acrobatic and dangerous feats of flying'. This led the British journal *The Aeroplane* to comment acerbically, 'It is clearly so much cheaper and

wiser to waste a few civilian lives on this sort of work.' It is extraordinary and somehow depressing that, even as a burst of innovation
held out the promise of a machine liberated to gambol in three
dimensions, 'informed' voices clung to the notion of an aeroplane as a
flying locomotive. At least *The Aeroplane*'s rival aviation journal, *Flight*,
exalted Pégoud for carrying out 'the most scientific flying exhibition
ever made'—and *Flight* had the right idea: manœuvrability would
prove the key to victory in aerial warfare. Also in 1913, when the
Russian pilot Lt Petr Nikolaevich Nesterov became the first man to
loop the loop, he was rewarded with close arrest for 'endangering
government property'. After he'd spent ten days in the can, belated
recognition of his achievement brought his immediate promotion to
staff captain.

Britain's best pre-war aerobat was Gustav Hamel, who was reputed
to have knocked off a policeman's helmet with his wing-tip and
whose loop-the-looping passengers included Winston Churchill.
Hamel's inverted flying skills were celebrated in January 1914 when
he was a guest of honour at the Hendon Aviators' 'Upside-Down
Dinner'. An inverted aeroplane was hung from the ceiling, guests sat
at upside-down tables whose legs gave the room the air of a
mahogany cloister, dinner began with coffee and liqueurs and ended
with soup, a music hall comedian performed standing on his head,
and the after-dinner speech began with the words 'And finally', and
ended with 'First of All'.

Hamel died in 1914, over the Channel. Petr Nikolaevich Nesterov
was to become one of the first fighter casualties of the war, when he
rammed his unarmed plane into an Austrian warplane, killing its crew
of two, and himself, on 8 September 1914. Adolphe Pégoud would
live to become a World War I Ace with six confirmed kills, and die
in aerial combat in 1915.

At the start of World War I, a pilot was more likely to be killed by
a stall-induced spin than enemy ordnance. The first pilot to survive a
spin was Fred Raynham, who in September 1911 accidentally put his
British-built Avro biplane into a near vertical dive, in which it made
two revolutions. He somehow escaped from the spin, but had no idea
how he'd managed it. The following August, Lt Wilfred Parke RN
accidentally entered a spin in another Avro. Displaying astonishing
presence of mind, he pushed the rudder away from the direction the

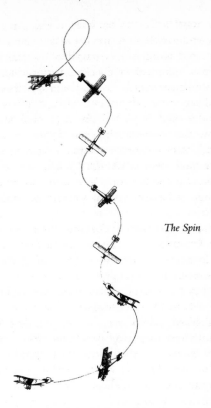

The Spin

plane was turning in—and 'broke' the spin. The Royal Aero Club Committee recommended investigating the phenomenon, but as *Flight* magazine commented, 'No one is going to risk voluntarily losing control of his machine in mid-air for the sake of demonstrating the facts.' Parke died in a crash soon afterwards and was unable to pass on in person a technique that would have saved many lives. In 1913 Geoffrey de Havilland accidentally entered a spin, but fortunately for him the spin 'went flat'—his aircraft began to revolve in the horizontal plane—and he was able to walk away from the crash. Few spin victims were so lucky; the frightening phenomenon continued to claim lives and to be the subject of superstitious awe.

As war began, pilots were still being advised officially to avoid aerobatics. They soon discovered that to survive in the twisting, zooming, aerial battles that became known as 'dogfights', they needed total knowledge of their planes. Aerobatic ignorance equalled death. The science of aerodynamics was still in its infancy, designers unable to offer any certainty about the flying performances of their machines. Pilots would energetically discuss the properties of aeroplanes—then take them up and try things out. Many deaths occurred in training, and more as pilots took the planes to their known limits of safe operation—then pushed them even further.

The first pilot *deliberately* to spin a plane was Harry Hawker, a young Australian who before the war had been one of the most gifted exhibition pilots in Britain. He became Sopwith's chief test pilot, where his emphasis on aerobatics helped Sopwith to create superbly manœuvrable aircraft which inspired a generation of wartime pilots. (After the war, Hawker was the first civilian to receive the Air Force Cross, and Sopwith went on to become, in his honour, Hawker Aircraft, builders of the famous Hurricane.) Pilots had their own theories about what made planes go into spins and what offered the best chances of recovery. Arguing one day in June 1914 about the probable spin recovery characteristics of Sopwith's new scout, the 'Tabloid', Hawker took the plane up and deliberately put it into a spin. His attempts to recover slowed the plane down enough for him to survive when it hit the ground. Determined, now, to master the secret of the spin, Hawker spent several days pondering the complex aerodynamics. His next deliberate spin was witnessed by the pilot Howard Pixton, who wrote,

I tried to dissuade him, told him it was plain suicide, but he took no notice.

The next day he took the machine up on what I expected was his last flight. He stalled, got into a spin and after several turns, the stall stopped and became a straight dive. He had conquered the spin simply by centralizing his controls. Aviation owes Harry Hawker a debt of gratitude.

In 1917 scientists at Farnborough finally worked out the spin's complex aerodynamics. Their recommendations: cut power, central-ize controls—as Parke and Hawker had already discovered. But by then, spinning not only held no fear for pilots, it had become a recognized technique for making a swift, vertical escape from an uncomfortable situation.

By 1916, an aerial arms race was in full swing. Aircraft reflected the intensive research and development both sides were putting into aerodynamics and armaments. Thousands of aircraft were being built and destroyed. In combat, inexperienced pilots were easy meat for experienced ones, and the Royal Flying Corps became the first force to set up a flying school which systematically taught aerobatics.

The School of Special Flying at Gosport was the brainchild of the extraordinary Major R. R. Smith-Barry. Against their will, aces were pulled back from the front line to give masterclasses. Smith-Barry's approach was brutally pragmatic: advanced pilots could fly however the hell they wanted to—the only limitations were their own nerves. Every known aerobatic technique was to be investigated and perfected. Every take-off and landing, every minute in the air, should simulate some combat or emergency condition, employing low-level flying and simulated damage to the controls. One Gosport graduate, Frank Courtney, recalled, 'I long ago gave up trying to describe the extreme degree of precision that we developed in doing everything with aeroplanes that could possibly be done—hardly anyone believes me . . . today, ten minutes of the old Gosport flying would cause any pilot to lose his licence.' Smith-Barry's unorthodox methods meant that fewer pilots arrived at the front with the near certainty of being dead within a fortnight.

Meanwhile, the designers' ideas about manœuvrability had resulted in the Sopwith Camel, an aeroplane one pilot described thus: 'totally unstable in all directions . . . a death-trap for an inexperienced pilot . . . [but] a skilled pilot could not wish for a better mount'.

After World War I, aerobatics were not only officially sanctioned, but codified. The test pilot Oliver Stewart wrote a *theory* of aerobatics. By the late 1920s the aeroplane held few mysteries for pilots.

I began by finding extreme attitudes both frightening and nauseating. By the time I had eighty hours of flying under my belt, putting the plane into a spiral gave me so much pleasure that when I thought about World War II pilots chucking a Spitfire into a dive my mouth began—literally—to water. (The closest I have come to that is sitting in the close cockpit of a Spit, an experience of man-machine intimacy so complete you feel it would be enough to *think* your intentions for the plane to fly.)

I have seen some of the greatest living exponents of aerobatics perform. Their routines make the strongest impression on a pilot; for the public, amazing aerobatic manœuvres are performed routinely in space movies, manufactured by computer geeks in California and Soho. But when, having painfully learned to coax a trainer horizontally through the sky, I saw other pilots make their tough little aerobatic planes zoom, tail slide in tight spins like tops, waddle down in flat, erratic spins like sycamore leaves, hover motionless, or tumble like burned moths, only to recover a few feet from the ground and surge skyward—I felt a profound awe. In fact, I felt tears in my eyes.

Six months after I had learned to fly, I sat in the observer's seat of that Fouga Magister over Auckland Bay, as Ken Walker put her through an aerobatic routine. The best experience you can have without taking your clothes off? Yes, but aerobatic flight is not really sexual—or not *merely* sexual; it takes possession of your entire being, it is overwhelmingly physical, but also rational, emotional and spiritual.

I have yet to study aerobatics—the vast majority of pilots never do; but can we really claim to be able to fly?

There is a photograph taken at the French National Air Show in 1951, which probably eclipses anything one could write about aerobatics. The show's organisers had decided to hold the show not over an aerodrome, but, for the first time, over the azure waters of the Med. The brilliant French aerobatic pilot Fred Nicole felt he could not let the occasion go by without producing something a little out of the ordinary. Before a huge crowd in front of the Carlton Hotel, he inverted his biplane and flew past the promenade with the tip of his tail fin cutting the water, leaving a wake of white foam.

CHAPTER XI

Happy Landings

Q: What's your definition of a good landing?
A: One you can walk away from.

Pilot's joke.

TAXIING UP TO TAKE-OFF one morning, the plane suddenly skewed to the left. I shut the engine down and went to look for Paul, the mechanic. I found him with his head inside the body of a dismembered Cessna.

'Paul, I have a situation.'

'Whassat?'

'Left brake locked on taxi.'

He pulled himself out of the fuselage, wiped his hands on his overalls and picked up a hammer.

'Is that what you need?' I asked.

'Fixes most things.'

He beat the brake pads and, achieving no result, grunted and stuck his head under the dashboard. I went to find a coat against the autumn winds. When I returned, Paul was smiling. 'Brakes had locked. You're lucky they didn't lock a couple of minutes later, when you were landing. Woulda spun you right off the runway.'

'Oh. Is it safe now?'

Again the inscrutable smile. 'Safe is a relative term, my friend. I used to have a flying licence; but then I wised up!'

Before you can qualify for your Private Pilot's Licence, you have to have done a long cross-country flight. You have to do this without electronic assistance from the technical miracle that's now so common place it's a feature in hikers' wristwatches: the Global

Positioning Satellite, or GPS. You fly cross-country the way a World War I flyer did, with a folded map on your lap and a compass.

Your first decision involves altitude: at 1000 feet it's surprisingly easy to confuse features in the landscape and get lost, so ideally you climb to something like 6000 feet, from which angelic perspective major features like lakes and towns can be read with the clarity of a giant map, spotted and identified thirty miles and perhaps twenty minutes before you reach them. But while it is forbidden to fly in low cloud, there can be other factors that impede navigation.

On this particular October day, you take off and discover that the entire surface of the earth is smeared with a yellow-white haze that makes rivers visible only at certain angles—when the sun ricochets off them—and only for an instant. Roads quickly merge into other roads, villages into other villages, and it's obvious that you're going to need to climb until you can see the big lakes. Up you go and there they are, oblate blobs you peer at and compare with the elongated forms on your map.

You have never ventured here before. You peer into the smear of glaucous mist for the precise web of suburban roads that will confirm that this town is Gravenhurst and not Uffington. You are not expected to land at Muskoka, merely to overfly the airfield. You radio the tower and, having left objective evidence of your passing, turn east.

Your track cuts through the southernmost shore of that inland sea, Lake Huron. Your headphones are a Babel of pilots' voices, some quiet and crackling—and therefore reassuringly remote—but others loud and even, chillingly, mentioning the names of airports you are close to. Nervously, you commit your own intentions to the aviation ether and keep your eyes open, while pilots who (unlike you) know what they're doing whizz by, busy, rapid specks. Here, fifty miles north of your departure point, the air is drier and the landscape concomitantly sharper-etched. Visibility. Thank God.

You have to land at the next aerodrome: Collingwood. You are carrying your Canadian Flight Supplement (an unexotic title for what is, in fact, your Bible, your *Bhagavadgita*, your green-jacketed Qu'ran, which, reissued bi-monthly, its 1000 pages of cheap paper rich-smelling of wood pulp, is fat with aerodrome maps, abbreviations, acronyms, runway lengths, crosswind limits, radio frequencies, radio beacons, information signals, military signals, details of the military interception of civilian aircraft, and all-you-need-to-know about ditching at sea and search-and-rescue—keep it by your bed, my boy, and read it every night, this cult book may not *change* your life, but it might *save* it). Your Supplement shows you a map of the drome. What you have to do is announce your arrival, approach from the correct direction and at the correct height—avoiding other traffic— enter the circuit, make your turns at the correct points, land, taxi, shut down, climb out, saunter into the clubhouse and drink a free cup of coffee. Cast a casual eye over the notice-board with its bland news of barbecues and car boot sales. But such mundane matters are not for you—you have to climb back into a small plane and pilot it through vaporous skies. You drink *another* coffee, go to the toilet, then, having no legitimate reason to delay, take off and fly south along the third leg of this cross-country trapezium, towards Toronto.

You are looking for power lines—and there they are, almost parallel to your track for ten miles. Where you part company with the lines, someone at Linvic told you, there should be a cottage—yes, there it is—and you look down and wonder if the owners know their rôle as a pilots' signpost, a lodestar.

As you head south, a smear of mist again coats everything like icing sugar. Your calculations have put you on target for your next trial, a touch-and-go (landing followed by immediate take-off) at Oshawa, a small commercial airport in east Toronto busy with air schools and charter planes, and complete with Air Traffic Control. You have descended to the correct height to enter the circuit; you request the Air Traffic Controller for permission to touch-and-go and he mumbles something back at you. Minutes later, as you prepare to enter the circuit, the Controller's furious voice barks out of your headphones: 'Echo Foxtrot, make an immediate 180-degree turn and turn right at the power lines for a direct approach on three-zero.'

What the *hell* is he *talking* about? (As you dip your wing and turn, highways and business parks revolve sickeningly in the weak, acidic sunshine.) Then the penny drops: he was *trying* to help you, giving you a direct approach from the north instead of making you join the circuit box and approach from the south like everyone else. But he *mumbled* his help, the fool! And now—which God- and Christ- damned *power lines* is he on about?

Luckily you've flown here once before and you remember that

'the power lines' are a local landmark. But you're in mid-turn, your sense of direction is uncertain, there are intersecting power lines everywhere—no, look, those ones are east–west, parallel to the Lake Ontario shoreline, it must be *this* ugly knot of struts and giant ceramic insulators he means. Keep your nerve! You are descending, suburban factory roofs and ant strings of cars are rising to meet you, remember how to fly, now: descend, descend, *round out*, touch down, steady, keep straight—*full power* and you're up again, climbing, turn left, away from the traffic, the charter jets, help-mumbling Mr Angry Controller, out into the empty green. In a few minutes you recognise the familiar landmarks of home—Lake Scucog, Sturgeon Lake. Your nerves are slowly calming. Sweet Jesus. Panic in the skies.

COMM		
ATF	tfc 123.2 3NM 3000 ASL	
CAUTION	Trees & marked hydro pole 40 AGL adj NE to thld rwy 13. Gliding area 4NM W.	

OSHAWA ON	CYOO	
REF	N43 55 22 W78 53 42 Adj N 11°W UTC-5(4) Elev 459′ VTA A5000 F-21 LO6 T2 HI5 CAP	
OPR	Muni 905-576-8146 Cert 1130-0330Z‡ O/T PPR.	
PF	B-1,2,6 C-3,4,5	
CUST	AOE-R/50 888-226-7277 PNR	
FLT PLN	NOTAM FILE CYOO Pilots are requested to open & close flt plans with Toronto/Buttonville Municipal FSS on 126.7/123.15 above 3000 AGL or by phone.	
FSS	W1 800-INFO FSS	
PATWAS	416-973-8973, 905-477-9219, 800-387-0444	
SERVICES		
FUEL	80, 100LL, JA-1	
OIL	All	
S	1,2,3,4,5	
PVT ADV	Enterprise Air Inc 131.05; Roaero 123.5; Shell Fuels 129.1	

Your Bible, your Bhagavadgita, *your green-jacketed Qu'ran . . .*

I burned the midnight oil and travelled, crippled with nerves, to the Transport Canada building in Toronto. 'Just relax,' Tim had told me. 'You probably know more than you know you know.' After the three-hour theory exam, I had a shock: I had got through, with 81 per cent—the pass mark is 60 per cent. Tim had been right, and my shock victory gave my confidence a meteoric boost.

But another impediment lay in my path. I discovered that the practical flying test had to be booked in advance, and if the weather on the day prevented flying, it might be a week before a retest could be arranged. And Penny would be arriving for the promised flying holiday any day. I had, as Tim had always said, backed myself into a ridiculous corner.

As it turned out, Penny had already been in Canada for three days by the time I was able to do the flight test. It was a miserable day of low cloud and drizzle, and I have not been so sick with nerves since A Levels. I flew much less well than I should have; I flew *badly*. As the test continued, my spirits plummeted. Towards the end the examiner, John Robertson, asked me to make an approach from the *opposite direction* to the customary one at Linvic—one-three (130 degrees) instead of three-one (310 degrees). A reasonable request, but I had only done anticlockwise, southerly circuits of the aerodrome, never a clockwise, northerly one. My mind went blank. John asked me with ominous calm to land as I normally did. It had been ninety minutes of sheer misery.

In fact, as with the theory exam, I had done far better than I thought. John told me I had a 'partial' pass. After two days of intensive circuit practice I did a ten-minute re-flight, landed impressively on one-three, and was pronounced a licenced—recreational—pilot. 'You're at pass level,' John told me, adding with feeling, 'But if you have any ideas about qualifying for a PPL in the near future, for God's sake get up there and practice!'

I had a licence—to kill, as the old flying joke goes. If Penny had any doubts about my ability to fly her safely after so few hours of instruction, she didn't show them. *I* had doubts. It was going to be my first flight where the person beside me in the cockpit wasn't a qualified flying instructor. I took off as smoothly as I knew how, and luck was with me—the air was preternaturally still that afternoon. I pointed the nose at the blue expanse of Lake Simco, and banked low over pocket-sized islands carpeted with trees flaming red and gold, with clapboard summerhouses and rowboats swinging at anchor. Suddenly I noticed Penny groping at the dashboard. She had located something I had not even known the plane possessed: a glove compartment and, within it, a specially placed greased-paper bag—into which she discreetly vomited.

At the end of our first flight I executed an equally deft landing. I *was* a pilot, dammit! We began a comparative study of different brands of air-sickness tablets.

It is no coincidence that recreational flying is largely a preserve of the wealthy. Consider the following two trips: the first was a Bank Holiday drive to Niagara Falls, eight hours in traffic jams and it rained. The same trip a week later by plane, in brilliant sunshine: we looked down airily on the clumsy, freeway-clogging cars, unable to comprehend why anyone would want to use one of the things. Air Traffic in Toronto directed us over the city centre (unthinkable in a small plane in London), towards the CN Tower—the world's tallest building—which we passed at merely 2500 feet, with half the structure looming over us. We flew then in precise circles over the Niagara Falls, with only helicopters, skittering like dragonflies, between us and the jade-green waters.

It is one thing to take off and fly a plane, quite another to land it. Sometimes I made perfect, smooth landings (it's called 'greasing it'), other times I fouled them up, meeting the ground with the aviation equivalent of a bellyflop; the process seemed unpredictable, patternless.

I was to learn that the perfect landing is the philosopher's stone of aviation. According to statistics, 40 to 50 per cent of accidents occur during the last few seconds of flight.

Landing is the principal activity commercial pilots get paid for. Few commercial runways are overlong and pilots are required to land within extremely exacting height and airspeed parameters. Commercial pilots are assisted in landing by technical aids not found at training airstrips; still, nervous passengers may not thank me for saying that the relative rarity of landing accidents in airliners is a reflection not of the boundless safety of commercial aviation, but of intensive pilot training and incessant refresher courses. Experience is everything. (And the bigger, long-established airlines generally have far more experienced pilots than, for example, the newer 'low-cost' operators.)

Trainee pilots build up their landing experience by flying endless circuits—rectangles around the airstrip, with half a dozen take-offs and landings per hour. To do a circuit (like the one described in Chapter VIII), you take off and 'climb out' to around 500 feet, make a 90 degree turn on to the 'crosswind leg' and continue to climb; approaching 1000 feet, you level off and make a second 90 degree turn on to the 'downwind leg' (you're now parallel to the runway, in the opposite direction to your take-off); a third 90 degree brings you on to the 'base leg', where you begin your descent; and a fourth 90 degree brings you on to 'final approach', where you're descending in the same direction from which you took off.

In the course of the turns from downwind to base and base to finals, you're putting down your flaps, which disturb the airflow over the wings and act like brakes. A good landing has already begun with these last two turns, because if the plane was positioned correctly, the finals should go well. But the medium through which you are moving is protean. The air temperature and humidity fluctuate; the wind's strength and direction change from minute to minute, and also vary at different heights. Even the plane's weight plays a rôle, since it is lighter when carrying no passengers and when it has burned off a significant amount of fuel.

Often, misjudged turns owing to slightly misjudged speed or power settings (I had a fondness either for putting in too much flap, or forgetting the flaps altogether) mean that your final approach begins not in line with the runway, but off to one side. The resulting need to veer back on to track, while maintaining a correct glide angle, turns your plans for the perfect 'greaser' into an uncertain crabbing grope towards the ground.

Assume, however, that the plane is perfectly aligned with the runway: you have to control its attitude (angle) and engine power to achieve the correct speed and angle of descent. There's very little visual information to help—your descent starts perhaps 8000 feet from the runway threshold and 1000 feet up, from which viewpoint the foreshortened tarmac is a tiny black rhomboid.

As that rhomboid swells, its proportions tell you about your approach: the runway should resemble a stolid capital 'A'; but if it's a very elongated **A**, you are overshooting—at risk of touching down in the middle or even at the end of the runway. A squashed **A** means an undershoot—the plane's glide path is too steep, terminating at the fence or trees before the runway threshold. Alan Bramson, the author of a classic textbook on landings, learned to fly in an open-cockpit RAF Tiger Moth. He had a bad habit of undershooting, until one day during a landing his instructor, sitting in the front seat, undid his seatbelt and stood up. These were the days before intercoms, and an alarmed Branson had to yell into the Gosport Tube (shades of a Victorian country house), 'What are you doing, sir?' His instructor replied, 'I'm going to open the bloody gate to let you in!'

Just before touchdown, the plane's nose has to be raised, a manœuvre called the 'round-out'. The height at which you do this is critical and—since altimeters are not accurate enough to be trusted—almost entirely intuitive. Come in too fast and you 'fly into the ground', bouncing, or, if you're really unlucky, 'ballooning' high into the air, only to lose all lift and drop like a pig. More hazardous is 'wheelbarrowing', where the nose is too low and the plane's centre of gravity pivots around the nosewheel, which can result in a wing-tip hitting the ground, or, even nastier, a somersault.

I think it's true to say that rounding out is the hardest (because most skilled) part of flying, the part tyro pilots most dislike. Barely a month into my training, trying to position the plane accurately as, at seventy knots, the unforgiving earth rushed up at me, seemed as much a question of luck as judgement.

Now that I was licenced to carry a passenger, I could go flying with other pilots and save the cost of instruction. One man I flew with often was Alastair, the former Belfast taxi driver. We'd spend an hour or two up in the air, then repair at dusk to the nylon snugs of The Grand, smoke some cigarettes and put away a jug each of beer.

It was Alastair who taught me how to land. I'd done about ten landings with him beside me, most of them OK, two or three of them terrible, and we'd sat in the café going through the gamut—coax the plane to *stop flying* at the precise moment you reach the ground, perfect combination of speed and engine power, don't stare at the runway ahead, peripheral vision for a three-dimensional sense of space. We went up again, did a circuit and I came down with an almighty thump. Dispirited, I took off again.

Alastair, who had been looking suitably miserable on my behalf, was suddenly pensive. 'You know,' he said, 'I've just remembered what my first instructor told me when I was having problems landing. He said, "Look at the end of the runway. Forget every other bloody thing, just look at the *end* of the runway." So, you see that brick box down there? Next time we come round, look at it. That'll get your eyes into the right, I dunno, focal length or some bloody thing. Jus' try it!'

It worked. I fixed my attention on the brick box at the end of the runway and suddenly the whole field ahead of me clicked into three-dimensional focus; I had the accurate sense of height that had always eluded me. Satori!

When I tried to share this epiphany with the other pilots at Linvic, they merely shrugged, as though I was communicating the most obvious and pathetic thing in the world, child's play, *they* had never had trouble landing. Well, they could go to hell. Landing held no fear for me now, and I was bloody happy about it.

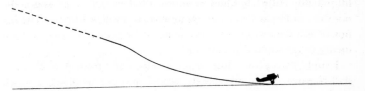

One morning, Alastair and I set off early by floatplane. He had his floatplane rating and was building up his hours. Landing on floats is a particular skill, because if you came down horizontal, the sudden increase in friction at the forward end of the floats might cause the plane to somersault. The technique, therefore, is to approach with the plane at a nose-up angle, dip the aft end of the floats in the water to slow you down, *then* let the plane settle forward. The other subtlety involves calculating altitude, since water can resemble glass, its reflectiveness sending out utterly misleading signals about height.

As Alastair explained all this, I felt relieved I was there not to fly, but to observe. We headed north, with our sandwiches and thermos, beyond the snowline. Sectioned and tamed rural Ontario yielded to a wilderness of glacially exposed rock, spare pines and fingery lakes. The blue sky glittered, the blue water glittered, the carpet of forest was splattered with gold and crimson. Reaching some remote lake far from any human habitation, we would overfly it under tree level, peering into the crystal water for submerged rocks. Then, on our second pass, Alastair would set the floatplane down. We'd take off again with a thrilling run the length of the lake, soar to just over tree height and fling a sharp turn to skim across the treetops in search of another sleek silver lake to perch on.

Winter was approaching inexorably. The days were growing shorter and breezier—less good for flight. The appearance of pumpkins on every porch told us that Hallowe'en was imminent.

My time was running out, as was my money. I had a recreational licence, but I had come to Canada to get a full PPL. I faced two final tests, which I *had to* get right: my Private Pilot's written exam and flight test. By now, I'd flown Cessnas hundreds of miles across Canada. I had landed on remote grass airstrips and large airport runways. With a sense of dread, I travelled back to Toronto for the full-length written test and again surprised myself by passing comfortably. Tim was right: I knew more than I knew I knew. The last hurdle was the flight test—was I going to be good enough? I did not intend to go home without a PPL.

I could fly a plane more or less competently from A to B, but I was nervous. With any activity where risks are involved, a touch of fear and adrenalin are inevitable and even useful, to ward off overconfidence. But I lacked self-confidence—I couldn't shake off the nagging feeling that it could all slip away from me.

The week before my flight test, I developed an ear infection. I assumed it was a recurrence of a nasty bug I'd picked up in the Amazon two years earlier, since which time an area of jaw beneath my left ear had been permanently numb. The symptoms came on in the course of an afternoon, and by evening, when I found a doctor, I was shivering with fever. The doctor concluded that the constant pressure changes of flying had caused the resurgence of the dormant infection. He scribbled a note for antibiotics and painkillers and told me not to fly for three weeks. Thank you, doctor.

For a couple of days it hurt like hell. On the third day, I went flying—the flight test was booked and I was damned if I was going to cancel it. I swallowed painkillers all day long, but what I could not control was the stream of yellow gunge that oozed out of my ear. At night, I slept with towels over my pillow; by morning, they were sodden and there was a stiff crust all over my cheek. After a flight, my shirt would be soaked. Naturally this situation disgusted and alarmed the instructors, so I tried to hide it. The pressure variations during flying were painful, especially anything involving rapid height changes—and I was trying to perfect my spins and spirals. My balance was affected, too, making landings difficult again.

For a week there was no apparent improvement in the infection. My flying was appalling. I would go up for revision sessions and land 90 or 120 minutes later feeling I'd done worse than before. I took my mock test on a brilliant, cold morning, with my head bursting and the left half of my face numb. My flying stank; the instructors were reluctant to sign the papers formally recommending me for the test.

On the day, I woke up and realised I was feeling a lot better. My head still throbbed, but there were pills for that; the ear still seeped, but a barrier of cotton wool was enough to staunch the flow. I took off for a two-hour refresher and found that my head was clear, and that my skills and confidence were returning. Elated, though still nervous, I shook hands with John Robertson, who knew I was going back to England in a few days, and had made an effort to fit me in at short notice.

I went into the toilets and swallowed a handful of codeine. We took off. My main problem was a tendency to gain or lose height beyond the acceptable hundred-foot parameters, and John brusquely drew my attention to this. Then he upset me profoundly by forcing me to take out my slide rule and calculate the distance to my next waypoint. It is far from easy to read figures on to the tiny scales of a slide rule while trying to fly a plane straight and level. John dismissed my protests with a curt, 'This is *real* flying—this could happen to you in an emergency one day, you need to be able to do it.'

As we taxied towards the apron at the end of the exam, I blurted some tentative heart-in-mouth utterance along the lines of, 'When are you going to tell me how I did?'

'Oh, you *passed*,' he said. He sounded surprised.

We went up to the café and ordered coffee. John looked straight at me. 'Martin, I'll be honest with you, I was not looking forward to this. After your flying the other week—frankly, I was expecting to fail you.' He studied his score card for a couple of minutes and his eyes widened. He grinned. 'This is a good score—nearly commercial standard. I never imagined you could reach private pilot level so quickly. Well—congratulations.'

Despite the halo of success which now, I was convinced,

shimmered around me, alerting every shop assistant and petrol pump attendant to the presence of that chivalric hero, a *licenced pilot*, I felt sheepish about my faltering progress. I was shamed by the extra-ordinary speed with which I'd seen youngsters of seventeen and nineteen get the feel of a plane, embarrassed that I'd had to sweat blood to master the complexities of slide rule, navigation and meteorology.

The day after I passed my test, I was sitting alone in the café when Adam, the chief instructor, came in and joined me. 'Heard you did it,' he said. 'Shake your hand.' He ordered a coffee and lit a cigarette. 'Got your test results there?' I handed the sheaf of papers over. 'Well done,' he said, having scanned them. 'You're a pilot now.'

'It was an effort, Adam. Far harder than I expected.'

He frowned sceptically. 'You knew nothing when you got here, right? Some joyrides?'

'Right.'

He plucked a speck of tobacco from his lower lip and pointed the two fingers holding the cigarette at me. 'You've absorbed a shitload of theory and got a good pass in the theory paper and got through your practical with a damn good score. From nowhere to a pilot in a month and a half. Fuck it, man, you can be proud of that.'

So I am.

My memories of Lindsay and northern Ontario are bird's-eye views. I became familiar with the winding courses of the marshy rivers around Lindsay, the pea-soup lakes. My most memorable flight was a few days after I had gained my licence, just before I left Canada.

It stirred me (it still does) to wake up and see the leather wallet with 'Pilot Licence' printed on it in gold, sitting on the bedside table. A deep layer of frost had dusted every surface white that morning, there was a bright and cloudless sky. I drove along roads blanketed with red and golden maple leaves, no one around but a cycling newsboy and the milkman. At the aerodrome I tugged my plane into the sun's first copper rays, and as they melted the fine layer of iced dew on the wings I completed the flyer's ritual, checking ailerons and rudder and poking a length of dowelling into the fuel tanks to be sure that the cockpit gauges didn't lie.

Climb in, headphones on, fire her up, taxi on to the runway. Add full power and the engine is almost brutally alive, the prop jerking the trembling fuselage forward as you accelerate to 2,200 rpm. At around fifty-five knots you ease back the stick—and weightlessness, gravity defiance, the instant miracle of flight; the landscape falling away from you, emerald streaked with early-morning gold.

PART II

CHAPTER XII

Night Mail I: To Stornoway

A T FIVE O'CLOCK on a frozen January morning, on the apron of Glasgow airport, I was standing under the high, strutted wing of a Logan Air Shorts 360, stamping my feet against the cold. A man appeared, a big bear of a man with a salt-and-pepper moustache, crinkly eyes and the reassuring presence of a priest—indeed, the black Loganair overcoat was so long it might have been a cassock. And Captain Morrisson was about to celebrate a rite: the pre-flight check. As he began patiently prodding the plane's nether regions with the beam of a pen torch and scanning its wings for ice, I followed him and his litany. Jack Morrisson emanated such competence and decency I somehow knew that with him at the helm, nothing could possibly go wrong.

We climbed aboard and squeezed into the cockpit, past scores of grey mail sacks trapped behind webbing. Morrisson told me to cram myself into the spare seat, the fold-down, groin-splitting 'jump seat' behind his left elbow, where my proximity to the plane's bank of circuit breakers gave me a spurious sense of importance. A few minutes later we were rolling at full power down the runway, its lights a flood of electric colour. At a hundred knots First Officer Mike Jardine took us up. The sodium rectangles of nocturnal Glasgow receded. At 500 feet, 120 knots, we banked tightly to the right. Soon we left the saffron glow of the city behind us and pointed our nose into the north-western darkness. Jardine set course for a place that's pregnant with Shipping Forecast mystique: Benbecula. At 3500 feet and 140 knots we settled into a cruise. Jardine turned to me. 'Lovely plane to fly, the Shorts,' he said. 'Looks like a flying freight container, but handles like a light aircraft.'

Short Brothers were the world's first aircraft manufacturers, and this, the Belfast-built 360, was the last plane to leave their production line. The company had been founded in Sussex in 1901, to manufacture balloons for military spotting. In 1908 the brothers Eustace, Oswald and Horace Short signed an agreement with Wilbur and Orville Wright to manufacture six Flyers under licence. The Wrights had always seen military spotting as the most immediate and profitable application of their flying machine, and hoped this link with the Shorts might be the start of a lucrative relationship with the armed forces of the Empire. But the explosion of aeroplane manufacture after 1908 quickly rendered the Flyer obsolete. By 1909 Short Brothers had launched a biplane of their own design and, while the Wrights' dreams of volume production went nowhere, Shorts became one of the world's principal aircraft manufacturers. They invented the air-launched torpedo and the folding wing that allowed aircraft to be carried aboard ships.

The company's apotheosis was its family of Empire flying boats, which linked the outflung limbs of the British Empire. These legendary leviathans included the much-loved Sunderland, which during World War II hunted U-boats and conducted search-and-rescue for downed RAF crews. After the war, however, a new generation of long-range airliners made flying boats obsolete almost overnight, and Shorts's fortunes plummeted. Today, the company still survives: it supplies fuselages for the glamorous Lear Jet and manufactures a missile called the Starburst, which, it proclaims, uses 'laser beam-riding guidance for enhanced lethality'. 'Lethality' may have improved with the years, but Shorts haven't built a complete aeroplane since 1991: the 360, a ribbed, square-section utility plane designed to carry thirty-six passengers in an unpressurised cabin at just 8000 feet. The rectangular fuselage provided superb headroom and Shorts commissioned the interior designer responsible for Boeing's 747 to give the plane a trendy look—lots of orange polyester. It also sold well to the US military as a troop carrier. By the time production ceased, 343 had been built and most of them are still flying, somewhere in the world.

'Look at that,' said Jardine. 'The full moon, just appearing behind the clouds.'

'You get very clear light up here in the Highlands, you know,' Morrisson added.

'Aye,' agreed Jardine.

An air of contentment had settled over the cockpit, as we scudded across the moonlit islands of the Inner Hebrides.

'We have one colleague who's just joined us after doing the Amsterdam–Caribbean route,' Morrisson went on, 'but he much prefers this. Can't get enough of it.'

Commercial pilots aren't *meant* to have fun; passengers like their flying *un*exciting, as predictable as pre-election tax cuts. I asked what made it so enjoyable.

'We're flying without autopilot. Up here, we fly VFR—Visual Flight Rules—which means flying visually, making your own decisions in terms of turning, climbing, descending. Ask an airline pilot: they take off, get a few thousand feet up and on goes the autopilot. Then they sit back and watch the instruments, making sure no one in the back gets a glass of Chardonnay in their lap. This is different. *Much* more fun than a 747.'

Earlier that night I'd travelled from London to Glasgow by British Airways, in an aircraft with the numinous words 'Royal Mail' stencilled on its fuselage. At 5 a.m. Glasgow's Western Highlands sorting office, a covered space the size of a football stadium, was alive with the unnatural intensity that accompanies work in the wee hours when everyone else is asleep. Fleets of red vans funnelled mail into whirling turbines, which sorted them centrifugally by size and weight. Addresses and postcodes were read electronically; any envelope with an illegible address was frozen before a camera which transmitted its image to a human team in a lab-white mezzanine. Mechanical caterpillars wound the sorted mail across the vastness of the sorting-factory floor, towards another rank of vans where postmen hurled them aboard, then—grateful to be off into the night and not prisoners of the caterpillars or the screens—hastened towards all points of north-west Scotland.

I, too, was soon in an overheated mail van, driving the deserted motorway towards the airport. I'd persuaded the Royal Mail to let me fly with their pilots to some of the remotest postboxes in the British Isles. Security was intense. At barbed-wired gates a gruff man known as 'Big Jim' squinted closely at my ID and insisted on double-checking with his HQ before issuing me a time-specific pass. A security escort accompanied the van on to the apron. Then, three waiting men began to hurl the Outer Hebrides' First Class mail into the plane's hold (second class travels steerage: by boat). The three worked like Furies—not least, to keep warm.

An hour later, the sky was starting to gain texture as the 360 began its descent on Benbecula. The airport runway had been aligned by some deranged surveyor with the only two peaks for miles around. 'It's ideal in fog,' observed Mike. There was ice on the runway as we landed, and we taxied gingerly to the apron where another triumvirate of postal workers, cheerfully whistling and swearing, attacked the grey sacks. By the time we had unloaded, the sky was rosy. Then we were northbound, the sun fiery off our starboard wing, across the waters of the Minch to Lewis.

Scotland is bisected by a gash running north-east to south-west, Lochs Ness, Lochy and Linnhe and the Murray Firth almost severing the north-west Highlands from the rest of Britain. Beyond this hard wedge of mountains is a strip of water fifteen to thirty miles wide—the Minch—and beyond it, the islands known as the Outer Hebrides. They depend on the declining industries of sheep-raising, tweed production and shipbuilding, and in summer on tourism. It is uneconomic for the Royal Mail to serve these islands by air; the reasons for doing so are political, with roots in the decision taken in 1839 to standardize the 'penny post' throughout Britain.

At Stornoway, I joined the van carrying the deliveries to the sorting office. I had arranged to meet the man in charge of the Western Isles mails.

A postman showed me into Eddie Mackenzie's office, and a cheerful man looked up from the desk. 'Good morning,' he said. 'You'll be wanting some breakfast, I suppose?'

I protested about interrupting his work.

'It's all right, I normally take a break about now.' He grabbed his coat. 'There's a place round the corner.' He held out his hand. 'I'm Eddie, by the way.'

We walked to a small square opposite the docks. 'I usually go to the *Coffee Pot*,' Eddie said. 'It's run by a family of Italians who came after the war.' We stepped into an atmosphere that could not have been less like an Italian bar. The *Coffee Pot* had adapted its decor, as well as its menu, to indigenous norms. We queued with our trays before a wall of glass cabinets containing white rolls. Urns steamed and ladies in catering tabards crashed white duralite cups on to saucers, scraped margarine on to spongy tablets of white bread and shovelled baked beans and deep-fried eggs.

Eddie greeted a group of men sitting with their mugs around a long table. He winked at me and murmured discreetly, 'Alcoholics Anonymous. They get together here every morning. Mutual support—help each other keep out of the pub.'

We sipped our un-Italianly watery coffee and stared through the steamy windows at the docks. It looked quiet out there.

'Oh, aye,' said Eddie. 'Not much fishing nowadays. It'll be busier when the tourists arrive.'

'But the rest of the year?'

'Like this. And everything stops on a Sunday, y'know. No ferries, no planes, no shops open. Hotels closed. Even the golf course is closed. No Sunday papers—they come on Monday afternoon off the ferry. Basically, everyone goes to chuch, observes the Sabbath.'

'Everyone?'

'Aye. Even those who don't go to church still observe the Sabbath.'

'It sounds restful.'

'It is, aye, Sunday's a lovely day. There's plenty that would like to change it, of course. The ferry company would. But the Church is strongly against a change and the ferries haven't been ready to upset the Church.'

'What about you?'

'I hope it stays the way it is. It has its inconveniences, but it's so much a part of life here. Everybody copies everybody else in this world. "Commercial pressures." I hope we stay the way we are.'

I wondered if the rise of the Internet had brought a decline in post services.

'No, quite the contrary, as a matter of fact. We deliver a lot of parcels, you see. There's a limit to what local shops can carry, so mail order catalogues have always been big up here. Nowadays, people are ordering stuff from the Internet. There may be fewer personal letters, but in terms of volume, we're doing better than ever before.'

The first aircraft to land in Stornoway was an RAF seaplane, which caused a stir when it settled in the harbour in 1928. At that time the only communication between islands was by boat, five hours to the Kyle of Lochalsh or fifteen to Glasgow. It wasn't until 1933 that a

conventional plane landed here, on the flat, springy turf of the golf links. Still no regular passenger service was inaugurated, and the Post Office did not think there was enough post to the islands to justify airmail deliveries.

Airmail was slow to start in Britain—as was aviation. After World

War I Germany, forbidden by the Treaty of Versailles from building military aircraft, found an outlet for national pride and technical progress in commercial aviation. Seven civil airlines were founded there in 1919, six more in 1920. The Germans were the first to introduce all-metal airliners, in-flight movies and sleeping berths. Forbidden to fly their planes in their own airspace, they flew them all over Eastern Europe. By 1930 Germany's innovative airlines were carrying 120,000 passengers a year—as many as Britain, France and Italy combined. France was Europe's second leader in aviation, with a policy of fierce subsidy it has pursued ever since. Britain, suspicious of subsidy then as now, lagged behind, to the consternation of many, including the air-minded Winston Churchill. But in 1924 Britain combined its struggling small airlines into a single, state-subsidised national carrier: Imperial Airways.

America also made a slow start in the aviation industry, but certain high-placed visionaries saw airmail as the potential vanguard of a new transport industry. In 1920 the US Post Office launched airmail services using its own fleet of aircraft, beginning with converted British de Havilland World War I bombers. The explicit aim was to work towards a coast-to-coast service, though the notion that these slow, low-flying aircraft might span an entire continent seemed far-fetched. The attempt to maintain regular flights across deserts and mountains was a perilous business. It gave rise to a breed of tough pilots who flew in relays, taking their inspiration from the legendary Pony Express. There were frequent accidents—for example, Charles Lindbergh had to bail out of his mail plane when he ran out of fuel in fog banks over Chicago. Purpose-built mail planes (like the cutely-named Curtiss Carrier Pigeon) began to appear, and by 1925 the US Post Office's fleet of a hundred aircraft had cut the time from New York to San Francisco to around thirty hours, knocking a full day off the rail time. There were commercial voices, however, which opposed the public subsidy of aviation. This led to the privatisation of mail flights and the birth of the American 'Big Four' airlines—TWA, United, Eastern and American. But Post Office subsidy had helped American aviation make a great leap forward. By the mid-1930s the USA could be crossed in just thirteen hours, in the revolutionary airliner that was to become a legend of World War II and the Berlin Airlift, christened by the RAF the Dakota: the Douglas DC-3.

The archetypal aeroplane: the DC-3 Dakota

In 1927, Pan American Airways was set up to fly international airmail. America was anxious about German and French transatlantic mail flights to South America. International postal services were now 'flag carriers', cloaks for governments to probe one another's spheres of influence as well as stimuli for domestic aviation industries. Britain, France, Belgium, Holland and all the imperial countries made communications within their empires a priority. Subsidized mail flights began to Brazzaville and Nairobi, New Delhi and Singapore, Hong Kong and Sydney. By the late 1930s vast new flying boats were rushing the mail across the Atlantic Ocean and even the vast Pacific.

In Europe, airmail began to replace rail on the longest international routes. By 1937, even the cost-conscious and reluctant British Post Office was forced to accept that some European airmail was inevitable. So it was that after the war, on 12 February 1948, deliveries to the Outer Hebrides began.

It was a BEA (British European Airways) de Havilland Dragon Rapide that inaugurated the service to Stornoway. There's a Tintin quality to the Rapide, a biplane whose sleek, art deco lines perfectly capture the spirit of early aviation. Hundreds of Rapides came on to the second-hand market after 1945, forming the fleets of many airlines, from KLM to Iraqi Airways. The first BEA flights to Stornoway also carried passengers, to subsidise the loss-making postal services. Today's Shorts 360 has seats fitted during the day, which are removed to make room for mailbags by night. The service still loses money—but then, so do the mail deliveries by boat. Carting post across storm-tossed northern seas is always going to cost more than taking a letter from, say, Pimlico to Shepherd's Bush.

I asked Eddie if anyone on the island might remember how life had changed with the introduction of air services. He frowned. 'There's Mrs Bannerman, who's been in the papers for her hundredth birthday. You could ask her.'

He took me among winding pebble-dash cul-de-sacs on the hill behind the town centre, to a semi-detached house. Mrs Bannerman was sitting on an upright Parker-Knoll with the bars of her electric fire full on. On the wall above the fireplace was her centennial telegram from the Queen.

She recalled how she had gone to work in service in London for a Sir Arthur Hamilton Grant, and how the journey to the capital by ferry and train used to take more than twenty-four hours.

'Was that your first job?' I asked.

'Och, no, dear. After leaving school I was a telegraph messenger. That was 1914. There was Peggy Matherson and myself and Maggie Henderson; the three of us had left school together and we got the job at the Post Office. I got the Admiralty, Peggy got the fish market and Maggie got the town. We'd to wear a uniform—it was dark navy with a red stripe all the way down and a leather belt with a pouch, a very thick navy skirt—and boots. Heavy boots, they killed me. I came home to my mother and I said, "Ma, they want me to wear a uniform and boots!" because, you know, I was beginning to get a bit stylish, like. "Oh, well,' she said, "you'll just have to do what they tell you to!" So I'd be given telegrams which went in the pouch and you hadn't to open it until you reached the Admiralty. Up the stairs to the Admiral's room, och, and put it in front of the Admiral. He had a big room on the first floor of the Caledonian Hotel, opposite the sea. There was a huge window, no blinds, just this window, full of the sea. It was the beginning of the war, and the fleet was in, the bay was full of ships. And that was the first job I had after school. I was fourteen.'

'Do you realise, Mrs Bannerman,' said Eddie, 'that you're probably the world's oldest living postwoman?'

He returned to his sorting office and I walked round Stornoway in the mild winter sunshine. At lunchtime I went into a near empty pub staffed by the dourest publican I had ever met, his thin face pinched into a permanent frown. I couldn't escape the impression that he actually *disapproved*—as every God-fearing islander no doubt should—of alcohol. I ordered a double malt and then, to provoke him further, I ordered another.

★

'Alpha one delta depart, flight level seven five, squawk five four four four, Logan six six five.' This was the Air Traffic Controller, from Glasgow. A new crew had taken over the Shorts, the passenger seats had been stripped out again and the stolid cargo plane was waiting for the night mail to Glasgow. I was squeezed back into the jump seat, beside the new crew of David Savage and Steve Cupples, both Scots.

'OK,' said David, 'Electrics. AIs, they are green and vertical, indications are normal.'

'Anti-ice?'

'Standards.'

'Reserve power?'

'Arm.'

This was a grown-up version of the checks I had learned to fly my little 152. The recitation was designed to get 26,000 lbs of aircraft with a possible payload of thirty-six passengers safely into the air.

'Oil Ts and Ps?'

'Four; in the greens.'

Although I had found the 152 pre-flight checks a dull business, they are not something that can be done on automatic. The 360's pilots went swiftly through routines they had rehearsed a thousand times, but their voices displayed concentration and alertness.

'Harnesses?'

'I'm secure; are you secure?'

'Secure.'

There is nothing supernatural about an aeroplane—flight is one of the most *rational* activities devised by human beings. At one level, an aeroplane is a kite; but to make possible the controlled and predictable flight of a modern aircraft, the laws of physics must be harnessed by complex combustive, mechanical, hydraulic, electric, electronic and aerodynamic systems. None of these must fail. There are fail-safe measures and 'built-in redundancy', but certain types of systems failure—like catastrophic engine or control surface breakdowns— could make our 26,000 lbs of metal and composites unable to hold the speed and direction that allow the wings to perform their trick of lift. Pilots' preparatory rituals always include a deliberate discussion of emergency options.

'Take-off will be a standard right hand departure . . . The wind is pretty negligible, any problems after departure we'll just climb straight ahead . . . so it'll be a visual left hand recovery back to land on three-six, er, once we've sorted the problem out. Failing that if the situation allows and it's pretty minor then we'll just take it back to Glasgow where we've got support. Any questions on that?'

'A've got nae questions on that.'

For take-offs with two crew, one pilot reads the crucial checks aloud for the other to verify. The checks are printed in large letters on laminated pages, usually spirally bound along the upper edge, sometimes attached to a small clipboard.

'D'you want to give me the board, Steve?'

'OK . . . Landing lights?'

'On.'

'Power levers?'

'Flight idle.'

'Props?'

'To max.'

'Fuel?'

'Flight.'

'Stopwatch?'

'Runs.'

'Ignitors?'

'Not required.'

'Then we're clear to go.'

As the plane rolls down the runway, the pilots do not sit smugly, holding on to their control columns, but monitor aloud the systems, the factors, that ensure that when the critical speed is reached, the plane will lift.

'OK—here comes the power!'

'We have air speed increasing both sides, warning captions are out, power is set.'

At the start of the run, the engines must be at full power, to ensure that the plane will reach take-off speed (a jumbo, for example, has 100,000 horsepower of thrust and needs to reach 180 mph to take off). After starting the take-off run, the pilots have only a few seconds to decide that everything is doing what it should be doing, or to abort if something's wrong. The co-pilot will say aloud, 'V1', meaning 'velocity one', or 'decision speed'. This is when the pilot makes the

commitment to take off. Up to this point, if an engine fails or a horn
warns of a systems failure, the take-off can be aborted, by applying
maximum brakes, retarding throttles, raising wing spoilers and engaging
reverse thrust. After V1 there's insufficient runway to abort: they *must*
take off. Moments later, the co-pilot will say, 'V2', meaning climb-
away speed has been reached. Then he will say, 'Rotate'. The pilot will
ease back the control column, lifting the aircraft's nose to an angle of
about 12 degrees. This change in the angle at which the wing meets the
airstream—its 'angle of attack'—will find the wing at its angle of
maximum lift. The plane will 'rotate'—take off—and climb.

'OK, it's my rudder.'

'Your rudder . . .'

The turbo-prop engines whine to a crescendo, the aeroplane
vibrates and when its brakes are released it surges forward, the
airspeed indicator needle spins, the runway ahead blurs.

'Indications normal . . . Seventy knots . . . V1 . . . V2 . . . Rotate . . .
Positive climb.'

We took off beneath a full moon. It was a fine evening: the air was
clear and still, the 360 glided along like a flying carpet. Soon the
rugged, snow-bright Northern Highlands were visible ahead.

'Is this typical January weather in these parts?' I asked.

'It can be perfectly smooth and you find yourself looking down on
the most wonderful scenery, like this,' replied David. 'And it can
change—so quickly—into the most horrendous flying conditions
you could encounter . . . Because we can't get above the weather,
we're limited to around 10,000 feet. We get snow, sleet, hail, ice,
fog—the lot. We carry a lot of anti-icing equipment on board—and
we need it.'

'What was your worst moment?'

He hesitated. Pilots do not like to discuss the dangers inherent in
the job. For one thing, they are not risk takers—in modern jargon,
they're 'risk-averse'. And out of professional sang-froid, or super-
stition, or a desire not to frighten their families and the passengers on
whom the airlines depend, it isn't done to harp on about hazards. But
in places like the Highlands, conditions are sometimes, inevitably,
unpredictable.

'Well . . . It was probably going out to Islay on a very dirty night—
black, rainy—thunderstorms about. And it's a Nondirectional Beacon

approach, and NDBs are not really reliable, especially during thunderstorms, when they point to the nearest electrical charge. So you're trying to find this strip, Islay, and it's surrounded by high ground in pretty well every direction. And the final approach on runway three-one is offset 21 degrees, and even when you do catch sight of the runway there's only some edge lines and two slope indicators. Black all around you . . . In conditions like that you do begin to wonder, "What am I doing here?" Aye. But it's almost as if something else is flying the aircraft at times, it must be like an inner consciousness, because there's a total focus and instinct—and this is, after all, what all your training has been for. And I emphasise, conditions have to warrant flying, we never deliberately take risks. But on evenings like this, it's the best job in the world . . .'

'That's Ben Nevis, with the moonlight on it,' said Steve Cupples, as we crossed the Grampians. 'You see, almost like a spiral going up to the summit? That's the track going up it.' Britain's tallest mountain stood out white against the planes and diagonals of the crumpled carpet of mountains around it. 'And look: there's the glow of Glasgow already, ahead of us.'

'What was *your* worst moment, Steve?' I asked.

He, too, hesitated. 'I got quite a scare going into Glasgow one night. It was about 2 a.m. and the wind was gusting up to fifty and fifty-five knots. Big jets were going into Glasgow before us, but we were struggling. We'd dropped off our cargo, so we were very light and the winds were bobbing us around like a cork. I think that's been my scariest moment—I was quite physically shaken when we got on to the ground. I just wanted to get away from planes, to go home . . . But a lot of the time the weather's stunning, very smooth, like tonight.'

Both pilots had ended their reminiscences on an upbeat. Neither wanted to dwell on the hazards of a pilot's life.

David said, 'This is *hands-on* flying, that's what it comes back to. Island-hopping up here we *have* to fly the planes ourselves and that's why pilots enjoy it. And it keeps you sharp. A lot of pilots who leave the company to fly charters really do miss it. They all say they'd rather be back here flying the Shorts, or the Twin Otter, or the Islander. Logan Air's small, close-knit. There's more money flying overseas, but you almost certainly have to move down south. With Logan Air you can live in Glasgow, and that's where I'm from, and I want to remain here. Piloting small planes about the islands seems to me to be about as close to the days of pioneer flying as you can get in British commercial aviation today. I love it.'

The buzzy immediacy of e-mail can make us forget that people still need contact with other people, as well as with artefacts, charms, tokens, handwritten notes, which we can send each other, to touch and keep. Airmail itself was a step towards instantaneity, as were mail trains when they replaced the horse and carriage. When long-distance mail flights began—to Montevideo, Kansas City, New Delhi, Tahiti—the initial toll of pilot deaths was so high that people said it would never work. How often, now, when we turn over a postcard, do we think about the nocturnal hives of sorting offices, the postmen and pilots who speed our mail from Bali or Benbecula?

A few weeks after I made those flights with Logan Air, a sister plane, Shorts 360 G-BNMT, experienced double engine failure shortly after take-off. It crashed into the Firth of Forth and both crew members were killed; 26,000 pieces of mail went to the bottom of the sea. The presumed cause of the accident was engine icing.

AEROPOSTALE

CHAPTER XIII

Night Mail II:
'St-Ex'

A s THE FIRST AIRMAIL services were starting, in unreliable planes through storm-tossed skies, a French author created the archetype of the mail pilot as hero in a novel called *Night Flight*. A postal pilot himself, he later found immortality as the author of a much-loved children's book. He was christened Antoine de Saint-Exupéry, but known to friends as 'St-Ex'.

Saint-Exupéry was sometimes attacked by pilots as a mystic scribbler with cavalier attitudes to flying, who ought to stick to his pen; but though Saint-Exupéry was no technophile, he *was* an authentic pioneer. Ironically, he was also attacked by literary critics as a pilot who had no business mixing with literature; but he wrote at least one modern classic, which puts him in very select company. If his struggle to unite the two contrasting *métiers* was to some extent his tragedy, it was also his achievement: to have been at once *homme de lettres* and *homme d'action*. And he was one of a tiny number of artists who have reclaimed from aviation's technical supremacism something of the aeroplane's magic. As one biographer put it, he was 'aviation's bard'.

For the French, two things make Saint-Exupéry a national figure, one who deserved a place on the fifty-franc note. His works are wholesome enough to be offered to schoolchildren as examples of grown-up philosophy; and he provided a country uneasy with its World War II record with the example of a self-sacrificing hero. To say that 'St-Ex' is a hero in France is a large understatement: he is totemic, immortal . . . It is not done to mention that in the last year of his life—1944—Saint-Exupéry was telling friends he feared that after the war de Gaulle might have him shot as a collaborator.

125

Like most people, I first came across Saint-Exupéry in his rôle as children's author. Later, his adult writing drew me to flying more than that of any other writer. Now, I wanted to make a homage, by flying from the airport in north-east Corsica from which Saint-Exupéry made his last flight. He took off from Bastia at 8.45 a.m. on 31 July 1944, on a reconnaissance flight over German-occupied Europe. He never returned, and despite persistent rumours, his plane and body have never been found. Like the death of the poet Wilfred Owen a few days before the end of the First World War, there was a pointlessness to Saint-Exupéry's death: Paris was liberated a fortnight later. That he may have *wanted* to die is a speculation his family and the priests of his cult have done everything to suppress.

It was a damp and freezing spring in England. I sulked under glowering unflyable skies, then fled south to Corsica, where it had been raining (unseasonably, the locals insisted) for a week. One morning, the sky over what is now the Aéroport Bastia Saint-Exupéry cleared briefly, letting me bum a joyride in an aircraft of the Aéroclub Saint-Exupéry (it had a Little Prince on its tailfin), only to be forced back by drizzle. 'No more flying today,' the club secretary shrugged apologetically. 'And possibly not this week.'

I went into the bar, had an *express* and leafed through a pile of old flying magazines. An older man walked in, cocked his head humorously at the sky and winked. Learning that I was English, he made the joke I'd already heard a hundred times: 'So you brought your weather with you?' He went behind the bar and poured himself a *pastis*. 'You should meet another member, Jo-Jo Alfonsi. He has an English aeroplane.'

'Oh yes?'

'A Europa.'

I'd heard of them: 'kit planes', manufactured in Yorkshire. You could buy the kit for around £35,000, and if you were clever enough to assemble it, you could end up with a plane worth much more.

'Have you been up in it?' I asked.

His expression made it clear that such a question could only be rooted in ignorance or madness.

'Why not?' I insisted.

'It has only one wheel!'

To reduce wind resistance and increase speed, the Europa dispenses with the usual tricycle undercarriage, employing a single main wheel which sits under the fuselage and retracts during flight. It makes for a very streamlined plane. 'A Europa's a lot faster than any of *them*,' I said, nodding towards the flying school's fleet of ageing conventional trainers.

He shrugged contemptuously. If I was foolish enough to put speed before personal safety, he was washing his hands of me.

Another man came into the bar. He had jet-black hair and wore a black leather jacket and a black Fedora. It was Jo-Jo Alfonsi. A few minutes later I was inspecting his private hangar, the rain pounding on the metal roof above our heads. All around us were machine tools and laser measuring instruments. A retired engineer, Jo-Jo handles such devices with total confidence. He assured me that the Europa's wings had been placed to within tolerances invisible to the naked eye. It had taken him 3500 hours to complete and he was clearly in love with his sleek little sports plane. 'Cruises at 150 knots,' he murmured tenderly, caressing her silken fibreglass skin. 'And she'll take you a hundred kilometres more cheaply than a car. I can pop over to Italy whenever I feel like it. Sometimes *madame* and I go to Rome for Sunday lunch. Venice is in range, or Spain—or Tunisia . . .'

'How does she fly?' I asked.

He smiled lasciviously and fondled her airscrew. '*Mais—elle est magnifique!*'

I had heard that their single wheels meant that Europas weren't the easiest planes to land. Jo-Jo protectively conceded that during landings his beloved still concentrated his mind wonderfully—as any demanding lover should. 'She did cause me some anxiety until I'd done a few hours with an expert on Europas, and I was confident I'd mastered the technique.'

After several more soggy days, the sky at last held out the possibility of a flight. It was still *grisâtre*, but the wind had dropped and there were a few breaks in the cloud. It was going to be my first opportunity to fly a plane at the cutting edge of contemporary design. We taxied the tiny Europa on to the apron of Bastia's under-used, but international, airport, waiting for a commercial jet to trundle down the runway. Then Jo-Jo applied full power. The Europa made a take-off run of barely forty feet, then darted into the sky like a bird.

'Look down to your left,' said Jo-Jo, 'see those marks on the grass just after the runway? That's where the airfield was in 1944. They had a grass runway. That's where Saint-Exupéry would have taken off from.'

We climbed almost vertically, then swung south. Soon we were shadowing the sandy Corsican coastline, at a speed that made it clear to me how different a proposition this was from the boring old aeroclub trainers.

'You take her,' said Jo-Jo. I took the joystick. The controls were extraordinarily light, with no play or vibration—every touch was translated into an immediate response. The Europa was to the creaky Cessnas I'd learned on as a Jaguar is to a JCB.

We continued south, occasionally flying over the remains of holiday homes that had been built too near the sea, ergo arsonised by Corsican nationalists. In the south, near Bonifacio, a pile of antique-looking ruins showed where an enormous discotheque had met a similar fate. 'The nationalists are living up to their violent reputation,' I said.

'That's all negative hype,' said Jo-Jo. 'People are *perfectly* safe on Corsica.'

I asked why, then, the North Corsican *préfet*, who happened to be a student pilot at the *aéroclub*, went everywhere with three body-guards—he even had one in the back of his plane during lessons.

'Oh, his predecessor was murdered a couple of years ago,' said Jo-Jo, with a dismissive wave of his hand. 'Look, the weather's turning nasty again, we'll have to head back.'

Our return flight took us through a French Air Force zone, where security devices suddenly jammed our GPS signal and the instruments produced gibberish. 'I was once flying through here on a landing approach when some low cloud abruptly came in, destroying visibility,' said Jo-Jo. 'I had a very nice time when my instruments went haywire. The air force seem to keep the jamming switched on permanently. Bloody inconvenient, but it doesn't do to argue with the military.'

Once past the military zone, our instruments began to read accurately again. Grey clouds were rolling, as they had all week, off the snowy peaks of Corsica's central spine and down the eastern slopes to the sea, bringing plenty of turbulence. The wind was starting to gust quite strongly and Jo-Jo took back the controls for the landing. Turbulence is not too worrying at 1000 feet, but during a landing a sudden gust could tip a wing down and, in the worst case, even cause a somersault.

As we began our descent, Jo-Jo returned to the matter of the plane's reluctance to return to earth. 'This will probably *seem* more dangerous than it really is,' he warned me. 'The Europa needs a particular technique.'

Landing on a conventional three-wheeled undercarriage is obviously easier than landing on a single wheel. Tricycles, where the plane sits stably on one nosewheel and two side-mounted wheels, were first used at the very dawn of aviation, but went out of fashion between the World Wars. By 1938 the Americans had reintroduced them, but most European World War II planes (Spitfire, Lancaster, Me 109 etc.) employed tailwheels. While nosewheel planes are forward-balanced, so that the fuselage is parallel to the ground, 'taildraggers' have their tails low and their noses high, so that a taxiing pilot, lacking forward vision, must weave to see ahead. Furthermore, taildraggers have an unpleasant tendency to 'ground-loop'—to swing violently back on themselves. This was so pronounced in powerful military machines that more British warplanes were lost to ground-looping than to enemy action. After the war, American airliners used nosewheel/tricycle designs, while British airlines chauvinistically persisted with tailwheels for nearly ten years, so that their cabins sloped steeply backwards and passengers felt like mountain climbers; one small example of why the British aviation industry, which led the world after World War II, subsequently almost died.

As the runway swelled beneath us, gusts were making the plane leapfrog gently. The Europa touched the runway and lurched back to around twenty feet—and not straight up, but off to the right (another consequence of the Europa's one-wheel configuration is that it's harder to keep straight than a three-wheeler).

'Nothing to worry about, nothing at all,' muttered Jo-Jo, as he added power to gain a little height, straightened the plane, tipped her nose forward to increase our speed and brought her back to meet the tarmac.

The Europa's modern design has another echo of archaic aero-nautic controversy. In the early 1900s most designers were obsessed with developing an aircraft that was completely stable at all times—an aerial motorcar; but a few fliers, like Lilienthal, Pilcher and the Wrights, saw that an 'unstable' design, where it was the pilot's skills that counterbalanced the forces of nature, produced a much more manœuvrable aircraft. This dichotomy is preserved today in the contrast between a commercial airliner, a paragon of stolid stability, and a fighter plane, which achieves its manœuvrability by being inherently *un*stable. A child could fly an airbus, but an untrained pilot would find it hard to keep a Eurofighter airborne for long. To the reader whose principal interest in aircraft is that they should be dull and safe, deliberate instability must sound rather unpleasant. But for the aviation enthusiast, a machine like Jo-Jo's Europa, delivering higher speed at lower cost—but demanding above-average skill—is alluring.

Jo-Jo brought the Europa back towards the tarmac, dropping our tail until the tiny tailwheel touched down, and we cycled down the runway. Owning his own hangar, Jo-Jo is in the privileged position of being able to drive—like a suburban husband home from the corporate coalface—straight into his garage.

Antoine de Saint-Exupéry died almost exactly a month after his forty-fourth birthday. When he took off on his last flight, he'd been a pilot for twenty-three years. The French have a sublime phrase: *baptême de l'air*—air baptism. Saint-Exupéry first flew in 1912, aged twelve, having tricked a pilot into believing he had his mother's permission to fly. The Saint-Exupérys had moved to Le Mans in 1909, exactly a year after Wilbur Wright's historic demonstrations of controlled flight over the local hippodrome, giving small boys in Le Mans even more reason to be aeroplane-obsessed than small boys anywhere else. After his *baptême* Antoine had, a school friend remembered, 'jumped for joy'. The plane was a Berthaud-Wroblewski, built by two Poles, the Wroblewski brothers. It was Gabriel Wroblewski who flew the young Antoine. At that time aircraft design was in its infancy and flight a risky affair—in 1914 both brothers were killed test-flying one of their planes.

Antoine had an enchanted childhood, living in a château outside Lyons where he and his two brothers and two sisters had the run of magnificent grounds. The enchantment was marred first by the death of their father—of a stroke, in the waiting room of a railway station—when he was just forty-one; Antoine was then almost four. When he was seventeen he lost his younger brother François to rheumatic fever, culminating in a heart attack. Antoine was at the bedside to witness his brother's painful last minutes.

When Antoine de Saint-Exupéry died, he had just published the ubiquitous children's classic which still sells in its hundreds of thousands. Many images and themes in *The Little Prince* have their origins in Antoine's childhood; they provided him with succour throughout his life. Childhood memories, he once wrote to his mother, were hopelessly more real to him than adult ones. 'I am not sure I have lived since my childhood.' The narrator of *The Little Prince* is lonely in the adult world—until he meets the Little Prince. All his life, Saint-Exupéry remained resistant to many of the dull *idées reçus* of adulthood. Characterised by teachers as '*un original*'—a one-off—he was untidy, sloppily dressed, vague, a window-starer. He would remain an obstinate abstractionist to the end. His childlike self-obsession, and expectation that others would indulge him, led to his being scorned as child*ish* and fey. But he clung, as a mystic to his moment of revelation, to the child's vision of life: vivid, secure, unmarred by hypocrisy and cynicism.

After his brother François's death in 1917, it was decided that Antoine's future lay not in the killing fields of Ypres and Flanders but in the Navy. He resolved that if he failed the entrance exams, he'd sign up for the air force. But as he turned nineteen and failed his exams, the Armistice was signed.

A bulky six foot two, an improbable æsthete, he immersed himself in the artistic riches of Paris, contemplating a literary career. He also began the long process of draining his mother's fortune: the series of generous allowances she made Antoine would ultimately lead the family to blame him for her financial ruin.

In 1921 he was called up for military service and joined the 2nd Fighter Group at Strasbourg as a humble private second-class, assigned to the ground crews known as *rampants*—creepers. The young aristocrat rapidly bent the rules, waiving military regulations so that he could have *private* flying lessons at a *military* airfield. He went solo in a British Sopwith after a couple of dozen circuits of the airfield and just two and a half hours of tuition—an impressive achievement. (I recently flew with a French flying instructor who informed me with pouting pedantry that 'Saint-Exupéry was a very bad pilot, you know'. Swallowing my astonishment, I asked him if *he* had gone solo in two and a half hours. He retorted, 'Oh, they had lower standards in those days.')

Saint-Exupéry now fell in love with Louise de Vilmorin, a society beauty. The couple became engaged, but Louise's parents considered an impoverished count an imperfect catch, especially given his fondness for an activity that almost guaranteed his early demise. Saint-Exupéry duly lost control of a plane at 270 feet and crashed (though the crash report described him as 'inspired' and 'born to be a fighter pilot'). He was pulled from the wreckage alive, but the de Vilmorins announced that the marriage was off unless he gave up flying. He agreed to do so, but soon afterwards 'Loulou' broke off the engagement. She went on to become one of the great seductresses of her age, an intimate of René Clair, Jean Cocteau and André Malraux. Near the end of her life, she listed the five men she had truly loved: Saint-Exupéry was not on the list.

Half a century earlier, however, she had broken Saint-Exupéry's heart. It would take him many years to get over Loulou. But at least he could go back to his first love: flying.

With his *service militaire* over, Saint-Exupéry drifted, spending what little cash he had renting planes at weekends. He was losing patience with what he saw as the glibness of the Parisian intelligentsia, turning increasingly to his interior world and to a belief that the only thing that mattered for a writer was actually to have lived and thought enough to have something worth saying. He briefly flew sightseers over Paris, then, in 1927, moved to Toulouse to become a mail pilot.

During the 1920s, France did a great deal to stimulate its aviation industry, partly for strategic reasons and partly because the land of the Montgolfiers believed (it still does) it had a historic tryst with aviation. A series of historic firsts brought France international prestige, and as Saint-Exupéry entered the mail service, pioneering transatlantic flights from West Africa to Brazil were beginning. The *Aéropostale* network would ultimately span the Atlantic and the Andes, reaching the Pacific. This was achieved with planes that did only 120 or 130 mph, at something like 15,000 feet. Yet by 1930, letters that had taken over a month to travel from Paris to Santiago were getting there by air in four days.

The first limb of the *Aéropostale* network led down the coast of Africa, through Morocco and Mauritania, to Dakar in Senegal. Saint-Exupéry was posted to Nouakchott, now the capital of Mauritania, but then little more than a French coastal fort on the edge of the Sahara. He would later remember his time in Mauritania as the most formative period in his life.

His memoir *Wind, Sand and Stars* opens with an incandescent description of Saint-Exupéry being inducted by the gruff veteran Henri Guillaumet into the ways of the sky. In 1927 aeroplanes were still primitive machines, their engines liable to fail without warning, making a noise 'like the crash of crockery'. The pilot had to hope that the cloud beneath him didn't reach down to ground level, and that the invisible ground didn't turn out to be a mountain range: 'Below the sea of clouds lies eternity.'

There were no radios, few airstrips. If you were lucky, you put down in a field, but even then there were fatal traps. The wind effect of a row of trees near a runway can hinder a plane's climb or descent (it's a persistent mystery to pilots why there are always trees near runways) and, if the aircraft struggles, the trees become a trap. Guillaumet's first gift was to bring the neophyte Saint-Exupéry's maps alive with information far more vital than the names of regions and rivers: 'Beware those trees. Better mark them on your chart,' and, 'Watch that brook: it breaks up the whole field. Mark it . . .'

Taking leave of Guillaumet, Saint-Exupéry walked the night streets of Toulouse in a sort of ecstasy. He imagined passers-by as separated lovers, who had no notion that he, the pilot, was about to carry their love letters through perilous skies to their beloved. These people, the earthbound, could never dream of flying as he would. As he passed *pâtisseries* that glittered with delicacies, he saw in his own celestial rôle a renunciation of such terrestrial pleasures. In the tram before dawn, en route to the airfield, he observed drowsy clerks and mused on how they had built edifices of work to keep the unpredictable at bay. They were now bound and gagged with red tape, while he, Saint-Exupéry, gloried in the freedom of the sky. Perhaps he would fight with the demons of a night-time storm over the mountains—but it was a fight with some hope of victory. And, more important, no one had *told* him to fight; he was where he wanted to be.

There are contradictions in all this. Saint-Exupéry sometimes venerated the humble worker or dutiful housewife, but at other times he expressed disdain for such domestic 'safety'. These sturdy types needed a Saint-Existential hero to perform the cosmic transactions— to transport the written tokens that gave their ordinary lives meaning. Saint-Exupéry was an élitist Romantic.

That morning of his first mail flight, he took off in drizzle. Five hours later, he landed in sun-splashed Alicante, the warmest city in Europe, the only one 'where dates ripen'.

Wind, Sand and Stars contains some of the most lyrical descriptions of aviation ever written. It is also a tirade against the dehumanizing effects of technology. Contradictions again: Saint-Exupéry loves the aeroplane, but hates machines and the way a mechanized society reduces its members to cogs. The book is intensely spiritual, chiefly in its observations of human beings at their best, transcending selfishness and greed, displaying charity and love. Much space is devoted to Saint-Exupéry's experiences of fellowship with other pilots, in particular Mermoz and Guillaumet, legendary pioneers of the mail flights, who risked their lives again and again, emerging miraculously from a kidnap by murderous tribesmen or from a crash high in the Andes. (Mermoz's luck ran out one night in the South Atlantic while Guillaumet was shot down during World War II.) But Saint-Exupéry was to have equally astonishing exploits. His initiation into the desert was a 70 mph collision with a sand dune—the first of many Saharan mishaps. Several times he sallied to the rescue of other downed pilots, experiencing armed attack from hostile tribesmen. His indifference to such dangers did much to forge his legend. In 1935 he would crash in the Sahara during the Paris–Saigon Air Race, miraculously surviving the accident and spending days without water, wandering the desert with his mechanic, until Bedouin discovered them.

No pilot can read about Saint-Exupéry's insouciance without a nervous smile. He was notorious for taking novels and a sketchpad with him in the cockpit. The pilot's *esprit de corps* might have demanded a studied indifference to personal safety, but St-Ex really *was* dangerously dreamy. In the Thirties, working as a test pilot, he spent one flight not monitoring the handling of the plane, but sketching a woman from memory. Another time he forgot to close a door, which was ripped from its hinges by the slipstream and fluttered down to land among bemused engineers on the airfield. During World War II, he once read a detective novel on a solo flight from Sardinia to Tunis. Of his many near-fatal crashes in twenty years as a pilot, more than a few were caused by inattention. Some of aviation's great heroes have been technically-minded and disciplined men with a fierce eye for detail; Saint-Exupéry was the opposite, an artist bored and even confused by technicality, though passionately in love with flying. Through the 1930s aeroplanes became safer and more complex—and Saint-Exupéry hated them.

In April 1931 he married. A big, jovial, sometimes brooding man, he was attracted to tiny, mercurial women. He had described Loulou, who turned him down a decade earlier, as a 'little girl' and a 'fairy', and all his life he had a tendency to see women as princesses or girl-children—frail, delicate, spiritual. The El Salvadorean Consuelo Gómez Carillo embodied his feminine ideal. She called him her lumbering bear, he called her his little tropical bird. She was tiny, exotic, dishonest and unfaithful. Some have diagnosed in Saint-Exupéry Ruskinesque difficulties—a problem with the physical realities of women. He had, especially towards the end of his life, a series of 'affairs', some or even all of which were physically uncon-summated. He also formed a curious relationship with Anne Morrow Lindbergh, the wife of that other legendary aviator, Charles Lindbergh. Saint-Exupéry had met them in New York in 1939. Although Anne spent only a single day in Antoine's company, when he was the Lindberghs' house guest, she seems to have fallen more than a little in love, sensing in him a soulmate. While Charles Lindbergh was vigorously anti-war and pro-German (it ultimately cost the superstar his huge popularity), Saint-Exupéry devoted himself after the fall of France to the cause of bringing America into the war. Secretly, Anne found that her own views chimed almost exactly with Saint-Exupéry's.

But his view of the war was about to cast an impenetrable shadow over Saint-Exupéry's relationship with the land of his birth. When the Germans invaded in 1940, France's armed forces stood no chance. France's lead in aviation had been undone by the political and economic chaos of the Thirties and by Hitler's shiny new air force. Saint-Exupéry joined up and flew reconnaissance flights over German-occupied France. It was near-suicidal work. His squadron was equipped with the French Potez 637, a plane far too slow to stand any chance of escape if German fighters spotted it—the Potez had a top speed of around 250 mph, versus the Me 109's 350-odd. The first plane to be shot down on the Western front was a Potez and losses over the following nine months were heavy.

Saint-Exupéry's book about his experience, *Flight to Arras*, sought to counter the widespread American perception that France had done little to resist the Germans. Published in New York in 1942, it was praised as a triumphant response to Nazism and soared into the best-seller lists.

Saint-Exupéry was determined that *Flight to Arras* should also be published in his homeland. But it won him only hatred there. The censors cut just one line, about Hitler's foolishness for unleashing the war (puzzlingly, it's still missing from the French edition). The book received a tiny print run and was denounced in the Vichyist press as 'another demented Judaeo-bellicose act', deeply insulting to France's German guests. For Gaullists, however, Saint-Exupéry had not insulted the occupiers *enough*—the mere fact of publication was an act of collaboration. Saint-Exupéry was no politician and his naïve (or stubborn) determination to express a humanitarian hatred of war *in general* earned him the loathing of the Gaullists, with Charles de Gaulle personally convinced that Saint-Exupéry was using his influence to turn the Americans against him. The two men became bitter enemies.

In fact, the American leadership and de Gaulle already had the opposite of a mutual appreciation society. In November 1942 American troops landed in North Africa, and Vichy French troops fired on them. De Gaulle, angry that Roosevelt had not informed him of the operation, spat, 'I hope Vichy throws them back into the sea.'

In April 1943 Saint-Exupéry sailed for North Africa, and was re-assigned to his old squadron, Groupe de Reconnaissance 2/33. He was greeted with joy, the squadron regarding the aristocratic author as a kind of mascot. But would he be allowed to fly? At forty-two, he was ten years over the age limit to pilot the planes with which 2/33 was being equipped. But Saint-Exupéry had influence; Eisenhower himself was petitioned to give the author wings.

The rapid reconstitution of the *Armée de l'Air* was made possible by the provision of modern British and American aircraft. 2/33 had been re-equipped with the Lockheed Lightning, a twin-engine fighter similar in concept to the Potez 637, but immeasurably superior (America's highest-scoring Ace made all forty of his kills in a Lightning). 2/33's Lightning F-5s were very fast and extremely high-altitude aircraft, ideal for high-level reconnaissance. Streamlined and sky-blue in colour, they were also sublimely beautiful.

To fly one of the most high-tech planes in existence, Saint-Exupéry needed to retrain. He had acquired his skills in an age of Romance—the Sopwith needed few controls and even mid-Thirties planes had only a handful of dials. The Lightning, at the apogee of aviation know-how, had two engines, eight fuel tanks, four cameras, electrical-everything and 148 separate controls. For Saint-Exupéry it was a 'flying torpedo that has nothing whatever to do with flying . . . with all its screens and buttons, it makes the pilot into a sort of chief accountant'. He had a tendency to misread his altimeter; on one occasion, having been told to climb to 2000 metres, he climbed to 20,000 feet—without oxygen.

Another time he opened the window at 30,000 feet, lost his oxygen mask and descended so quickly he damaged the P-38's wings. The Americans were unimpressed with his flying, while he declared himself unimpressed with their miracle of technology.

In addition to his age, Saint-Exupéry suffered from injuries sustained in a dozen major accidents, including a permanent humming in one ear. He woke every morning in pain and could not bend to the floor, or lift anything heavy. Within two inches of being too tall to fly the Lightning, he had to have his bulk shoe-horned into it. The effects of high-level flight on pilots were known to get worse with age, and he was training for high-altitude reconnaissance. But there is a streak of defiance in the French character. On his forty-third birthday, Saint-Exupéry was cleared by the French medical examiner for high-level flight.

At last, the weather had cleared. It was a bright, calm day. 'Lunch at the Tower of Pisa?' asked Jo-Jo. The Italians were just removing the cables that for a decade had been retumescing the celebrated tower.

As we prepared the Europa, a police wagon pulled up and a *douanier* climbed out with a large Alsatian. 'I'm not running drugs, this time,' Jo-Jo told him familiarly, '—but contrabrand. Martin, could you get the bottle?'

I went to my bag and took out the bottle of home-distilled liqueur he'd presented me with the previous day. The label proclaimed (I translate):

Country Acqua Vita
Illegal Manufacture Guaranteed
Distilled Out-of-Sight of the Gendarmerie
All Rights Reserved
53%   37.5 cl

Printed at the Illegal Manufacturers'
clandestine printing works, Corsica

The gendarme read this and nearly collapsed with laughter, struggled back into his car seat and drove off still guffawing, with his puzzled-looking dog beside him. Corsica is another country: they do things differently there.

We climbed into orange life jackets, as we'd be crossing seventy miles of open sea. 'Pull this toggle to inflate,' said Jo-Jo. 'And this is your whistle.' I wondered idly what chance we'd have of getting out alive if the single-engine plane did conk out mid-Med.

A few minutes later we were grazing the rocky edge of Elba, the miniature kingdom-in-exile where the deposed Emperor Napoleon did so much during his short stay to improve the drains. Ahead lay the Isola di Capraia, still a home to hundreds of Italian prisoners. 'They're very particular about not being flown over,' Jo-Jo said.

'They always think you're crooks trying to whisk away a Mafia capo or something.'

We were navigating by Jo-Jo's GPS, a posh model that represented us as a small aeroplane icon crawling over a densely detailed map. For me, the advantage of knowing my precise location was diminished by the display's revelation of my uneven pilotage—the dotted line of my track resembled the meandering of a drunken beetle.

As we approached the Italian coast, Jo-Jo radioed our destination, only to be informed that the aerodrome was—*eccezionalménte*—closed for the day.

'Why's that?' I asked him.

Jo-Jo shrugged. 'With Italians, who knows? Maybe for maintenance, maybe they just felt like it. Perhaps the controller fancied a morning with his mistress. It doesn't do to be too efficient in Italy, you know. *La vie est pour régaler, pas la règlementation.* [Life is for having fun, not following rules.]'

'But you couldn't have landed anyway,' the voice on the radio went on. 'We're fogged in.'

Fogged in? On a day like this?

We peered ahead. Sure enough, miles of coastline were disfigured by a shiny smear of grey. Hurriedly, we swung the plane through 180 degrees on to the reciprocal of our previous heading, back towards Corsica.

'Surely we can land at the main Pisa airport,' I said.

'Hm . . . The thing is, it's a commercial airport combined with a military base.' The prospect of *pizza al fresco* was receding rapidly. 'But nothing ventured . . .'

He got through to Pisa air traffic control, and his eyebrows arched when they gave us immediate permission to land. We crossed the Italian coast over the mouth of the River Arno and turned north towards the airport, descending among the aggressive, olive-grey shapes of military aircraft. But Pisa was colder than Corsica. We ate our pizzas indoors, a few feet from the Leaning Tower.

As we returned to Corsica, Jo-Jo pointed at the jagged spine of the island. 'I saw a German plane crash up there, you know. It's one of my most vivid childhood memories. I was up in my village, in the north-west. It was dark, but we saw the plane, chased by an Allied night-fighter, the streaks of tracer. The German plane went straight into the mountainside—boom—a great cloud of flame. That was the war for Corsica: not on the ground, but up in the air.'

We overflew Erbalunga, the coastal hamlet six miles north of Bastia where Saint-Exupéry had been billeted during the final fortnight of his life. It is still a small village, just beyond Bastia's suburban sprawl. No one knows precisely which house Saint-Exupéry stayed at. It is a matter of record, however, that on the last night of his life he did not sleep in his bed. A romantic interlude? A dark night of the soul? He should not have gone up the following morning, either—his erratic flying had made his superiors anxious, and with the end of the war in sight, there was official concern for the celebrity's safety. When Lieutenant René Gavoille learned that Saint-Exupéry had taken off, he yelled at his subordinates, 'In the name of God, why did you let him fly?'

The last year of Saint-Exupéry's life had also been the unhappiest. The poet of solidarity, he rediscovered his hatred for the uniformity of military life; and when he wrote off one of the hugely expensive Lightnings on his *second* mission, the Americans grounded him.

In desperation, Saint-Exupéry launched a charm offensive. He threw a lavish banquet for a hundred French and American officers, inebriatedly beating his fist against his chest as he told Colonel Frank Dunn, Roosevelt's second-in-command, 'I want to die for France.'

'Fine,' Dunn replied, 'but not in one of our planes.'

Eisenhower was petitioned again. Having just read and liked (partly because de Gaulle disliked it) *Flight to Arras*, he was sympathetic. But Saint-Exupéry's many attacks on de Gaulle now returned to haunt him. The General, who had by now politicked his way into control of the provisional French government, publicly implied that he regarded the author as a collaborator, and had his books banned. Saint-Exupéry was watched, his mail was intercepted, his requests for active service were blocked. Eight months went by, with him unable to take any active rôle in the war effort. Saint-Exupéry began to feel he was the last survivor of a lost race of aviators. Even to casual acquaintances he often seemed to be on the verge of tears. Darkly, he foresaw himself being shot as a collaborator after the Liberation. He drank heavily and chain-smoked, he despaired. When clear evidence emerged that de Gaulle was personally blocking him Saint-Exupéry heaped yet more counter-productive abuse on his tormentor.

String-pulling was to come to his aid one last time. A social meeting with the head of de Gaulle's air commission gave Saint-Exupéry an opportunity to proclaim his undying patriotism. He was granted permission to rejoin 2/33. For the squadron, the return of their mascot was a cause for celebration. On 24 May Saint-Exupéry made a refresher flight in a Lightning.

But he was now frequently and visibly distracted. On one occasion he deviated from the mission itinerary to overfly his sister's house, which he heard had been destroyed by the Germans. His colleagues gave a collective sigh of relief each time he returned to base safely. News came of the Allied landings at Normandy, but, as the war neared its conclusion, Saint-Exupéry brooded about the world of vulgarity and ant-like uniformity that would follow it. He felt as bitter about France's internecine squabbling and the sullying of his own reputation as he did about Hitler's war. Observing his fragile mental state, Saint-Exupéry's superiors looked for reasons to keep him on the ground. René Gavoille, an old friend and the commander of 2/33, attempted to broach the subject one day. Saint-Exupéry replied that he would not survive being grounded again, and that since it was clear that he was going to disappear one way or another, he'd rather it was on a war mission. He handed Gavoille all his papers, plus detailed instructions on what to do with them in the event of his death. He gave away his much-used chess set. In a number of letters he described his indifference to life.

Saint-Exupéry took off at 8.45 a.m. on 31 July, crossed over the French mainland a few minutes later, disappeared from Allied radar and was never heard of again.

Jo-Jo had a friend, François Marchisio, who was Corsica's greatest expert on Saint-Exupéry. We had dinner one evening in a restaurant overlooking Bastia harbour. The story of the last flight, François told me, was deeply mysterious. 'It's not only that St-Ex didn't sleep in his bed that night and no one knows where he went. The next morning, he apparently took a mission that someone else should have flown. But the military, who supposedly keep records, were unable to say for sure if St-Ex had a mission, indeed if *anyone* had a mission, which could have meant that St-Ex swapped with them, or intimidated a subordinate into letting him fly. The whole thing is a tissue of half-remembered details and contradictions. The Germans, who were fanatical, indeed morbid, record keepers, still insist that no one shot down a Lightning that day. St-Ex simply disappeared—vanished into thin air.'

'Do you believe any of these reports that keep coming up that his plane has been found in the Mediterranean?'

With a melancholy smile, François pulled his bulky 'St-Ex' file from his briefcase. 'There's a huge St-Ex disappearance industry. Conspiracy theories, allegations of cover-ups, supposed discoveries of his plane underwater . . . Allegations that his identity bracelet was dredged up in a net and deliberately "lost" by his family . . .'

'Nothing in it?'

'A lot of people stand to gain financially from discovering St-Ex's remains—writers, TV stations, day-trip organisers, diving companies. In my opinion, it's all hype. His disappearance is still a total mystery.'

'Well, then—do you think he committed suicide?'

'I'd prefer to think not; but sadly, when you consider his mental state, it does seem a strong possibility.'

It was raining again. Jo-Jo and François told me there was an Allied war grave outside Bastia. I went to visit it, a neat, wooded grove where sixty Commonwealth servicemen lie. As the Allies pushed the Germans north, Corsica escaped involvement in the ground war. Almost all of the men in the war graves are aircrew. Their average age is around twenty-two. One grave was unidentified, an airman of the Royal Air Force, 'Known unto God'. The five crewmen of another plane were buried together, their gravestones touching, shoulder to shoulder in death as in life. The inscriptions on the graves provide painfully brief glimpses into lives cut short:

Tell England we died for her and here we rest content.

The only son of . . .

Remembered by your loving wife and baby daughter . . .

Sleep well, darling.

In the afternoon, the sky cleared. Jo-Jo and I took off an hour before sunset and flew straight at the mountains, as St-Ex would have done. North-west of Bastia a mountain pass miraculously gapes and you almost scrape the rock walls with your wing tips. Then you see the glittering sea, the sun streaking low and golden across western Corsica, the French coast ahead.

As I had left England, Penny had pushed into my hand a box containing the petals of a dozen red roses which held a certain memory for us. In tribute to St-Ex, I had wanted to release them over the sea beneath which many believe him to lie. Other lost lives were now in my thoughts, too. As I opened the small flap in the side of the Plexiglas canopy, a 110 mph jet of air rushed into the cockpit. Three times I thrust my fist with a handful of petals through the aperture. Each time I opened my hand, the petals simply vanished.

CHAPTER XIV

A Montgolfière *over the Mara*

I HAD FLOWN straight from Europe to East Africa, instead of following, as I had intended, the old Aéropostale route down Africa's west coast. That coast is not somewhere you air-hitch; I had driven it the previous year. South from Morocco into Western Sahara, the ex-Portuguese colony annexed by Morocco in 1979. A thousand miles and more where the Sahara is a great golden enigma in the east, with a chopping, sapphire ocean in the west. The hot easterly wind meeting the ocean's westerly breeze.

I met some fishermen living in threadbare tents on the edge of the desert, clambering on ropes down sandstone cliffs studded with gigantic scallop shells, to the narrow and battered strand where they fish with rod and line. They are proudly Moroccan, they tell me, these men wearing rags. Inland, somewhere inside that golden enigma, live the original, displaced, discontented inhabitants of this place, the men whose great-grandfathers shot at Saint-Exupéry and who have struggled without success through the United Nations for restitution of their birthright. In Dakhla, where *Aéropostale* once had a staging post, I met sullen Moroccan bureaucrats, living lives of colonial civilization far from the heart of their culture, from Marrakesh or Casablanca, grateful for the good government schools for their children and the bussed-in meat, but suspicious that some terrorist bomb might turn them into soot. Friendly, fresh-faced young officers from Austria and Sweden seconded to UN peace-keeping missions told me off the record that Morocco will talk until eternity in the UN, but will never return this territory, with its mineral and fishing wealth, to the nomads.

I continued south, across the Tropic of Cancer, through the

minefield on the Mauritanian border. Confirmation that the lurid warning signs did not lie was the shattered wreck of a Land Rover in which some British travellers executed a fatal three-point turn a couple of years earlier. The meandering track through no man's land has patches of soft sand where cars get bogged down and travellers drive in convoys to help each other out. From Nouâdhibou, just inside Mauritania, there are two routes south: one the coastal track, where you drive long stretches along the beach at low tide, the other an inland route, across desert. I took the latter. And further south to Nouakchott, the capital of modern Mauritania, where since I had last passed through—two years earlier, on honeymoon—new buildings had sprouted and Internet cafés were feeding the mercantile aspirations of a newly confident middle class.

Finally I left the Sahara. A car ferry crosses the Senegal river into Senegal and a landscape of boabab trees, those tubby, waxen, almost leafless forms so lovingly depicted by St-Ex in his *Petit Prince*. The first town is St Louis, a spit-shaped island like its namesake in Paris, reached by a Gustave Eiffel iron bridge that once spanned the Danube and was transplanted here in 1897. Today the town's main hotel, the *Hôtel de la Poste*, trades heavily on its *Aéropostale* connections. Saint-Exupéry and all his flying colleagues put up here, for during the 1920s this was the first outpost of civilisation you hit south of Morocco. Today there are tour parties and disconsolate prostitutes. The town of St Louis is run-down, but far-sighted visitors are turning the shuttered colonial French houses into holiday homes, and hideous holiday resorts are springing up along the beach.

There is no private aviation down this entire desert coast and few non-military airstrips. But a friend of mine who worked for Air Maroc had arranged for me to fly to Dakhla in one of the fifteen-seat Fokkers that cross the desert once a week. A fortnight before I was due to leave, the Dakar Rally, whose participants see the desert as a culturally inert racetrack, confirmed its intention of passing this way. Western Saharan independence fighters saw this as a de facto recognition of Morocco's legitimacy and announced their intention to use ground-to-air missiles to shoot down any passenger flights in 'their' airspace. Air Maroc cancelled all flights.

I could not wait months for the threat to be rescinded. I flew to Nairobi.

Demonstrating that the sun has not finally set on the British Empire, the Aero Club of East Africa is decked with varnished propellers and sepia photographs of Englishmen in pith helmets posing with biplanes. The Club makes a congenial alternative to hotels in down-town Nairobi, and most of its guests have some kind of connection with the diverse (but largely white) world of African aviation. One morning a man was staring at the Merlin aero engine (fabled power plant of the Spitfire, Lancaster, Mustang . . .) that reposes like a fallen sarsen in the Club's entrance hall. 'That's my plane,' he said, as I walked past.

He was a large, full-bearded man, with a jovial presence and public school vowels; late fifties, perhaps—but no World War II veteran. I stepped closer.

He was wiping his wire-rim glasses on a handkerchief. He pointed at a small framed photograph that stood on top of the Merlin, clamped his glasses back on and leaned closer. 'It must be a still from the film,' he said. I frowned, uncomprehending. '*The Battle of Britain*, they made it in the Sixties. I was one of the stunt pilots, you see. MH 434—that was my plane!' Radiant with nostalgia, he returned the glasses to his nose and peered at the photograph. 'I flew the Messerschmitts too. You know the controversy that goes on about which was *really* the better plane? I'm probably one of the few people who's flown them both, who can actually give a genuine opinion.'

'And?'

'Oh, the Spit, no question. You know the famous quote—they used it in the film—when Göring asks the Ace, Adolf Galland, if there's anything he needs to fight the British; and Galland replies, "Yes, sir—give me a squadron of Spitfires." Well, he was quite right about their superiority—absolutely right. Faster at almost every altitude, tighter turning circle, responsive, predictable; the Spit had the edge, all right.'

It may be strange, even reprehensible, that half a century after the Second World War men are still having such small-boy conversations, are still in thrall to the vampish charms of a war machine. But the Spitfire is not simply one of the most beautiful machines ever made; it is an example of a technology that critically shifted the balance of power in a global conflict. In World War II British forces were rarely better equipped than their opponents, but the Spitfire was the best fighter-interceptor in the world, brought into existence by weird serendipity, the development of a fast seaplane for the British team in the Schneider Trophy races. Victory for the *Luftwaffe* in the Battle of Britain would have exposed Britain to invasion and certain defeat. The victory of RAF Fighter Command not only prevented invasion, but created the conditions for Britain's survival and for the eventual defeat of Nazi Germany. It was Hitler's first reverse since he had begun hostilities and the turning point in the entire war. It can be argued that the Spitfire and its Merlin engine were the two key Allied technologies of the war. What's certain is that the legend of the Spitfire will never fade.

Every day there's to be found in the Club bar one of its oldest members, Bill Armstrong, a man with a more direct perspective on World War II, since he served in the RAF as a bomber pilot. One day, I invited Bill for lunch. We sat in the enclosed veranda built on the side of the Aero Club's original 1932 wood pavilion. Bill has an elderly man's slightness, and precise, neat hands. He dresses immaculately, in jacket and tie; he is civil, but sharp—no fool and not one who tolerates fools, and he is not going to spill his guts to a stranger just for the hell of it. Our conversation began hesitantly, with Bill talking in his clipped, slightly scornful Thirties style. But as lunch progressed, he became friendlier.

'I was born here. My parents were farmers, but when my mother died of blackwater fever in '26 my father sent my brother and me to England. I came back in the slump, in 1933, finished school here and joined the RAF in 1941. This, where we're sitting, was my first station—Nairobi West, as it was in those days. I trained as a pilot in Rhodesia and was posted to the Mediterranean theatre.

'I flew Glenn Martin Baltimores. Know them? Glenn Martin was an American pioneer—associated with the Wrights for a while. Anyway, at the start of the war, Martins built a thing on spec called the Maryland—a twin-engine light bomber—and the Yanks said no bloody thanks, but the French ordered loads of them, so did the RAF. The French didn't get many of theirs before the Germans rolled in in 1940. Then the RAF issued a spec for a specially modified version— bigger, faster, more powerful engines—and that became the Baltimore. Built by the Yanks, flown by the Brits. The engines were Wright Cyclones, 1660 horsepower radials—and 1700 horsepower in those days was something else, my God. A powerful, very manoeuvrable aircraft.' Bill's eyes glittered. 'Very, very good machines. We got the MK IV. Four seats and carried 2000 lbs' worth of bombs.

'I flew in Italy, mostly hitting the front line, the Gustav Line, the Sangro river. Started in Brindisi, then moved to Foggia and on up the east coast. They used us for close support, to attack targets the army were chasing—we broke bridges, bombed troops, things like that. We'd be there and back in two and a half hours, then wait to see if there was another target they wanted bombs dropped on. They were short ops, so we did seventy in a tour, which would have been the equivalent of twenty ops on Bomber Command into Germany. We had it easy, really. Their chances of survival were less than one in three, you know. They lost 47,000 men in Bomber Command, more than the infantry. Bloody hell, they had a rough time.'

'Didn't you?'

'Well . . . Our opposition was mainly flak—there was a hell of a lot of anti-aircraft stuff, but not many fighters, because most of the time we had fighter escorts. Kept the Germans away. But we did lose quite a lot to anti-aircraft fire.'

'What chance did you have of getting out if you were hit?'

'Depends *where* it hit you—if it was your petrol tank, of course, you were blown up. But a friend of mine who used to be a member of this club, I actually saw him being shot down over Isernia in Italy. I saw him bail out, and three months later he was back with his squadron.'

'But not everyone was that lucky?'

'No; you'd go into the mess at night and you'd think about the chums who'd been there the previous night and had been buggered up that day. I lost friends. We all lost friends.

'One of the worst times, I remember . . . We used to drink ruddy Italian wine, and most nights it would be Johnny or Jo's gone today and his crew, well, tough luck, whatever, you could get yours tomorrow, you hoped not, but there it was, raise a glass. But on this day a chap had been hit by a bit of flak and he wasn't sure how bad the damage was, so he told his crew, "Stand by ready to bail out." But the intercom was bad and all the navigator heard was 'bail out'. And he jumped—but his chute didn't open. And the plane did manage to get back safely after all. Well, I've never known anything so quiet as the mess that night. The chaps felt far worse about that than anybody being thumped by flak and going down in bloody flames. Being shot down was accepted, you see, it was normal. But the idea of that chap jumping out for no bloody reason and then his chute failing . . . so damned unnecessary. The mess was utterly silent that night.'

Bill was quiet for a few moments. 'All this is going back a few bloody years, isn't it? How's your grub?'

I had ordered fish and chips, and they tasted extraordinarily English. We sipped our beers. 'Did you fly after the war?' I asked.

'Never.'

'Yet here we are, sitting in the Aero Club . . .'

'People who fly talk the same bloody nonsense as each other. They get on extremely well, whether it's a boy of fifteen or a chap like me who was flying sixty years ago. You always have a common theme. The youngsters are interested in the older planes, and so it goes . . .'

'You gave up flying?'

'I came back here and I've been here ever since. In farming initially, because my father was a farmer, then I became a property valuer. I've sat in plenty of cockpits, but never flying the blooming thing. I didn't come back to Nairobi until 1963, mind you, and I hadn't flown for twenty years. Too much water under the bridge. This was still Nairobi West then; after Independence they decided to christen it Wilson Airport, after Florence Kerr Wilson. Heard of her?'

'The founder of Wilson Airways?' I'd done my homework.

'Exactly. It's quite something, you know. It's usually the other way round, they change British names to African ones. But they recognised what Florence Wilson did to get aviation established in this country. She started in 1928—had the mad idea of setting up Kenya's first commercial airline. Mad, because she was a fifty-year-old widow and she started with a Gypsy Moth biplane that carried one bloody passenger! And Wilson Airways grew into what is today, Kenyan Airways, the national carrier . . . And then there was Beryl Markham, know her?'

It would be hard not to: the Aero Club has a virtual shrine devoted to Markham's memory.

'First woman to fly from England to America. She learned to fly here, you know. Drank at this bar, probably sat in the same bloody chair you're sitting in.'

Africa's wide-open skies and vast landscapes welcomed the 'air madness' that swept the world during the Roaring Twenties. In 1927 Lindbergh crossed the Atlantic solo, to tickertape and stardom. As aeroplane engines achieved new levels of reliability, sleek, streamlined models were targeted at the classes who would otherwise be buying Bentleys and Bugattis—or, in Markham's case, racehorses. A member of the Nairobi 'high set', she became a professional trainer when still in her teens (her horses were ridden by the likes of the Prince of Wales). The high set's amusements included hunting elephants from the air. When Markham discovered flying, gaining her licence in 1933 at the age of twenty-eight, she gave up breeding horses to become a commercial pilot (she kept just one horse, appropriately named Pegasus).

Aviatrices were powerful symbols of female liberation at the time; tall and slender, capable yet glamorous young women. By 1936 Markham had been married twice and divorced twice, was a mother, and was ready to attempt to be the first woman to fly from England to North America. She took off from Abingdon in a Percival Vega Gull, a 150 mph, single-engine plane, which ended up on its nose in a Nova Scotian swamp twenty-one and a half hours later when its fuel tanks iced up. Markham had, however, defeated the Atlantic.

She moved to California, published the book that is now considered an aviation classic, *West with the Night*, and flew for the Hollywood studios. There is a photograph of Douglas Fairbanks Jnr looking quizzically over her shoulder into a biplane cockpit. Markham, dressed in a short Prince of Wales-cheque jacket, is half-turned, amused, poised, Garboishly good-looking. She stayed in Hollywood until 1952, when she returned to Kenya and to training racehorses.

East African aviation can boast one other notable figure. A few years ago a British TV channel asked viewers to vote on the hundred most memorable moments in cinema. Near the top came the scene from *Out of Africa* where Karen Blixen, played by Meryl Streep, is flown in a biplane over the verdant vastnesses of Kenya. Her lover, played by Robert Redford, was the Englishman Denys Finch Hatton. Blixen wrote,

[To Denys] I owe what was, I think, the greatest, most trans-porting pleasure of my life on the farm: I flew with him over

Africa. There, where there are few or no roads and where you can land on the plains, flying becomes a thing of real and vital importance in your life, it opens up a world. Denys had brought out his Moth machine: it could land on my plain on the farm only a few minutes from the house and we were up nearly every day.

. . . you are sitting in front of your pilot, with nothing but space before you. You feel that he is carrying you upon the outstretched palms of his hands, as the Djinn carried Prince Ali through the air, and that the wings that bear you onward are his.

The Hon. Denys Finch Hatton was born on 24 April 1887, brought up on a 300-acre estate in Lincolnshire and educated at Eton, then Oxford, where he was a member of an élite group of intellectuals who called themselves 'The New Elizabethans'. Even then, Hatton announced his intention of leaving England, which he found 'small, much too small for me. I shall go to Africa.' In 1910 he attended one of the first air meets ever held in England and fell in love with flying. In 1911 he arrived in Kenya and by 1912 had bought a farm and was running cattle from Somalia to Nairobi. When war came he seized his opportunity to learn to fly and joined the Royal Flying Corps. Ten years later he was earning enough from his farm, and from big game hunting, to buy his de Havilland Gipsy Moth.

Hatton adored the freedom of flying; he once flew to London just to see the Ballets Russes perform *La Boutique Fantasque*, returning to Kenya immediately without even telephoning his family to say he was in London. It is the stuff, is it not, of High Romance. His life is immortalized in the writings of his lover Karen Blixen, whom he taught Greek and Latin, and to read the Bible. Blixen acknowledged that she would not have become the writer she did had she not met Hatton.

The cause of the accident that killed him was never known. His friend J. A. Hunter remembered his taking off from Nairobi at 8 a.m., after repairing his propeller. Hunter then saw a plume of black smoke. 'Denys had crashed . . . The plane was a blazing inferno and we were held off by the intense heat . . '. A few blackened oranges rolled out of the wreckage.'

The Aero Club has changed a lot of late, according to its chairman

Harro Trempenau. 'We're proud of our heritage, but the bastion of colonialism image has gone for good, I hope. Some Kenyans probably think we're a racist anachronism, but as you can see, there are plenty of black pilots at the bar. I'll tell you one thing, though: ten years ago, they wouldn't have had *me* here: a *German*. It was all old Spitfire pilots talking about the Messerschmitts they'd shot down. And you wouldn't believe how petty some people can still be.' He pointed at a framed print of a Messerschmitt Bf 109. 'That was a gift from myself and another German pilot. The day after we put it up, some people took it down—and replaced it with a picture of a Spitfire!'

There are 351 aircraft in Kenya, 110 of them private, of which half belong to white farmers. In recent years the Kenyan authorities have waged a subtle campaign against them, levying taxes and compulsory fees that have brought the cost of flying a small plane up to European levels. It has put the squeeze on private aviation.

'The other thing killing us is the government's attitude to airfields. There are 520 airfields in Kenya, many of which were funded by the World Bank to open up remote areas. Almost fifty are nice, tarmacked, regional airports. But the Kenyan Airports Authority has decided to accept responsibility for only ten of them. We've argued that they have military value, that banks use them for transferring

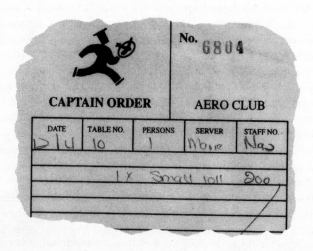

cash, air ambulances need them—it falls on deaf ears. Most of them are being left to rot.'

Simultaneously, there is pressure for Wilson Airport's prime real estate to be used for housing. Similar pressures threaten the adjacent national park.

'The immediate future's bleak,' Trempenau said. 'A couple of medium-sized private airlines are owned by politicians; they'll survive. But the logic of politics at present is against the small operator and the private pilot. It's absurd, because the skies are almost empty! At the busiest times, there will only be eighty planes in the sky in the entire country. Kenya is vast and aviation offers the best way of opening it up. At least, it could . . .'

I was strolling along the half-mile wall of hangars at Wilson Airport. It was a hot, dry morning, the sky still and cloudless. Standing beside a Cessna 152 outside one of the hangars was a young Asian woman, who I assumed was learning to fly. I was astonished to discover that she already had 1200 hours in her logbook. Reshma Shah was, at twenty years of age, a flying instructor.

Asians play a major rôle in the Kenyan economy, but are not known for encouraging their daughters to become pilots. 'Yeah, I guess my parents would have liked me to be a lawyer or something,' Reshma told me. 'But I've always been the odd one out—attracted to things girls aren't meant to be. Cars, planes . . . I learned to fly at sixteen and I knew right away that this is how I wanted to spend my life. They don't like it, of course. A daughter doing something so *dangerous*, as they see it. And once I'm in the airlines I'll be away a lot. Maybe I'll have to leave Kenya altogether.' She sounded as though she could hardly wait.

We took one of the 152s from Reshma's school and flew west, out over the Longonot crater, where the idea for this book was born. As we circled over it, I remembered a spectacular sunset five years earlier. The last thing I'd expected then was that I'd next see this crater from a pilot's seat.

Pilots criss-crossing Kenya had picked up Reshma's voice on the radio. 'Reshma, how's that cool new car of yours going?' 'Didn't see you on Saturday, *yaar*!' 'Hey, what are you doing tonight?' I wondered how such aerial flirtation would go down with the overworked and dour air traffic controllers of Europe. But then, Kenyan aviation is *not* anonymous or remote.

'Pilots in Africa', Doug Morey told me, 'aren't mere extensions of somebody's computer, we're not mollycoddled. Flying here is an antidote to a world that's getting too centralized, too samey. We may not be as high-tech as Europe or the US, but it means that we actually have to think for ourselves, that we look out for each other. I like that.'

He flies with Air Kenya, which sounds like a national carrier, but is in fact a medium-sized private airline, whose fleet includes a Shorts 360 like the one I'd flown to Stornoway.

With his luxuriant moustache and lived-in face, Doug would be many people's idea of how a veteran pilot ought to look. He started flying in the Sixties in the US Air Force at the height of the Vietnam War. 'But I was mostly flying freighters across the Pacific and a few VIPs. Nobody ever shot at me—I had a pretty easy war. It was a good life for a young guy.' By the mid-Seventies his VIPs had included President Carter, but when he left the USAF he found charter work dull. 'I fancied some adventure, so I came to Africa for six months. I never left.'

He offered me a spin into the Maasai Mara, Kenya's principal game reserve, 400-odd square miles of undulating grassland swarming with wildlife and dotted with exclusive game lodges. Prosperous tourists eschew a 4x4 ride over rutted tracks into the Mara, choosing instead to drop out of the sky.

Doug was flying a de Havilland Dash 7, a four-engine, fifty-passenger plane, well-known for its STOL abilities—Short Take-Off and Landing. STOL is a phrase you hear a lot in places where aircraft operate out of unmade airstrips. Conventional airliners need long runways to build up speed for take-off, but bush airstrips are often short, rutted, or even quite steeply sloping. STOL aircraft have big-bladed propellers and specifically-configured wings to achieve lift at low speeds. Some can take off in just a few times their own length.

I was about to see for myself what STOL meant. A second or two into a take-off run from one of the Mara dirt strips, a herd of antelope burst from the long grass halfway down the strip and began to leap across it. As we thundered towards them at maximum speed, a collision seemed inevitable. Instead, the fully laden plane went up like a lift. Doug turned to me and winked. 'Now you know why pilots love the Dash 7.'

I had heard that some people in the Maasai Mara offered balloon rides. Doug didn't know the pilots, but a friend of his, Murray Levit, was standing in for the manager at the camp which operated the balloons. Doug suggested he leave me in Murray's hands and dropped me at a place called Little Governors Camp, arranging to collect me two days later.

Little Governors is a Hemingwayesque former big game hunting camp, where tourists sip tea in front of tents (luxurious rooms that happen to have canvas walls) around a lake in which hippos wallow among lily pads. The animals of the Mara have acquired a fairly relaxed attitude to humans, but they aren't tame. Strolling outside the camp is dangerous and forbidden. Hippos and other creatures occasionally wander through the camp. Maasai *askaris*—lanky men armed with semi-automatic rifles—are posted every few yards and keep a keen lookout.

Murray Levit trained as an artist in London, but now makes a living designing and building these re-creations of some colonial Eden. He invited me to the bar at 3 p.m. and we kept drinking until bedtime. I woke the next morning with a hangover and faint memories of a story about a medical student who stole a penis from a jar of formaldehyde and took it into a crowded pub urinal on a Saturday night, where he shook it vigorously in front of his fly, then dropped it in the trough.

Murray had introduced me to two VIPs—'Very Irritating Pilots'. If his existence as creator-god of these Edens seemed agreeable, these men surely had the best jobs in the world. Robin Batchelor and Greg Russell were the balloon pilots, the men who wafted across the Maasai Mara every day at dawn, en route to a champagne breakfast in the bush.

As we sat down, Murray asked the barman for four chilled Tuskers. I explained that I hadn't ever been in a balloon. 'Call yourself a pilot and never been ballooning!' Robin huffed. 'The ancient art of Joseph-Michel and Jacques-Étienne Montgolfier—218 years old, to be precise—the first and still the most elegant form of manned flight!'

Here was a man whose fanaticism matched that of Peter Morrow, whose passion got me flying in the first place. Shamefaced, I wondered if a spare place aboard one of the balloons might allow me to make amends.

'Love to, old man,' said Robin, 'but unfortunately they're all fully booked. Costs a bomb, you know. Long waiting lists. Highlight of the Maasai Mara.'

'Murray's probably got you thinking people come here to gawp at wildlife,' added Greg, 'and maybe do a balloon ride on the side. He'd love that to be the case, but of course he's got it all the wrong way round.'

'Cheeky bastard,' said Murray.

'People come here', continued Robin, 'to drift in the world's biggest balloon across one of its most magnificent landscapes, as the first rays of the sun are turning the early-morning mist pink and gold.'

'Of course, we throw in a few animals,' said Greg breezily. 'As a matter of fact, they're the most intimate views of animals you'll ever get.'

Like Doug Morey, Greg Russell had found that his stay in Africa proved longer than he expected. 'I used to work in Sydney—sightseeing over the Opera House, that sort of thing. I decided to come here for three months. That was thirteen years ago.'

A hippo climbed lazily out of the lake and waddled past us, observed by several armed guards.

'Four more Tuskers?' asked Murray.

It was not difficult to get Robin and Greg to talk about their favourite subject—more a question of light the blue touch paper and retire.

'If it's windy on take-off, it's hairy. You've got to really passion-ately want to do it. Which is why you choose ballooning in the first place.'

'We hit a sudden windsheer one morning. Overburn and we'd end on the rocks in Tanzania. Underburn and we'd hit the ground hard. And we both greased it perfectly. That is job satisfaction.'

'I'm not rich, but I've flown in thirty countries and kissed death on the mouth three times, I reckon.'

'I had a hairy moment once. I was at 3000 feet and there was a jumbo jet on collision course at 4000. Well, *I* couldn't give way. I could see his nose on the glass as he banked away.'

'But the balloon is the only aircraft in the world where you can have a mid-air collision and keep going.'

'One day in Johannesburg I'd gone past the perfect landing site and suddenly I went straight up in a thermal, then dropped like a grand piano. I was giving it full heat and we were dropping. It was a choice between landing on telegraph wires or the motorway or a railway track and I knew I was going to die, and I was that terrified I swore that if I ever got out of it I would never get in a balloon again. And somehow I landed in a cemetery. There was this six-foot-five black man praying. And I ran up to him and threw my arms around him.'

'I don't see how *anyone*, let alone a pilot, can *not* go ballooning. I mean, they must look up into the sky and these majestic globes are sailing serenely through the sky, offering a perspective on the world

that men have dreamed about for millennia. And it's available, it's an option, all they have to do is lift the phone and book a flight. And they *don't*. Why? *Why*? Why this enfeeblement, this crippling absence of simple curiosity? Don't they *want* to feel awe? Don't they *want* to wake up and come to life, for goodness' sake?'

'We at Governors are Kenya's principal consumers of propane and champagne. The champagne comes by *container*. At the millennium we were doing thirty-six bottles of Moët a night.'

'Balloons and champagne are inextricably interlinked. I've had a glass of champagne almost every day for the last twenty years. I get withdrawal symptoms when I don't.'

'Basically it's showbiz.'

'We're paid to entertain a dozen strangers.'

'Hangover, gut-rot or malaria, the show must go on . . .'

Murray stood up. 'And when they don't fly, they get very fucking grumpy. Four more Tuskers?'

It was late. Lunch had long since been cleared away and the camp's guests had disappeared in 4x4s to gawp at crocodile and lion.

'Are you sure there's no chance of squeezing one more person aboard?' I asked.

The ancient art of Joseph-Michel and Jacques-Étienne Montgolfier? In France, there are many who like to believe that aviation is somehow French property, part of that chauvinist fantasy, *l'exception française*. They protest too much. There has been no national destiny in aviation. But it's probably true that the French have been more in love with aviation, for longer, than any other nation. It is also true that a Frenchman was the first to ascend in a lighter-than-air machine.

Everyone knows the engraving of the Montgolfiers' balloon, a plump inverted teardrop classically decorated with fleurs-de-lis and wreaths, aloft over Paris. But the principle of the balloon was not invented in France.

In the two centuries after Leonardo's death, virtually the only new insight into aviation came from an Italian Jesuit, Francesco de Lana, who published a design for an 'aerial ship' that would sail through the air supported by four evacuated, wafer-thin copper globes. Being lighter than air, the spheres would rise. The weakness in de Lana's theory was that in practice, the pressure of the surrounding air would crush the fragile copper spheres. De Lana did, however, have the distinction of being the first recorded man to predict the use of aircraft as weapons: 'No city would be proof against surprise . . . iron weights could be hurled down . . . houses, fortresses and cities could thus be destroyed.' So great, de Lana felt, was the destructive potential of the aerial ship, that 'God would surely never allow such a machine to be successful'.

In chapter III I mentioned the first person to demonstrate a *functioning* balloon—another of those intellectual Jesuits, the Portuguese Bartolomeu Laurenço de Gusmão, born in Brazil in 1686. By the first decade of the eighteenth century the young Father Bartolomeu was

De Gusmão's design for a manned balloon

already a well-known theologian and 'natural philosopher'. In 1709 he applied to the King of Portugal for a patent for an ornithopter, which was duly granted. The machine was rapidly built and scheduled for flight-testing in Lisbon on 24 June 1709. It goes without saying that like every other ornithopter, it remained on terra firma. A ludicrous illustration of his creation made de Gusmão a laughing stock in the eyes of later generations, but he was an early victim of journalism: the boa-like wings and magnetic lodestone power were figments of the illustrator's imagination.

De Gusmão did not deserve such derision. Like Leonardo, he seems to have understood that birds do not only flap their wings, but also *glide*. It appears that during the summer of 1709—perhaps in an attempt to restore his dented reputation—de Gusmão launched some sort of glider, probably from the heights of the Castillo de São Jorge in Lisbon. Unfortunately, no witness left a written record. But three months later, on 8 August, Father de Gusmão launched a miniature hot air balloon, in the presence of King John V of Portugal and several men of letters. 'Various spirits, quintessences and other ingredients' were placed in a small trough-shaped bark, with a globe-shaped canvas cloth over it. When the spirits were lit, the hot vapours caused the bark to fly. It rose gently to a small height, before setting fire to some of the Salla das Exbaixadas's wall hangings, 'and everything against which it knocked. His Majesty was good enough not to take ill.'

To have experimented publicly with an ornithopter, a glider and a hot air balloon in the space of a few months, before he had reached the age of twenty-five, suggests a consummate scientist utterly absorbed in aviation. Manifestly de Gusmão was a genius. There's one other piece of evidence that confirms the breadth of his vision: a drawing showing a full-sized, manned balloon. But no one saw fit to set about constructing it. Indeed, de Gusmão was exhibiting aero-nautical insights at a time and place when it wasn't really safe to do so: there were murmurings of sorcery, of the Inquisition. There is no evidence of an interrogation, but he appears to have left Portugal for Spain under somewhat mysterious circumstances.

In 1766, the English chemist Henry Cavendish read before the Royal Society a paper describing his experiments with the little-known substance he described as 'inflammable air': hydrogen. At sea level, hydrogen weighs 5.3 lbs per 1000 cubic feet, compared with 76 lbs for air. In other words, it rises. If Cavendish ever considered the possibilities of enclosing hydrogen in some kind of envelope which would ascend, he didn't mention it. But when Dr Joseph Black of Glasgow University read the paper, he provoked laughter among his students by suggesting that someone could fill a bladder with gas and make it float. He later recorded honestly that it never occurred to him to construct 'large artificial bladders, and making these lift heavy weights, and carry men up into the air'. Nevertheless, his playful suggestions reached the ears of another natural philosopher working in Britain, the Italian Tiberius Cavallo, who in 1781 did set out to make a floating bladder. Unfortunately, he found the available materials—animal guts and paper—too heavy or too porous. He succeeded in filling soap bubbles with hydrogen, but found that, being 'very brittle and altogether intractable, they do not seem applicable to any philosophical purpose'. Having become 'tired with the expense and loss of time,' Cavallo gave up.

The Montgolfier brothers were papermakers from Annonay, near Lyons in France. They were not masters in the science of lighter-than-air gases (in fact, they were quite the opposite, though they knew pioneering works like Joseph Priestley's *Experiments and Observations on Different Kinds of Air*). But having noticed the way that a burning fire carries feathery fragments into the air above the flames, the Montgolfiers asked why should they not, as they put it, 'enclose a cloud in a bag and let the latter be lifted up by the former'. From an early stage, their aim was to devise a form of transport.

The first experiments were made in November 1782 and must have been similar to those of Laurenço de Gusmão. Starting with a silk bag, the brothers experimented with various materials, adding glued paper linings to make them airtight. They quickly showed that they were not going to be content with mere models. By the following June, they were ready to make a public demonstration at Annonay of a balloon thirty-eight feet in diameter. Made from triangular pieces of linen buttoned together and sealed internally with paper, it was tethered over a fire of wool and straw. As the structure filled with hot air and swelled, it was released. Rising into the sky, the world's first full-sized hot air balloon provoked an amazed silence, then loud cheers, from an assembled crowd of officials, savants and countrymen. It rose to 6000 feet and drifted 7000 feet before returning to earth. Oddly enough, the Montgolfiers didn't realize they had invented the *hot air* balloon; they believed it was a gas created by their patent combination of wool and straw that caused the balloon to ascend (they had also explored the smoke-producing potential of old shoes and raw meat).

Jacques Charles's hydrogen balloon

When an account of the Montgolfiers' achievement reached Paris (in the form, to counter metropolitan scepticism, of a sworn affidavit), it caused a sensation. The *Académie des Sciences* was galvanized into raising a subscription to finance research into lighter-than-air flight. Jacques Charles was engaged to carry out the work, and from the sketchy information available to him he concluded that the 'gas' used at Annonay must have been less efficient than the 'inflammable air' recently described by Cavendish. By 23 August Charles's hydrogen balloon, a spherical, rubberised silk construction thirteen feet in diameter, was ready to go. Despite being transported by night to avoid crowds, news got out and the flammable balloon was accompanied to its launch site by a boisterous crowd carrying lighted torches perilously close. It was launched at five o'clock on 27 August. It rose for two minutes before disappearing in cloud. Among those present was Benjamin Franklin, scientist (he had made electrical experiments with a kite in a storm in 1752) and Paris representative of the newly independent American states. 'What's the use of a balloon?' some sceptic asked him, after the demonstration.

'What's the use of a newborn baby?' Franklin is supposed to have replied.

A little later that afternoon, at Gonesse, fifteen miles from Paris, Charles's balloon abruptly dropped out of low cloud—much to the alarm of villagers whom no one had prepared for the advent of aviation. They spent an hour creeping fearfully up to the monster, until at last someone fired a shot, and it began to deflate. The victorious peasants tied the defeated balloon to the tail of a horse and galloped it around the fields until it was torn to shreds.

While the *Académie* was moving to stamp the imprimatur of respectability on the discovery, the provincial papermakers, not to be deprived of *gloire*, had travelled to Paris and were constructing and testing balloons in the garden of a friend and fellow papermaker (careful to conceal the straw and wool combination they knew to be the secret of their 'gas'). For all the success of the Establishment's M. Charles, the achievements of the Montgolfiers could not be gainsaid—especially as their vast balloons began to blossom above the rooftops of Paris. On 19 September they were at last able (after a first attempt was rained off and the sodden balloon collapsed) to give a demonstration before the King and Queen, and countless men and women of rank and influence, at Versailles. To go one step further than Charles, the brothers wanted to put living creatures in the balloon, but, unready to risk human lives, they sent aloft a sheep, a cock and a rooster, dangling beneath the balloon in a wicker cage. *Le tout Paris* was duly amazed, the brothers were awarded the Order of Saint Michael, their father was granted a patent of nobility and gold medals were struck with the brothers' profiles and the words, '*Pour avoir rendu l'air navigable*'.

The successful balloon was now reconstructed, with an onboard brazier and a circular wicker gallery capable of taking human weight.

But who would be chosen as the world's first balloon pilot? The King was said to believe only a criminal should be used for such a hazardous undertaking, until it was pointed out that in the event of a successful flight, they would have conferred an unprecedented honour on a murderer or thief. The successful applicant was a doctor, Pilâtre de Rosier, whose enthusiasm for the revolutionary mode of transport is demonstrated by the fact that he had been the first on the scene when the animals touched down after the Versailles flight. On 15 October de Rosier climbed into the gallery and the balloon rose, tethered, to a height of eighty-four feet. He kept himself airborne by stoking the brazier with straw and wool, returning after four minutes twenty-four seconds to earth, to a place in the history books and to the acclamation of the onlookers,

> . . . having shown the world the accomplishment of what had been for ages desired and attempted in vain . . . to ascend into the atmosphere with a machine, to which, a few years hence, the most timid woman will perhaps not hesitate to trust herself.

The brothers Montgolfier made few flights (the most brilliant aircraft designers have rarely been enthusiastic aviators themselves), but de Rosier made many, most notably on 21 November the same year. This is the balloon which we all hold an image of in our heads, from that engraving showing it classically decorated with garlands and putti. On this occasion de Rosier was accompanied by an infantry

The wool-powered Montgolfier

major, the Marquis d'Arlandes. Taking off at 1.54 p.m., they ascended to 280 feet, removed their hats to salute the crowds, then drifted south-east over Paris, crossed the Seine, passed between the Invalides and the École Militaire, and landed 'very gently in a field beyond the new Boulevard' (near Gobelins). But according to the account left by d'Arlandes, the flight was far from serene. Perched on either side of the smoke-belching brazier, unable to see each other, their conversation went something like this:

Pilâtre: If you don't do anything, we're not going to go up.
D'Arlandes: Oh—sorry. (*Throws a lump of wool on the brazier.*)
Pilâtre (*slightly testy*):   Don't worry, *I'll* do it. (*Stokes vigorously. A heavy jolt is felt.*)
D'Arlandes: What are you doing, *dancing*?
Pilâtre: I didn't budge. It's the rising gas from the new combustion.
D'Arlandes: Ah; good; let's hope it gets us across the Seine. (*Pause.*) My God, this basket isn't tied on very securely, is it?
Pilâtre: Oh. No, I suppose there could be a bit more lashing . . .
D'Arlandes: Crikey . . .
Pilâtre: Look, we're right in the heart of Paris!
D'Arlandes: Frankly, I'm not interested in sightseeing. Are we about to hit anything? Is it clear on your side?
Pilâtre: Yes. Well, we are a bit close to the tower of the Saint Sulpice, actually. Yes, I think we could hit it.
D'Arlandes (*urgently*):   For Goodness' sake put some more wool on the fire, then, and let's get up over it!
Pilâtre: Well, why don't you put some of *yours* on?

On 1 December the *Académie*'s man, M. Charles, took to the air in a large hydrogen balloon. This flight is far less famous, but in truth, even more impressive. Carefully calculated according to wind strength and direction—checked by a small pilot balloon—and monitored by a variety of instruments, the flight allowed Charles to rise to an extraordinary *9000 feet*. It also gave him the experience that even today's aviators especially cherish: seeing the sun set twice. Charles did all this less than six months after the Montgolfiers' first unmanned flight! One of the world's great aviation pioneers, Charles made this epochal flight—after which, nothing more is known of him.

The following year, 1784, the records rapidly mounted: the first ascent by a woman (Madame Thible at Lyons, 4 June), the first American ascent (at Baltimore, 24 June, made by the thirteen-year-old Edward Warren when the balloon proved incapable of lifting the weight of its builder, Peter Carnes), the first Briton to make an ascent (James Sadler, a confectioner, on 4 October, from a spot a few hundred yards from where I'm writing this, Christchurch Meadows in Oxford); soon would follow the first international flight, the first crossing of the English Channel, the first ascent *on horseback*, etc. Several '*Montgolfières*' were destroyed by fire and the far more predictable and practical (if inherently dangerous) hydrogen balloons, or '*Charlières*', became the norm.

In 1785 Pilâtre de Rosier designed a hybrid balloon that combined the essential 'buoyancy' of a hydrogen balloon with a hot air element to allow the pilot to ascend at will. The hydrogen section was a perfect sphere, with a long cylinder beneath it, and the brazier swung under that. With hindsight, it sounds suicidal; but de Rosier set off to cross the Channel in the device on 15 June 1785. Twenty-five minutes into the journey the heat from the brazier ignited the hydrogen sphere and de Rosier and his co-pilot plunged to their deaths on the French shores of the Channel. The world's first pilot had become the first aviation fatality.

Miraculously, after a long and largely liquid lunch, Greg and Robin had found room for one more passenger. The following morning I got up at five and watched as two of the world's largest balloons were inflated. In the moonless dark it was a scene out of Dante—the burners laid horizontally, roaring and vomiting orange flames into the hooped open mouth of the envelope, illuminating its rainbow stripes. In the silences between each roar came the clacking nocturnal noises of the bush. Slowly each vast pod swelled, taking on some pale external colour as the pre-dawn sky grew grey. At last the balloons were inflated, pregnant, potent, ten storeys high. I clambered into Greg's wicker basket, which was itself the size of a small bus. He heaved on a rope, an eight-foot tongue of flame leapt vertically into the striped canopy and we were aloft.

The sky grew rapidly pink, revealing the Mara river shrouded in silver mist. Suspended at 1500 feet, we watched the rising sun cast long shadows across a landscape of emerald marshes and honey-coloured grasses, awakening flocks of birds, and herds of buffalo and antelope. We could also see the ground crew, their Land Rovers tracing our course with their cargo of eggs and bubbly. In silence, we watched a male leopard slinking through tall grass close to a small herd of impala. Ours was a supernaturally privileged perspective. An American woman beside me murmured aloud, as though putting it on the record, 'This is the best experience I have ever had.'

After ninety minutes aloft Greg asked, 'Where shall we land?'

'How about parking next to Robin?' suggested an adolescent wag. Robin had already settled ahead of us and well off to our right—and everyone knows that balloons can't be steered.

'I'll do my best,' said Greg enigmatically. For ten minutes he felt his way forward, intuitively working the light airs that at different altitudes blew in slightly different directions. Sometimes we rose high, at other times the basket was so low that leaves and grass heads caught in its wicker weave. To our astonishment Greg brought us precisely alongside the other, now flat, balloon, laying the enormous basket to earth without so much as a bump. As I climbed out, I could hear corks popping, and smell eggs and bacon on the still morning air.

CHAPTER XV

A Flying Incident

'THIS ISN'T REALLY A good day for you, is it?' I asked, settling into the sticky velour passenger seat of Bernard Terlouw's ageing Datsun.

'No,' he replied candidly.

Mission Aviation Fellowship, the missionary airline of which Bernard Terlouw was the Kenya Director, had just suffered its first crash in a decade. The accident, in neighbouring Tanzania, had landed the plane's five occupants in hospital and flung Bernard into a wave of frantic activity. Today, Sunday, day of rest, he was trying to air ambulance two victims to Europe, coping with stress, red tape, a long-arranged VIP visit, a family that was fast forgetting what he looks like—and me.

Bernard's tall, bony, blond-crew-cut figure had not fitted the mental picture of the theologian I was expecting to meet. Just turned forty, he looked all of twenty-six.

'So what *is* your mental picture of a theologian?' he asked.

'Severe. Hunched. Pedantic.'

'Just wait a bit—you don't know me yet.'

I'd heard I might be able to hitch with MAF pilots in East Africa—with the permission of their boss. Bernard had told me on the phone he *might* be able to help. He even offered to let me stay at the MAF guest house for a few days. Today, it seemed, he was having second thoughts.

Bernard's 'vipps', as he called them, were the directors of the Christian Blind Mission. 'They've chartered us to take them to the opening of a hospital in Tanzania in Dar es Salaam. This is the very rare occasion that we fly on a Sunday—as a Christian mission, we naturally observe Sunday as a day of rest.'

MAF's Nairobi HQ sits in splendid isolation at one end of the

Wilson apron—the far end from the Aero Club. The building is a large hangar with sun-baked offices built into its façade. Bernard's office was an oven. He threw open a window and turned on a fan.

'No air-conditioning?' I asked.

He grinned. Please, 'we're a *mission*, we're supposed to suffer a bit! The fact is, the building is *naturally* air conditioned, there are shafts that let air circulate, the architect got an award for it. The trouble is, he also gave the building this glass wall . . .

'Now, my vipps.' He reached into the drawer of his desk and pulled out a time-dulled black polyester tie. 'Always prepared, you see.'

I was beginning to see another side of Bernard Terlouw, a playfulness. Douglas Kimanthi, the MAF Operations Manager, put his head round the door and told Bernard his vipps had come early and gone early and were now halfway to Dar es Salaam.

Bernard shrugged, pulled his tie off and stuffed it back in the drawer. 'Suddenly I have an hour to spare. You want to look around?'

Behind the offices, a mezzanine gangway overlooked a cavernous and spotless hangar containing four planes. Bernard pointed at the larger ones. 'Cessna Caravans. Licensed to carry nine passengers in America, or fourteen in Kenya. Interesting statistic, no? The relative wealth of the first and third worlds denoted in terms of human fat.'

Outside the hangar stood a de Havilland Beaver, sold by MAF and waiting for a ferry pilot to deliver it to its new owners in Canada. 'He has to fly it across the Atlantic, via Iceland and Greenland,' said Bernard with a shudder. 'Freezing waters. A small, single-engine plane. It's in good condition, but it hasn't been in regular use for months. Quite a breed, those ferry pilots.'

Just beyond the MAF hangar was an aerial graveyard, dozens of aircraft carcasses. Bernard threw out his arms. 'Behold, the prehistory of aviation: rusty, half-winged, no engines, flat tyres. I wouldn't be surprised to find a Swastika or some bullet holes. Happily these aren't our aircraft. It's where they store the airport's eyesores.'

'Why next to your hangar?'

'I'd love to know. We had asked for some space over there and were amazed when bulldozers arrived immediately and started to level it. Our wonder turned to horror when every wreck on the airfield was dragged into our backyard.'

I pointed at a small regional airliner, with gory tangles of red cable where its engines had been. 'I reckon you could get that twin-engine job going without too much effort.'

'Pah! It's a twin *no*-engine,' retorted Bernard. 'If you think that can fly again, you must have vision. You are a visionary.' We wandered deeper into the graveyard. 'But no, they're not all antique. At Wilson there are mysterious fires aboard aircraft in the middle of the night. People are forced to leave planes because of unpaid debts and other reasons into which I'm told it doesn't pay to dig too deeply. The planes get dragged here and looted, and left to rot. Maybe they think that as missionaries we can give them the last rites.'

I laughed. 'Someone even keeps the grass cut.'

'Oh yes, it's a well-preserved graveyard.'

Birds fluttered from wing-tip to tail fin, nested in empty engine nacelles. Cicadas kept up a rhythmic creak. This was a paradoxical place, clashing everything an aircraft symbolises—modernity, physical perfection, financial value—with a tangle of corroded aluminium.

A great silver plane stood before us. I ran my hand down its aluminium tail section. It was a Douglas DC-3/Dakota, the revolutionary Thirties airliner and stalwart of the Berlin Airlift. Around 13,000 DC-3s were built and some are in commercial use even today, the thirsty radial engines 'retrofitted' with modern turboprops. This Dakota's wings were half missing, its engines gone. But nearby was another, plump-tyred and gleaming, as though waiting for a couple of cheery pilots to jump into the cockpit, fire up the Pratt & Whitneys and climb into the African sky. The Dakota is the archetypal aeroplane, purposeful yet cuddly, illustrated on luggage labels, in tourist brochures and children's books. The entire graveyard, in fact, was a magnificent children's playground and it made children of us. 'What do you think "No Step Here" means?' asked Bernard, balancing on a silvery wing.

In a far corner stood a rotten biplane, with strips of fabric hanging from its wings. We pulled open the cobwebbed doors and edged past pendulous hornets' nests. 'Sixteen seats,' Bernard counted. 'Funny: it's a wreck, but it still smells exactly like an aeroplane.'

Gigantic hornets circled slowly among the beams of afternoon sunlight that penetrated the glassless portholes. The rudder creaked in the wind, causing the rudder pedals to work as though there were a ghostly pilot at the controls. I saw stout leather straps that could have been tightened to lash the pilots' feet to these pedals and shuddered to imagine what conditions could necessitate such measures.

We peered at the mass of dials and riveted plates: they were marked in Cyrillic. On the control columns were the letters 'AH-2' and I realised it was an Antonov AN-2. I had read about these Russian biplanes, so sturdy and reliable that they had remained in production until the collapse of Soviet communism.

The AN-2, fondly known as 'Annushka', was a sort of Russian Dakota. It came from the pen of the brilliant Russian aircraft designer

Dying DC-3 with Annushka in background

Oleg Antonov. After World War II Antonov had an idea for a flying jeep and the commission eventually came from the Agriculture Ministry. Antonov christened his baby the 'Colt', but its first official designation was the less romantic *Selskokhozyaistvennyi-1*: Agricultural-economic-1. Its biplane layout (in the West it was joked that the letters 'AN' stood for 'Anachronism') had been dictated simply by practicality: biplanes have lower wing loadings and lower structural weight, and in the Soviet Union, unbreakable simplicity counted for more than fashionable modernity. In production terms, Annushka was an outstanding success. Over 25,000 were built, in Russia, Poland and China. They have served as crop sprayers, firefighters, air ambulances, executive aircraft, paratroop carriers and, in Cuba, as airliners.

Bernard knelt down and picked up a ring-bound sheaf of mouldering cards. 'Look, these must be the pre-flight checks the pilot used on the last flight. "Remove all external control locks, remove drain bung from exhaust . . . Tips for landing downwind: 130 km/hr, 15% of flap if required."' He pointed at the metal rods holding the control columns in place. 'They even put the control locks on when they left. They thought this plane was going to fly again one day.'

Back in the office, I asked about MAF's recent accident. Bernard's good humour disappeared. He showed me some pictures, taken both from the air and the ground, of a white Cessna resting on a cultivated, gently sloping hillside. Its nose was fifteen feet from the fuselage.

'Basically, it was a hard landing,' Bernard said.

I tried not to smile.

'Yes,' he went on quickly, 'a very, very hard landing. But to be pedantic, it was an *incident*, not an accident. I want to insist on that. The pilot was in control all the way through. There were four passengers and everybody survived. They have some back problems and head injuries, but they're alive and doing relatively well.'

'But the plane *was* destroyed.'

'No, it's still very much an aeroplane, the, er, prop and engine have, of course, fallen off because of the landing and the nosewheel is gone. But the cabin is intact.'

'How did it happen?'

'He was on the way from one mission hospital to another and the weather worsened—low cloud. Small planes can't climb over the weather, of course, a Cessna 206 is really a grasshopper that has to keep out of the cloud—*under* the weather. He was trying to find his way through the mountains and he got into a downdraught and was forced to land.'

'How did he get into the downdraught?'

'Well, I'm not a pilot. As I understand it, there was cloud at the end of the valley, preventing him from crossing into the next valley. He had to turn and at that moment the downdraught got hold of him. It had a force of around 2000 feet per minute, far more than the plane's climbing rate. If you're already low, you don't have many options. And I understand from other pilots that he did a very brave thing by not turning further, which you'd be inclined to do. That would have been fatal, because turning would have lowered the plane's speed even more and possibly caused a stall.'

How often have low cloud and mountains proved a fatal combination for aircraft? So this crash *was* a success story: the Cessna's engine is designed to spiral away in the event of an impact. And everyone had survived.

But an investigation was inevitable. If a pilot suspects that conditions are worsening beyond the point of safety, he must turn back; but as the pilots of slow, low-flying aircraft have discovered ever since the days of Saint-Exupéry, the weather can close in behind you. Some meteorological events cannot be predicted—or even seen. Nevertheless, downdraughts—violent down-rushes of wind often sweeping off the ridges of mountains—are a known hazard that pilots are meant to take into account.

I imagined myself piloting the fully laden Cessna, trying to pick my way through valleys cut off at the height of the passes by clouds that were now descending like portcullises. The plane strays close to a valley wall, where a current of air is plunging like a cascade of water at 2000 feet per minute. As the ground rushes up, you search for a patch of relatively flat land, desperately scanning for any obstruction—a fence or an irrigation ditch—that could cause the plane to somersault. You crash-land, the landing gear collapses, you're knocked momentarily unconscious; the whirling propeller bites the ground, its enormous torque rips the engine from its mountings and cartwheels it away. But the cabin is intact. There's no fire, thank God. There are gashed knees and foreheads and compacted spines, but the bloody occupants are able to undo their seat belts and limp out.

'I'd stress', Bernard was saying, 'that as a mission, we still feel God protected him, because this could have been a lot worse. The fact is, this is the kind of flying we do, in rough parts of Africa where missionaries and medical teams have to go—and it's our job to take them.'

As we left the airport, we encountered at its gates a car crash, two ageing Japanese cars entwined almost affectionately in puddles of glass and chrome. A couple of policemen carrying antique carbines forced us, unnecessarily, to wait.

'I'm not going to argue, I don't want them dragging these wrecks behind our hangar.' Bernard was recovering his habitual droll form. 'But I think we should have started this trip with a prayer. Our pilots always say a prayer before flights.'

'Doesn't that make some passengers nervous?'

'But others would get nervous if there weren't any prayers!'

After the initial cool reception from Bernard, we seemed to be getting on. I broached again the question of my flying with MAF. He gave me an ironic look. 'You know the parable of the good Samaritan? Well, without his donkey, he couldn't have carried the injured man he found at the roadside. MAF is a donkey; people do aid, relief and mission work all over the world and we exist to carry them, fly them over war zones, take them into places it would need days to reach by land.' He gave a slightly lupine grin. 'Do you do any good works, Martin?'

We reached the gates of MAF's walled residential compound.

Bernard gave a sigh. 'You know that joke? "What do your children say when you get home? Mummy, there's a strange man at the door."'

We went into the house, a typical colonial bungalow, with cool, airy rooms and plenty of varnished hardwood. He introduced me to his wife Margriet, a pastor. Three sunny children piled into Bernard, grabbing legs or, in the case of the elder ones, reaching up for his long arms. Four years ago, the Terlouws had the calling. Now they work for a missionary organisation created in the late 1940s by Murray Kendon and Jack Hemmings, an Englishman and a New Zealander, ex-RAF pilots who wanted to turn their wartime skills to good. It began with a research trip to East Africa via Egypt and Sudan—the long-established East Africa route that avoided the vast open spaces of the Sahara. The plane they used was a de Havilland Rapide, the same art deco biplane that first flew the mails to Stornoway. Today, an MAF plane takes off somewhere in the world every four minutes—a record no commercial airline can equal.

I ran my eyes over the Terlouws' library of books and a music collection which included every piece of music Bach composed, 145 CDs. Bernard was telling me of some of MAF's recent operations. Their medevacs (medical evacuations) had ranged from a nomad boy who'd been accidentally shot with an arrow, to a tribal hunter gored by a tusked wild pig. Recently, they'd airlifted from a village in Sudan a woman suffering from a breech birth, saving both her life and her baby's.

Margriet brought in a tray with a pot of tea and biscuits and handed me a cup. She gave me a frank, appraising look. 'So, you hope to— hitch-hike with MAF?'

And suddenly I lost all my confidence, my request seemed out-rageous. Here they were, ferrying missionaries into war zones and plucking the victims of homicidal pigs from rain forests, in the course of which they sometimes crashed in remote, cloud-veiled valleys. And I turn up with the entirely frivolous and egoistic expectation of being chauffeured around for free.

After tea, Bernard took me over to the guest house, a Victorian gingerbread confection standing under flame trees full of screeching birds. It was late afternoon, the air warm and static. After marvelling briefly at the cottage's crazed Royal Doulton sinks and brass Birmingham fittings, I succumbed to a siesta.

Bernard had arranged for St John Ambulances to collect two of the injured Cessna passengers—Norwegian nurses—and take them to the airport at 8 p.m. 'I'm going along, just to make sure everything runs smoothly. Someone may ask for a pink slip . . .'

'A what?'

'They tell you you need a green and an orange slip, which you have duly obtained—but suddenly they say you need a pink slip. And it's out of office hours, or the official who needs to sign it is attending a wedding today. Basically it's colonial bureaucracy—the fault of you Brits.

'Also, I'm hoping St John send two ambulances this time. Last time they sent only one for two patients and they had to sort of hold them in, which they said was perfectly fine and of course I have absolutely no reason to dispute their professional competence . . . But this time I've insisted on *two* ambulances.'

A few minutes later we were standing at the bedside of the injured pilot, Andy Fothergill, a Briton in his mid-thirties. He was lying flat in bed, for his back. Bernard greeted him cheerfully and introduced me. Andy looked apprehensive.

'Can you remember anything about the accident?' I asked.

His pained expression became even more dolorous. 'I . . . can't talk to you. Until the insurance company make their decision, I can't put anything on the record.'

So we went to see Marit Bu Oppedal, one of the injured nurses. She looked up with a welcoming smile as we entered her room. She was a tall, big-boned Nordic woman, her body bound up with surgical straps, her face as red and swollen as an August sunset. I was struck by her good humour and complete unselfconsciousness, the way she inhabited those most intimate of spaces—bed and bedroom —as though she had no more proprietorship over them than we did. As she recalled the accident, her eyes glittered.

'We were flying down a valley under the cloud and then the pilot couldn't keep the plane in the air. It only took seconds; we were near the base of the valley and suddenly the ground was very close. I can't remember the actual impact . . .' She laughed. 'The pilot told me that after the crash I looked at him accusingly, as though to say, "Why did you *do* that?" Then I stood up and climbed out.'

The ward matron entered the room. She was a mountainous woman, who seemed, like many of the hospital's physical artefacts— its curvaceous iron beds and bronze 'Britannia' hydraulic door-closers—to come from a forgotten English past. She promptly ejected us from the room.

Minutes later two St John ambulances arrived and the Norwegian nurses were strapped in. The vehicles careered through the bumpy streets of Nairobi, blue lights flashing, with Bernard racing to keep up, muttering angrily, 'Don't the drivers realise these people have *back injuries*?'

'This is called ambulance chasing,' I said.

When we reached the airport, the ambulances were already parked. Bernard approached the driver of the first one. 'Did you used to be a racing driver?'

The man looked up from his crossword puzzle. 'No,' he said, 'I aspire to be one.'

'Trust me, my friend, you already are. What was your fastest speed on the way here?'

'120,' the driver replied, unabashed.

Inside the ambulance Marit was sitting up on her stretcher, looking terrified. 'I do not want to survive a plane crash only to die in a car accident. I want to get home, now. *To go home.*'

'Don't worry,' Bernard said soothingly, 'in less than twenty-four hours you will be home.'

She sank back on to the stretcher. 'It's funny, I wasn't afraid either before or after the crash. But there was no pain—I was so hurt that the nerves sort of cut out.' She smiled again, the brilliant smile that made it seem that the accident had been, for her, a sort of epiphany. 'I remember climbing out of the plane, drenched with blood. A lot of people came rushing up—villagers. They covered us with blankets and gave us water and I remember thinking, "Yes, human nature is essentially good." A priest appeared; he asked if I was a Christian, then I felt water on my head and I wondered if it was raining—' She laughed again.

'He thought you were dying,' said Bernard. 'He was trying to give you the last rites and Andy told him, "I don't need the last rites, my sins are forgiven. Besides, I don't think we're going to die." But the priest looked doubtful and said very tactfully, "Well, let's do it, just in case . . ."'

Marit laughed again. 'It *was* funny, believe it or not. And all the time there were voices in the background, the village women were singing a kind of lament, on and on, without stopping . . . I felt like an actor. It was someone else lying there and yet, still me. And I felt peaceful; in fact, I felt *happy*: OK, I'm covered in blood, I can't speak, or see out of one eye—but I'm alive . . .

'A very close friend of mine lost her husband and her brother in a helicopter accident two years ago, in the Norwegian mountains. Her son of seven and the pilot survived. I went through that with her and during this crash, I somehow seemed to be sharing their accident. So in a strange way, there was something good about it. You have to see the good side of every experience. It was—the intensity. But it's impossible to communicate . . .'

There was a medevac doctor in attendance, a heavy-set Dane with a brooding manner. Returning from Customs he handed Marit back her passport, joking lugubriously that she looked better in her passport photograph than she did now. We all laughed, not at his joke, but with relief that five people were still alive.

He went on to talk with sinister relish of a job he'd done in

Namibia the previous year. 'I had to pick up two wounded women. One of them was a mother, the other her friend. They'd been on the border with Angola and encountered some so-called "rebels". The husband, wife, two children and this friend were lined up and shot. Only the two women survived. "Survived", I say. You can probably imagine the condition they were in.'

At last, the nurses were transferred on to British Airways stretchers and wheeled across the apron, where they ascended on catering lifts to the 747's First Class compartment.

As we drove, at a slower pace, back to the MAF compound, our headlights picked out of the darkness a dented car slewed at an angle across the central reservation. We saw a man, ripped apart and strung out along the road like fallen luggage, his arm thrown out behind him in a mockery of relaxation.

Bernard braked and pulled over and reached into his glove compartment for a pair of surgical gloves. 'We're likely to be in contact with blood,' he said.

As we climbed out, another car pulled up behind us. Crowds were gathering, voices were raised.

'He was obviously dead, wasn't he?' said Bernard.

'He was dead, all right.'

After hesitating for a moment, we climbed back into the car. We sat in silence for a few moments.

'It's a shock, isn't it?' said Bernard. 'But there are a lot of accidents like this. There are people walking everywhere, you see. Sometimes they cross the road suddenly and you don't see them. Other times they're drunk. Sometimes cars drive without lights . . .'

He started the engine.

'Do you always keep surgical gloves in the glove compartment?' I asked.

'Yes; my first thought was to help, my second to put gloves on. But I'm not going to touch blood here. It's very likely that anyone you touch will be HIV positive and you cannot disregard that risk. We do a lot of medevacs and we have to clean the aircraft carefully afterwards. 500 a day are dying of AIDS in Kenya. The front pages of the papers talk about bus crashes and fires, fifteen dead here, twenty there, but they never mention the enormity of the AIDS epidemic. It's a collective denial—a terrible blindness.'

At the next roundabout, a car veered around the wrong side of the island, coming straight at us with headlights blazing and Bernard had to swerve into the roadside gravel to avoid it. 'It seems everyone's a little mad tonight,' he said.

We drove on in silence, passing a parked Land Rover with a number of uniformed men in it. 'Security back-up,' said Bernard. 'Armed guards. The compounds have panic buttons and in the event of a break-in these guys show up in minutes to chase the thugs away. The UN has recently downgraded Nairobi to a "C"-rating for security, which means the diplomats get better paid because it's more dangerous. Very unpopular with the government, which wants to present Nairobi as Africa's capital city, but violent crime is rising. People say it's the same level as Colombia. Car-jackings are particularly common at the moment. That's why I drive this very undesirable old Datsun: the car-jackers prefer the latest 4×4s. But if we do get stopped, don't undo your seat belt. They tend to think you're reaching for a gun and they shoot you. It happened to someone we know very recently, he was shot in the head.'

We pulled up at the compound gates. 'People even get hijacked right in front of their gates, that's why we have the bushes cut back low, to see if anyone's hiding.' He greeted the guard, '*Asante sana, Bwana* . . .' The gates closed behind us. 'Well, that was my free Sunday; I don't know about you, but I could use a beer.'

(The pilot, Andy Fothergill, was flown back to Britain later that week and found to be more severely injured than had been believed. As this book goes to press over a year later, he is still making a slow but steady recovery.)

CHAPTER XVI

A Desert Storm

T HE FLIGHT BEGAN with a prayer. 'Dear Christ our Master,' said Captain Marcos Habtetsion, 'We ask for Your blessing on our journey today . . .' I was sitting beside him, in the First Officer's seat. The plane was a Cessna—the ubiquitous Cessna found all over the world, those little high-wing planes, but this was a 210 model, a Centurion, whose retractable undercarriage, 300 horsepower engine and unstrutted wings made for a slippery top speed of 170 mph. The 210 was as close as stolid Cessna came to making a sports model, winning class records for round-the-world speed.

'. . . in the name of our Lord, Amen.'

'Amen,' I said.

'Amen,' said the four passengers.

We took off and climbed over one of the tendrils of raw nature where the Nairobi National Park miraculously penetrates central Nairobi, abutting the boundary wire of Wilson Airport.

'You see that buffalo?' asked Marcos, '—he's a big fellow.' An extravagantly horned and probably very old bull buffalo plodded through the long grass underneath us.

We turned towards our destination, Marsabit, an oasis near the Ethiopian border, 250 miles north-east of Nairobi. Our route took us past the densely vegetated equatorial slopes of Mount Kenya. The 'Little Rains' were just beginning and the sky that spring morning was an armada of cumulus clouds 15,000 and 16,000 feet high. Unable to climb over them—above 13,000 feet you need oxygen-breathing equipment and the 210 was unpressurised—we levelled at around 12,000 feet and flew along cloud canyons between billowing walls of radiant white. The bases of the clouds touched and only an occasional break beneath us offered a glimpse of the level desert, copper-red and polka-dotted with stunted shrubs. The trick was to fly down the canyons, staying as much as possible out of the cloud. This was largely to minimize turbulence for the passengers—each time we entered cloud the windows turned a dirty shade of grey and the plane made a nauseating lurch—but it was also because to enter cloud meant disorientation. At Lindsay I'd done the compulsory exercises wearing 'foggles' (an opaque visor that simulates fog, forcing the pilot to fly on instruments) and I knew how rapidly one's sense of balance betrays one. It's calculated that a pilot who loses touch with the horizon becomes completely disorientated within thirty seconds. You can turn almost upside down and not know it till you feel the harness bite into your shoulder blades—by which time it may be too late. The slightest inadvertent left or right pressure on the stick will put the plane into a steepening bank, which can rapidly become a terminal spiral. (This, apparently, was the fate of John Kennedy Jnr, son of the late President, who died with his wife and sister-in-law in an air crash in 1999. According to the investigation, he experienced spatial disorientation when haze and low light over Martha's Vineyard prevented him from seeing the horizon. Kennedy had ventured into these perilous conditions even though he had no qualification to fly on instruments alone.)

In the absence of visual references and because we had no autopilot fitted, the Cessna had to be flown on instruments. We were using the artificial horizon, a gyroscopic device that shows a horizontal aeroplane icon bisecting two hemispheres, the sky and the ground. The plane icon is always horizontal, while the ground and sky wheel around it, exactly representing the plane's ascent, descent, or bank angle. For the pilot to keep the plane straight and level using instruments—mostly the artificial horizon, the altimeter and the rate of climb/descent indicator—requires constant adjustments to the control column and immense concentration.

It was also difficult to maintain our direction, because the cloud canyons weren't orientated in the direction we needed to follow. Every six or seven minutes we would break out of a cloud mass into an open space, like emerging from a narrow loch into a broad lake, where the points of exit on the far shore are obscured by mountainous islands rising out of mist. We needed to scan the space for a likely way out that not only returned us to our chosen course, but corrected for the deviation we had just made. If, for example, you fly 10 degrees east of your intended course for the first ten minutes of a thirty-minute flight, flying 5 degrees west for the remaining twenty minutes will bring you to your destination. Or so the theory goes. As I was soon to discover, bush flying in Africa is less about theory than about experience.

After an hour, the big clouds broke up. For a few minutes the sky was a clear blue band and then we saw in the distance something ominous and astonishing: a cloud mass of titanic proportions, a maelstrom of grey-purple vapour extending from the surface of the desert to a height of many thousands of feet.

The passenger behind me, a logistics officer with the UN's World Food Programme, leaned forward and yelled, 'What the hell is *that*?'

'It's a sandstorm,' Marcos yelled back. He pointed to his weather radar. A pattern of red-cored concentric circles showed the storm to be more than thirty miles across and alive with electricity. To the eye, the storm appeared to have a distinct curvature, the overall form of a flattened orb, like a Dutch cheese.

As we drew nearer, we saw something wonderful: the mass of bruised cloud was carrying before it an apron of orange sand thousands of feet high, which it seized and churned and threw back to earth behind it as it rumbled across the desert.

Our aircraft was a tiny black speck, a flimsy man-made device hovering irrelevantly just beyond the blind and brutal force of nature. Fine veils of moisture splattered the windscreen with raindrops, which burst and cross-hatched the screen. Occasionally, our wings rocked with turbulence. Close to the sandstorm now, we stared in awe.

'I don't want to get any nearer,' said Marcos.

A pilot who enters a thunderstorm is courting death, whether the plane is a tiny Cessna or a colossal 747. Thunderstorms can contain almost every meteorological hazard known to aviation, including turbulence, tornadoes, squall lines, icing, hail, lightning, static, heavy rain, low ceilings, low visibility, violent updraughts and down-draughts. This one looked likely to have the lot.

I asked Marcos if he'd seen anything like it before. 'Only twice,' he replied. Marcos Habtetsion is an experienced pilot. Before joining

MAF in the mid-1980s, he served with the Ethiopian air force for eleven years. He frowned and called the MAF control room, telling them he was going to deviate forty miles west.

We banked away from the boiling cloud and began a long detour over the burnt-orange desert. After thirty minutes we saw on the horizon the peaks of Marsabit, an isolated outcrop of volcanic plugs rising from the desert. This miniature mountain range is a visual shock: a cluster of flat-topped peaks so tall and slender they suggest a desert Manhattan.

Marsabit was where we were planning to drop the two World Food Programme officials. Drought had made northern Kenya the UN's third-largest recipient of food aid and the distribution centre for the region's suffering pastoralists was Marsabit. The aid workers' choice of air travel over road transport was not merely a question of convenience: the road south was lawless and could only be used by heavily armed convoy. Even then, security wasn't certain. Of late, bandits had taken to shooting first and asking questions later— spraying vehicles they wanted to ambush with bullets before approaching. Anyone who had a choice took the plane to Marsabit.

By now, we had another reason for needing to land here: the long flight north, combined with our lengthy detour, meant that we would soon be cutting into our fuel reserves.

The Marsabit hills rise high enough to enter cooler air and attract rain. As we crossed the thick woodland of the lower slopes, the World Food Programme man behind me leaned forward. 'This forest is supposedly protected—Marsabit National Park. There are meant to be elephant, lions, leopards down there. But no tourists come any more, the park is badly supervised and there's poaching. God knows what's left.'

The red roofs of Marsabit town were visible as we began our descent towards the airstrip. The sky over the hills beyond the town was overcast and we could see a layer of mist perhaps two or three miles to the north. But as we continued our descent, we suddenly realised that the mist was advancing towards us—*rapidly*. It was the projecting tongue of a vast wall of cloud that, even as we watched, broke over the bluff behind the town and swept onwards, towering over it and us. It was evidently part of the storm we had gone so far to circumvent—but which had reached Marsabit just as we did.

We were on final approach, so low I could easily distinguish individual houses and trees. Marcos had split seconds to calculate whether he could hope to land safely before the cloud engulfed the strip. 'I'm aborting the landing,' he said tersely.

We were closing on the wall of cloud at over 100 mph, but it too was advancing with astonishing speed, starting to immerse the town and about to swallow us. Marcos threw the plane into a steep right bank and from my right seat I looked straight down at treetops and rooftops that seemed almost close enough to touch. Then, everything became grey.

It's a well-known paradox of navigation that a map is no use unless you know where you are—unless you can orientate yourself to some visible landmark. A pilot lost in cloud, of course, cannot do this. He suffers the additional disadvantage of being unable to stop and look about—he's moving rapidly and in three dimensions (hardly surprising that the majority of fatal aircraft accidents take place in low cloud). Finger-wagging lectures at Lindsay on the mortal dangers of cloud flashed through my mind: pilots in Ontario are at the mercy of a fickle weather system—vapour swirling around those inland seas, the Great Lakes—but they have on tap one of the world's most sophisticated weather information services. Marcos's only information had been a radio call to the aid workers at the Marsabit airstrip to confirm the wind direction and speed. No one had known about the storm closing like a banshee from behind the mountains.

So: we were flying half inverted, blind, at around 300 feet, with Marsabit's peaks looming invisibly around us. Had I been the pilot, I would have attempted to do what Marcos did. But I was not the pilot, I was a helpless spectator. I stared out—down? up?—at grey. I could feel the proximity of the ground and mountains through my very skin. I was too startled to be afraid. I'd spent a good few training hours doing instrument flying and I was *almost* confident of my ability to execute a steep turn on instruments, without losing too much height, and return on the reciprocal—the opposite compass heading. But that does not describe what Marcos did. He knows Marsabit well and he's an ex-fighter pilot; but it was superb flying to fling the plane through that tight, fast, but perfectly controlled turn blind—completely on instruments.

When a plane is moving fast, it takes a few seconds and several hundred feet to turn safely, to avoid dangerously high wing loadings and possible damage to the airframe. It may have only taken seconds to flick the Cessna round, but my experience of time was elastic. I do remember that my mouth fell open like a trapdoor (it's humbling to realize that if death ever claims me unexpectedly, I'll be wearing an expression of imbecile stupefaction). I gazed avidly through my side window—but there was nothing to see. I flicked my eyes helplessly at the artificial horizon, the altimeter, the vertical speed indicator in front of me.

After an age or two had passed, we emerged from the blanket of grey. We were still enveloped in cloud, but it had retreated a hundred feet on either side of us and we seemed to be flying through a bright white tunnel, about to be spat from the mouth of an angry anthropomorphic cloud on the edge of some fifteenth-century map. Marcos pushed the Cessna 210, the sports plane with its powerful engine and slippery wing, towards its top speed of 170 mph. At the end of the tunnel was a lozenge of sunlit desert, like a filmic vision of Paradise, and we stared at it hungrily. I kept peering for some glimpse of the ground and then I saw trees through a break in the cloud and understood that we were well above them and safe. When the trees appeared, a common emotion swept over the occupants of the plane. We didn't need to look at or touch each other, it was a shared wave of relief, or telepathy, or maybe a subconscious registration of the static electricity in one another's skin—who knows? But it felt as definite and intimate as if the five of us had been holding hands.

With the high winds of the storm behind us adding to our speed, we burst from the cloud like a ball from a cannon. As we flew out across the desert, I looked back: a billowing cap of bruised cloud had engulfed the whole mountain range. Marcos headed for the alternative Marsabit strip, a rough-marked rectangle of orange sand some fifteen miles into the desert. Even here, the winds were strong, but Marcos overflew the strip, concluded that it was safe to land and did so.

As he shut down the engine, he turned to me and grinned. 'So, Martin, you got your baptism into the life of a bush pilot a bit earlier than you expected.'

We tumbled out of the plane into a thirty-knot squall that whipped the orange sand into our teeth. There was much relieved laughter and shoulder-slapping. We turned to look back at Marsabit. The entire range was invisible, now. All we could see in the north was a mass of glowering purple cloud.

CHAPTER XVII

Sudan

G UY BROOKING pointed through the windscreen.
'Loki's just off the end of that ridge—can you see it?'

There were several ridges, rising indistinctly from the dazzling sheen of the desert, like the backs of water buffalo from a pond at dusk. Then I saw the airstrip: a filament of runway, and minute windows that spangled with pixels of light when the sun caught them.

After crossing the deserts of north-eastern Kenya for three hours, we'd begun our descent within sight of the Sudanese border. We would refuel here, in Lokichoggio, then fly on into southern Sudan to drop three missionaries at a remote medical centre.

We landed, and taxied past a clutch of old prop-driven cargo transports. 'They're supposed to be under repair,' said Guy, 'which means they're unlikely ever to leave.'

Hercules and Buffalo transports were lined up with their aft ramps open, waiting for their big bellies to be filled with palettes of food. Behind the main apron were enormous brown tents, canvas warehouses bearing the turquoise logo of the UN. They held mountains of aid: sacks of maize and drums of vegetable oil. All were colourfully marked, in English, with the names of the donor countries—give to the hungry, but take the credit.

For the people of this arid region, existence is little different today from 100 years ago, except that tribal struggles are now carried out with automatic firearms picked up from wars in neighbouring Ethiopia and Somalia. These days tribal score-settling results in many deaths, and on occasion the massacre of entire villages.

A few days earlier, I had flown into the semi-desert of northern Uganda with a MAF flight. When we landed on a tiny, rocky airstrip to drop a missionary doctor, a herd of bony cattle wandered around the plane, quickly joined by their herders, a collection of similarly bony men, dressed in brown tunics, with rifles balanced across their shoulders. When I raised my camera, one of them became enraged, and shook his Kalashnikov at me. Queasily I put the camera down, and looked away.

Lokichoggio is five degrees north of the equator, where Kenya's Chalbi Desert dissolves into dusty savannah, and the borders of Kenya collide with those of three other countries—Uganda, Sudan and Ethiopia. These frontiers were drawn by colonial administrators, riding roughshod over the tribal realities of the region. The legacy has been permanent instability.

To the west, Uganda was in chaos through the 1970s and '80s. To the east, there's the crazy mosaic that is the Horn of Africa. Many separate factors led to the instability here—Britain's encouragement of Italian colonial ambitions in Ethiopia and Somaliland as a way of frustrating the French; the support of the US and the Soviet Block for puppet regimes or Marxist-Leninist independence movements; and long-simmering Christian-Moslem resentments. It is a history of regular coups and rampant warlordism, and would be farcical if it weren't drenched in the blood of millions.

To the north is Sudan, where for almost half a century civil war has raged between the Moslem Arabs of the north and the black, animist tribes of the south. The British had seen these proud and warlike Dinka tribes as a potential threat. So they did almost nothing to 'civilize' their territory, to introduce modern infrastructures into a fertile farming area twice the size of France. Southern Sudan was preserved, in the words of one historian, as 'a sort of human game reserve . . . an abyss of backwardness'.

During the 1940s, in a belated attempt to accelerate development, the British pursued integrationist policies. The southern black tribes and the Arabs joined together in an effort to be rid of the colonial power. But soon after Independence in 1956, the southerners foresaw their assimilation into Arab culture, and pushed for autonomy. They were put down by the north, with great severity. Slowly, the south split into warlord-ruled fiefdoms which have fought among themselves with almost unbelievable barbarity. This ethnically unviable nation state was surely one of the worst blunders in British colonial history, resulting in two million deaths during fifty years.

The routine destruction of crops and herds in the south has led the United Nations and a galaxy of aid organizations to pursue a massive aid programme to stave off the threat of famine. Sudan's Khartoum government has claimed that aid provides succour to the secessionist militias, but the relief agencies maintain that the issue is apolitical, a humanitarian crisis impossible to ignore. An uneasy truce has permitted dozens of charities to keep pumping aid into Sudan's beleaguered south.

For security reasons, these NGOs are based just outside Sudan—in Lokichoggio. The aid effort is entirely airborne, and Loki is entirely an aviation town. If Sudan had not been at war, Loki would be an obscure frontier trading post for the local cattle-rearing tribes, a raggedly picturesque back-drop for handfuls of tourists who passed through en route to wildlife lodges in the nearby uplands. As it is, Loki has the surreal atmosphere of *M*A*S*H* or *Catch 22*, an air of being *of* the war, yet not *in* it. Everything costs a fortune—the lawless roads to the south mean that goods only arrive in irregular army convoys. Close by the great marquees of donated foodstuffs are two hotels offering semi-permanent accommodation to aid officials, some video shops and a hut offering intermittent internet access. There are discos and prostitutes. Every few minutes the sky rumbles as a heavy transporter takes off or returns from a food drop in Sudan.

As soon as we had taken on fuel, we were off. Within minutes we'd crossed the border with Sudan. 'This is a war zone,' said Guy, 'but theoretically we're not in any danger.'

'Theoretically?'

'Well, we're ferrying aid workers, which makes us non-combatants. We have a UN call sign that's okayed with Khartoum, and gives us immunity. So we shouldn't be targeted by fighters or anybody.'

Later, I'd hear about all the instances of aid planes being bombed and shot at in Sudan. A couple of weeks after I left, a Red Cross plane was destroyed and its crew killed in Sudanese airspace, a few miles north of Loki.

For an 18-year conflict waged in Africa's largest country, the Sudanese civil war has been oddly under-reported. This makes doubly surprising the recent declaration by the USA that Sudan is a foreign policy priority. Why should Washington have discovered Sudan? One answer is the alliance of right-wing senators, Christians and social activists, including the Congressional Black Caucus, which has been lobbying for action. It has been widely alleged that there is state support for slavery in Sudan, and a concerted effort is underway to make the country a *cause célèbre*, like South Africa in the days of Apartheid.

America is in fact already *in* Sudan. Our three passengers were female missionaries from rural Oregon, taking Christ to the Dinka. They were typical of hundreds of aid workers and missionaries in the country. The southern Sudanese have often claimed that the Khartoum government is fighting a *jihad* against them, and such rhetoric does not make the missionaries uncomfortable: theirs is also a Crusade, for peace and democracy, yes, for education and health-care—but perhaps, above all, for Christian conversion. The potential harvest of souls is enormous: Sudan is claimed to have the fastest-growing Christian Church in the world—and Khartoum threatens that. Some have even accused the Church of *exploiting* the war in Sudan, to convert more of the animist tribespeople to Christianity.

If it's hard to believe that the spiritual and moral plight of the Sudanese has given Washington's power brokers sleepless nights, there is a more pragmatic reason for America's interest: oil. Ample reserves were recently discovered in southern Sudan. And securing oil supplies is perhaps America's main policy objective in the Middle East.

We were crossing a table-flat landscape on which the only visible mark was the fatly meandering snake of the White Nile. The ground beneath us was a faint orange-pink in colour, on which occasional patterns of black dots were the huts of small settlements. There are few tarred roads in thousands of square miles of prairie, no bridges, no buses, trains or taxis, little formal civil administration, and only the sketchiest healthcare, provided by far-flung charity dispensaries.

After flying for three hours, we were approaching our destination, not far from the Front Line—or rather, in a war of shifting boundaries, from one of the areas that have seen sporadic fighting in recent years. It was Guy Brooking's first flight to the tiny settlement of Liethnom. It would be almost impossible to locate a particular spot in this undifferentiated landscape without a satellite navigation reference point. We dropped to a thousand feet above ground level, and squinted into the fawn haze. I was first to see it, a narrow dry dirt clearing. Guy brought the Caravan low over the strip, to check for pot holes and scare off wandering cows.

By 'Caravan', Cessna are evoking not the placid working-class pleasures of an English seaside campsite, but the Arabian romance of the camel caravan. It's ironic, then, that Sudan is the one place on earth where that idea still strikes terror into people. 150 years ago, before the British abolished slavery, the Dinka tribespeople when they wanted to chide their children would say, 'The camels are coming to take you away!' Half a century after Independence, the caravans are back. Reports suggest that thousands of men, women and teenagers have been abducted and forced into slavery. A recent report accused the government not only of tolerating the practise, but of deliberately using the raiding-parties as a terror-weapon.

Guy made another turn, lining the Caravan up for landing. We could see a large group of people beside the airstrip. One of flying's revolutions is its ability to propel us, with all the speed of a movie, into a world wholly different from the one we left two hours earlier. The culture shock is immediate and total.

As we climbed out of the plane, there were broad grins from those orchestrating the reception for our three Oregon missionaries. The women were surrounded by a gaggle of stick-thin young children dressed in ragged, dust-caked pinafores and shorts, chanting 'Welcome, Alison'. In fact, none of the missionaries was called Alison—it turned out that the children had learned the phrase to greet a previous missionary, and now used it generically for all white visitors. I took my bag, as men heaved crates of medicines and religious paraphernalia out of the Caravan. We slowly processed up a gentle slope into a compound with a dozen *tukuls*—grass-roofed huts—and a larger central meeting and eating room. I was allotted my own *tukul*, a very luxurious version of the indigenous structure, since it featured a cement floor and fly screens.

Three years ago the American Christian charity, World Relief, set up this healthcare centre. It has had a huge impact, in particular on infant and maternal mortality. There's nothing of strategic value here, yet the staff vividly recall the two times they have been bombed. 'The last one was on a Sunday morning,' Stephen Kanyia, the Manager, told me. 'We were all at Church. Suddenly there was the roar of engines, and the sound of explosions, and everyone was diving for cover. There were a lot of craters, but nobody got killed. We've got to know the sounds of the different aeroplane engines really well now. We're always listening out for an Antonov, and getting ready to run.'

In the morning, I went to see the missionaries at work. They were teacher trainers, staging a sort of seminar for a group of teachers who'd travelled here from miles around. The 'teachers' were in fact pastors, touchingly bony, adam's appley young men, all wearing neat, cheaply-tailored shirts, and cupping black Bibles in their palms in the way preachers are wont to do, suggesting either possessiveness or dependency—I'm never sure which. Several had walked for more than a day to be here, as the only vehicle in a thousand square miles was the dispensary's 4×4. They sat in a grass-roofed hut on the crudest of wooden benches, made from narrow branches laid across forked staves driven into the earth (chairs were found for the four white visitors). From a large plastic crate the American women produced, like gifts on Christmas morning, a series of primary-coloured English-teaching aids, all geared to the eternal truths of the Bible (they are forbidden to bring the Good Book itself into Sudan). There was more than a touch of the revivalist meeting about the atmosphere. The men were touchingly grateful for the garish gifts, pitifully eager to please. The American women were naïve, gauche, culturally out of their depth. This is how white civilization propagates its values, I thought. One of the teaching aids was a five-colour laminated card, where red represented the blood of Our Lord, gold was Heaven etc. White was clean, 'How we all want to be'. Black was Satan. During a break in the proceedings, I asked one of the women if it had occurred to anyone that the southern Sudanese have among the blackest skins of any race on earth. She stared back at me with utter incomprehension and mild hostility.

That evening the youngest of the three women, who was in her early twenties, had a touch of diarrhoea and a slight fever. She staged a Garbo-like death-bed scene, her colleagues clustered around her, clasping hands and murmuring support. Then a satellite phone was produced, and to my astonishment, her father in Oregon was telephoned for advice. Should a medevac be summoned? Given the poverty and desperation of the place, this seemed to me an utterly frivolous suggestion. Stephen Kanyia was convinced that the girl was fine, but anxious that it would reflect badly on him if she *should* prove to be seriously ill. The fundamentalist Protestants of the Bible Belt were, after all, his dispensary's lifeline.

The next day, when the air ambulance came to take her away, she was well on the mend, and sheepishly aware that it was obvious to everyone. But her relief to be returning to civilization a week early over-rode all other considerations. This was her first time out of the USA. From fitted carpets, oversprung automobiles and McDonalds to a village of mud huts: it was just too much.

The following day, I went out into the local countryside, where I met some men labouring with a bullock-drawn plough. One of them told me his whole family had been abducted by raiders twelve years ago, never to be seen again. He stared at me intently. 'You must tell your people what's happening to us,' he ordered. He had a haunted face. His ribs were prominent under his torn shirt. All the Sudanese I met were thin, in contrast with the well-fed Kenyan aid workers. The farmers told me the war's disruption of their planting meant that food would soon be running out. Indeed, in Loki, the aid workers were predicting famine and gearing up for another vast relief effort that autumn.

Power in Liethnom takes the form of the local Commander of the breakaway Sudan People's Liberation Party. My nosing around had by now attracted his attention, and Stephen told me it would be best for me to request an interview. 'Please be very diplomatic,' he said.

Late that afternoon, we went to meet the Commander. I found myself confronted by a sort of soviet—eight hard-faced apparatchiks scowling with undisguised hostility. What, they asked, did I want?

I took a deep breath. Permission to visit this area, I said. (I already had a *laisser-passer* from the SPLP 'embassy' in Nairobi, but it evidently wasn't enough.) Was it possible that they might be kind enough to let me stay for a few days?

There was a round of formal introductions. The Commander was the only man in uniform. The others were lower in the pecking order, members of the military faction's civilian wing—in effect, the local civil administration. Politicians to a man, they deferred to the

Commander, and answered any direct question from me by looking in his direction and mumbling non-commitally.

The Commander had received some of his education in the UK. In fact, he had trained to be a pilot, at Oxford Airport. He spoke impeccable English, and retained for the British a fondness, mixed with scorn. 'You were the colonial power, and supposedly our friends,' he told me. 'But you left this country in the grip of an Arab élite. And we in the south, the more fertile part of Sudan, the place where the oil is—we are exploited and abused. What's our crime? Being Christian? Being *black*? All we know is that we have no rights, and are forced to fight in order to survive.'

The man who seemed to be his Number Two added forcefully, 'This government is perpetrating a *jihad* against the south.' Another man remarked, *a propos* of famine, that he didn't like the flavours of the UN's sunflower oil and yellow maize. As he spoke, his mouth twisted as though he could taste the alien flavours. 'We're poor but proud,' he said, 'and perfectly capable of being self-sufficient. It's this war that makes the world think of us as starving beggars. When is the West going to intervene to support us?'

'If anyone has a responsibility to intervene here,' the Commander resumed, 'it's Britain. When is your Prime Minister going to speak out for the southern Sudanese?'

Eight sets of eyes regarded me keenly.

I floundered. 'Well, what can I say? We're totally in the wrong . . . Er, on behalf of Britain, I'd just like to say I'm very, very sorry.'

It was what they wanted to hear. A meaningless apology from a non-entity on behalf of an entire people, an entire imperial epoch. There was a palpable relaxation of tension—especially from the Commander, who suddenly smiled, and began to speak nostalgically of his time up at Oxford. There were smiles all round, lots of male joshing, and a polite request from the cash-strapped Commander, whose command had little in the way of materiel, to get a lift somewhere or other in Stephen's 4×4. This request was politely declined, but did nothing to blunt the Commander's humour, as he segued into another favour he was sure Stephen could oblige with. Laughter filled the air. Slapping me on the back, the Commander told me that what he and his army really needed was aeroplanes. 'I want to pilot an assault aircraft. Give us some Harriers, and we'll smash those Arabs.

You must tell your Tony Blair to help us!' I promised that I would.

The British did keep southern Sudan as a human game reserve, and as Independence loomed, dithered for a decade before settling on the Arab/black union that has guaranteed hostilities ever since. The south has been fighting *itself*, but there's no question that government-funded militias have waged war on the south. They have used scorched earth tactics to force southerners to vacate thousands of square miles of land so that Canadian, Swedish and Chinese drilling companies can have unimpeded access to new oil fields. The windfall revenues have been used to buy vast quantities of high-tech weaponry hitherto unseen in Sudan. The Arab government now has the kind of hardware it needs to prosecute an irresistible counter-insurgency campaign.

The need to stabilize Sudan and secure its huge oil reserves has caused the Americans to knock heads together. Recently there was a US-brokered cease-fire in Sudan. But is real reconciliation between the north and south, a united, multi-ethnic and multi-religious Sudan, truly possible?

The MAF Caravan that came to collect the two remaining missionaries was piloted by a strikingly handsome Nordic type. He had a sardonic look about him, offering the hope, I thought, of a sensibility closer to Bernard Terlouw's trenchant wit than the fundamentalist religiosity of some of MAF's missionary pilots. As we began the six-hour flight back to Nairobi, he asked me if I considered myself a religious man.

'Well . . . somewhat,' I replied.

'Are you a Christian?'

'Y . . . yes . . .'

'Have you been born again in Our Lord Jesus Christ? Have you accepted him into your life as your Redeemer and Master?'

'N . . . Not as such, really.'

'Then you are *not* a Christian. If you die, you'll go to Hell. Doesn't that prospect frighten you?'

It was going to be a long flight home.

CHAPTER XVIII
On the Piste

PEOPLE WHO REMEMBERED Sir Henry ('Harry') Wigley told me he was a gent. In photographs, he's invariably natty, wearing a tweed jacket with a silk hanky in the breast pocket. Wigley's mystique had a lot to do with his way of using aeroplanes the way other people used Land Rovers—to probe the remotest corners of New Zealand.

He caught the flying bug as a schoolboy. One day in 1920 Harry was called from class to the headmaster's office and found his father, an automobile importer, waiting there. Did he fancy taking the day off school to see the test flight of a plane his father had bought? The plane was an Avro 504K, the two-seater biplane in which thousands of RAF pilots had learned to fly during World War I. Many of the 8000-odd 504s built during the war were coming on to the second-hand market, ending up as far afield as Chile and China.

New Zealand is an elongated country bisected by the sea and further broken up by mountain ranges. New Zealanders were quick to seize on aviation as a means to overcome these natural barriers. Harry Wigley's autobiography is a gung-ho account of those early days of civil aviation. In the 1930s the Mount Cook and Southern Lakes Tourist Company Ltd began the first hazardous tourist flights over the glaciers around New Zealand's tallest peak. The erratic behaviour of air currents in mountains was little understood in those days and Harry's flying alternated between enthusiastic barnstorming and trying to learn enough about the mountains simply to stay alive.

> The air that day was so calm that my passengers had undone their safety belts and were really enjoying the flight, when without warning we struck a downdraught which must have been in the

vicinity of 4000 feet a minute . . . The passengers all hit the roof, as did the luggage, and stayed there for what seemed like minutes. It was certainly quite a number of seconds, and I can remember wiping the skirt of my front seat passenger out of my eyes . . . When we hit the bottom of the air pocket, she came down on top of me with one leg through the spokes of the wheel . . . The rear passengers were semi-recumbent, with suitcases on top of them . . . We flew on to Timaru without a trace of a bump, but my passengers did not relax again and I doubt they have ever flown since.

In 1939 Wigley volunteered for the Royal New Zealand Air Force. He began as a flying instructor, but by 1942 the Japanese threat in the Pacific had become serious, and he was posted to the Solomon Islands as a fighter pilot flying Curtiss Kittyhawks.

It was decided that the aircraft should be flown to the islands. Before this, flights across the vast spaces of the Pacific in single-engine aircraft by Jean Batten, Francis Chichester and others were hailed as heroic enterprises, as indeed they were, so it was not without misgivings that we set out . . .

He survived both the crossing and armed combat. After the war he bought an old Tiger Moth biplane, and would leap into it and fly wherever the hell he liked, on shooting, fishing and skiing trips, or—if no other pretext could be found—simply to see where his wings carried him. In the early Fifties, he had the idea of strapping skis to an aircraft to land on the glaciers of Mount Cook National Park. The plane he chose to use was an Auster, a British World War II workhorse, but Harry had the brainwave of coating its skis with a brand-new plastic called Teflon. As he began exploratory flights, he became familiar with a curious optical phenomenon of the mountains —that light reflected off snow or ice can make it impossible to know if you're 200 or 2000 feet above it. During his first tentative approaches he threw branches out of the Auster, watching where they fell to gauge his height above the snow. In September 1955 he landed at 5000 feet on the Tasman Glacier and slid smoothly to a halt. A year later, he was ferrying Ed (Sir Edmund) Hillary into the mountains to train for his Antarctic expedition.

The peak Wigley's airline took its name from is 12,500 feet high and permanently white. Today's ski-plane pilots fly long, scenic routes around Mount Cook, but are most famous for continuing the Wigley tradition of landing, on skis, on glaciers.

Mount Cook airfield is built on the sedimentary valley floor. It's surrounded by scrub and terminal moraine, with the brilliant Alpine light that seems to find a speck of quartz in every stone, making the entire landscape sparkle. Beyond the level valley floor is the snout of the glacier, then several lower peaks and, towering over everything, Mount Cook itself, like the prow of some celestial liner.

The year's first snows were falling. I had left Africa in early summer, but arrived in a southern hemisphere where winter was setting in. It was my most successful hitch yet: a friend with contacts in Air New Zealand had persuaded them to let me occupy a vacant seat to Auckland. I continued with Mount Cook Airlines into the Southern Highlands. My bags and I were left at the tiny airport under New Zealand's highest mountain.

The ski-plane pilots are a down-to-earth and taciturn bunch. Between flights they hang out in a dingy room where you make your own cup of instant coffee and sit with the local paper at a Formica table. I asked one of them, Gary Rowe, if, as Wigley claimed, it could be impossible to tell your height above ground level.

'Oh, sure. When you get a "bright-out", where the sun's directly overhead, the snow becomes a white mass. You can't tell whether you're a thousand feet or ten feet above the surface. It's like looking down into a huge bowl of milk. The other problem is a flat light, when everything just turns to a white haze. They say there's forty-nine different kinds of snow, y' know—icy, soft, sticky . . . Anyway, when there's new snow, somebody will go up and do a landing to feel it out, assess which sort it is . . .'

The most experienced Mount Cook pilot is Ross Anderson, who's been flying there for two decades. He's a man of the tall, bony type, a chain-smoker, someone who seems happy with his own thoughts—which, as often as not, have something to do with flight. I sat beside him in a red- and yellow-painted Pilatus Porter, a long-snouted utility plane. The Porter takes off on tyres, then the pilot works a hydraulic pump to lower the skis.

We climbed quickly up the valley's eastern wall. Just as down-draughts can be found on the lee side of valleys, there are often updraughts on the far sides, which pilots can ride—a bit like walking up a moving escalator. It allows them to fly safely close to the valley walls. 'It all depends on knowledge of local conditions,' I told myself, as I peered at grass tufts on the mountainside and had the uneasy impression that I could count every blade.

The wandering veins of the Tasman river passed beneath us, then a dirty-looking mass of terminal moraine. Finally, at 6500 feet, we reached Climber's Col, the near horizontal névé or snow field where the ski-planes land.

Circling over a vista of luminous white, Anderson jabbed a finger down. 'You see the other planes?'

I could not. Then I did: the other two Porters, looking like minute toys, were much further below us than I'd expected. The surface of the snow *seemed* about 250 feet away, but evidently the real distance was more like 1000 feet. Disorientated, I peered into the haze as Anderson began the circuit that would bring us in to land beside the other planes.

I have tried in this book to keep 'planehead' stuff to a minimum, but a little machine fetishism must find its way in. Even a reader who can't see the aeroplane as a machine touched with magic, who's immune to the mystique and pulse-raising beauty of a Spitfire or a Mustang, must be intrigued by aircraft simply as artefacts, as extra-ordinary technical solutions to questions of fluid mechanics, engineering, physics. Such an artefact is the Swiss-built Pilatus Porter. An aerial jeep, it can be fitted with wheels, floats or skis to accomplish almost every conceivable aviation task, from air ambulance to crop-dusting or water-bombing. Like the Dash 7 I'd flown in Kenya, the

Porter is a STOL aircraft, Short Take-Off and Landing. It can take off in barely twice its own length and land on a postage stamp. Like all STOL aircraft, it relies on long, specially configured wings and a powerful engine within its immense, borzoi-like snout.

A steep bank brought us round and down, across a network of gaping crevasses and seracs. Anderson eased the plane towards the ice and made an uphill landing so frictionless we still seemed to be flying.

Porters on ice

The three planes' passengers were twenty-one gleeful Japanese, all throwing snowballs as discreetly and self-effacingly as they could. Anderson walked a few feet from the plane. I saw his hands go up and his head dip forward and an instant later a plume of cigarette smoke rose into the sharp air.

The dusting of snow on the glacier was pristine, the silence imposing. Jagged black peaks rose above us like some palace out of Tolkien.

When it was time to leave the glacier, I had an even more dramatic demonstration of what a Porter can do. We skied downhill, straight at the network of crevasses we'd crossed on our approach. No time, I thought apprehensively, for engine failure. The Porter lifted off and climbed over the gashed ice, heading directly for the vertical valley side ahead. At last, as the blue ice wall hung before and above us like some gigantic cinema screen, Anderson brought the Porter steeply round. So that's how you fly a ski-plane, I thought.

'Not much space before the mountainside,' I said.

He gave me a look of genuine surprise. 'What?'

'We seemed to be practically on top of it before we turned.'

'No, no, it just *appears* that way, there's much more room than it seems.'

'*Much* more?'

'Miles. Miles of valley. It's a visual phenomenon—there's loads of room.'

We flew on, over the epically sundered and boulder-scattered surface of the Tasman Glacier.

'I was just wondering', I said, 'where you'd land if there was an engine failure?'

'There're several places, all the way along the glacier. If you have a problem, you know where you're gonna go—it's all been worked out. And down-valley, the glacier's descending at almost your glide rate—you could virtually glide right out of here. Don't worry, we come up and do simulated engine failures. We make sure it works.'

The following morning, cloud obscured the peak of Mount Cook. Although there was plenty of blue sky and the winds on the runway were within safety margins, the speed of the scuttling clouds didn't augur well for flying.

On such mornings, a helicopter climbs to the top of the Tasman Glacier to check the winds. The Captain, Richard Desborough, asked if I wanted to go along.

It was an exhilarating flight, the more so for knowing that we were the only aircraft in the sky. Below the summit of Malte Brun on the south-eastern flank of the Tasman the chopper hovered over a shelf about the size of two tennis courts.

I asked Desborough if I might jump out to take some pictures.

'All right,' he said. 'But don't fall over the bloody edge. We're not insured for kamikaze writers.'

'I promise not to,' I said complacently.

'Well, I'm sending Tony with you anyway.'

I skipped around the patch of ice, peering through my viewfinder for a shot of the hovering chopper with Mount Cook in the background.

'This is what he was worried about.' It was the voice of the co-pilot, Tony Delaney. I looked round. He was standing just behind me. A few feet behind *him* was a vertical drop of 2000 feet to the Tasman Glacier. Left to my own devices, I would very likely have backed into the abyss and felt profoundly stupid for the five or six remaining seconds of my life. As it was, I merely had to cope with a hot feeling of embarrassment as I crunched back across the ice to the chopper.

The next day the winds had moderated and I bummed another ride with Ross Anderson. He was going up with a colleague for his annual 'Check Flight', a formality if ever there was one. But the rules required him to demonstrate a series of emergency manœuvres.

We climbed away from the usual Tasman flight path, until we were suspended between two plummeting walls of blue-white ice. Seated in the back this time, I couldn't hear the talk on the RT. Ross turned and yelled, 'We're going to do some steep turns—all right?'

'Great!' I yelled back.

'Make sure your harness is on tight!'

A second later the plane fell sideways and I slid like so much sand from a wheelbarrow, only prevented by my harness from smashing into the far side of the cabin.

What followed was a sort of aerial tango, apparently performed with one wing pointed at the ground. It left neither me nor the check pilot in any doubt about Ross Anderson's ability to handle a Porter.

After these aerial diversions, we climbed the Tasman Valley. We had an appointment high on the glacier, to collect a mountain guide and two English mountaineers, who'd been skiing up high for several days.

We landed on the ice and the three mountaineers, their ski suits lurid against the white snow, plodded towards us. The guide greeted Ross, with whom he'd often flown, phlegmatically. By contrast, the other two climbers began to babble ecstatically about their days among the perpetual snows.

'We've had an incredible time, man,' one told me.

'I mean, like—*totally* spectacular,' grinned the other.

As they stowed their glass fibre gear, Ross turned to me and said quietly, 'Adrenalin junkies, these mountain boys. We'll see if we can give them something to think about. You can do a beta approach in a Porter. Know what that is?'

'No.'

'You put the prop into zero thrust pitch range so that it provides air *resistance*, acting like an air brake. Lets you do a controlled dive.'

The climbers stuck their sun-blistered noses to the windows as we flew down the valley. The flight was magnificent, but hardly adrenal. And no dives. But as we approached the airstrip, Ross yelled over his shoulder, 'Hold on tight, everybody!'

The plane tipped forward until the threshold of the runway filled the windscreen—then we plummeted. It was like the view from the nose-cone of a missile, as the runway swelled alarmingly before us. At the last possible moment, the plane abruptly levelled, touched down and stopped dead.

Ross slipped a discreet glance at those of us in the back seats. Our popping eyes and astonished grins proved that the demonstration had been satisfactorily adrenal.

During the 1960s, the Pilatus Porter was built under licence in America. Given the presumably ironic name 'Peacemaker', it served in counter-insurgency in Vietnam. Vietnam was where the world first met the term 'COIN': COunter-INsurgency. The American military have invented a large number of acronyms to describe the un-Wellingtonian nature of modern warfare. COIN is held to encompass, among other things, 'psyops' (psychological operations designed to influence attitudes and behaviour), 'MCA' (military/civic action, in which armed forces attempt to seduce local populations with economic or social assistance) and 'UW' (unconventional warfare inside territory held in practice, if not officially, by the enemy), as well as direct attack with ground-to-air missiles, etc.

All very Vietnam, though the history of COIN probably began around 1920 in Somalia when, as one history puts it, 'the Mad Mullah's crazed regime required the RAF to . . . restore law and order by using air power with skill and finesse'. Sayyid Muhammad Ibn Abdulla Hassan was an outspoken critic of British imperialism, who declared a jihad against the British when the colonial administration permitted the opening of a Christian school. The RAF's three-week campaign against him cost a mere £77,000, leading Winston Churchill to praise it as 'the cheapest war in history'. The RAF's 'skill and finesse' in using the latest technology to kill tribesmen armed with matchlocks and sabres eliminated a problem that had troubled the British army for twenty-one years. The concept of 'Air Control' was born.

After the defeat of the Ottoman Empire in World War I, Britain's mandate included Mesopotamia—Iraq. British forces were soon put to the test by a variety of indigenous groups, chiefly the Kurds and the Marsh Arabs. The RAF, fighting its domestic corner in the midst of post-war defence cuts, argued that only air power could guarantee the security of the colonies. It duly bailed out the struggling army in Iraq, and in 1922, in one of the oddest episodes in aviation history, the RAF officially took control of Iraq. Eight squadrons of bombers were installed, the primary objects of punitive operations being the Kurds and the Marsh Arabs (whom Saddam Hussein, in a continuation of British policy, tried to break). The RAF administered the Iraqi mandate for ten years, with the loss of fourteen killed in action and eighty-four wounded. For British governments it was an outstanding success. However, in the words of the British historian Peter Slugett, air control 'developed into a substitute for administration'. When the British left their colonies, all the simmering socio-political tensions they'd used bombs to suppress came to the boil again. Britain was only interested in creating a stable environment for the operation of trade. Dramatic demonstrations of air power, rather than the brute use of ground forces, were the chosen instrument. Without the advances in air technology that came about as a result of World War I, it is almost certain that Britain would have lost control over large chunks of its baggy empire of 13 million square miles and 450 million people.

Between the World Wars the RAF became Britain's imperial policeman. Its means of subduing 'recalcitrant Arabs' may have included the dropping of poisoned gas on Kurds in 1920. When I grew up, I was taught that one of the crimes of the German people in the twentieth century had been the deployment of gas in World War I—my paternal grandfather died from the after-effects of chlorine or phosgene gas. Saddam Hussein's 'evil' is demonstrated by his use of nerve gas to kill perhaps 5000 Iraqi Kurdish citizens at Halabjah in

1988. In fact, during World War I gas was used massively by *both* sides. General revulsion at the effects of gas poisoning led to the Geneva Protocol of 1925, but this did not stop various signatories of the Protocol using chemical weapons, including Italy in Ethiopia in 1936–7 and Japan against the Chinese in 1937–41. During the Iran–Iraq war, both sides used gas.

The Soviet Union was probably the first country to use air power against its own citizens, to stamp out resistance to the collectivisation of farms during the early 1930s. It was also the first to develop specifically counter-insurgency armaments like fragmentation bombs, and it was the USSR that designed the world's first dedicated COIN aircraft. Fifty years later, the fearful Mil Mi-24 helicopter gunship would be the Soviet army's principal weapon during its brutal war in Afghanistan.

After the French departure from Indo-China in 1954, America became involved in Vietnam. The Americans soon realised that insurgent guerrilla operations were being carried out by people who seemed to be peaceful villagers. In 1961 the US Air Force created a counter-insurgency unit, the 4400th Combat Crew Training Squadron. It rapidly outgrew mere squadron strength, mushrooming into a Special Operations Force with a training school and two wings of aircraft deploying twenty-nine different types of aeroplane. COIN targets were not traditional battalions armed with heavy weapons, but small, highly mobile groups carrying small arms. Jets played little part in COIN; it was a task for slow, old-fashioned, prop-driven aircraft. Their work ranged from directing bombing to firing their own rockets from 200 feet, dispensing leaflets, or delivering psyops propaganda via directional loudspeakers that were audible 9000 feet down. COIN aircraft didn't need speed so much as the ability to hover almost motionless over a given spot. High altitudes were unnecessary, but the ability to fly low and land in bumpy wet fields without damaging undercarriage, occupants or armaments was crucial.

Subsequently, the world's aircraft manufacturers have made a good living from providing deadly anti-insurgency aeroplanes and helicopter gunships to a variety of client states in both East and West, who have used them to suppress dissent within their populations. General Pinochet of Chile was a big customer, likewise the rulers of Argentina, Iraq, Oman, Indonesia, Burma, Turkey, Morocco, Niger . . .

Every sizeable aircraft manufacturer has benefited from military contracts—even cosy Cessna made the A-37 Dragonfly, a twin-jet light-strike aircraft, which flew with the USAF and the South Vietnamese air force. Military contracts have driven forward research and development into aviation far more than any commercial programme. The vast majority of books, films and TV programmes about aviation are stories of war.

The earliest manned kites were war weapons. The Wrights saw their principal market as military. The First World War honed the modern aircraft, the Second brought Dresden and Hiroshima. The Cold War drove supersonic research and put men on the moon.

We have been inspired by birds, but the birds we imitate are the predators who bring death from the sky.

CHAPTER XIX
Top-Dressing

'IF YOU WANT to know about Kiwi flying, you want to do some top-dressing,' one of the ski-plane pilots told me.

'"Top-dressing"?'

'It's the Kiwi version of crop-dusting. They dump fertiliser all over the hill country. Practically bloody aerobatics at 150 feet. These guys are reckoned to be among the best pilots in the world.'

I sat in the pilots' minibus as they drove along the shore of the opaline Lake Pukaki, then wound through rusty highland scrub to Twizel, where most of the pilots live. It's a small community of 1500 souls, built on a circular grid around a handful of struggling shops.

They dropped me at a motel that had closed for winter, save for one permanent resident, a Maori man called Jimmy, a slight, shy fellow in his fifties, who drove a cement truck at a mine thirty miles away. He had warm eyes and an unguarded, un-European smile that revealed missing front teeth. We shared the kitchen-living room, the only place with heating, where we sat by the big wood-burning stove. For kindling, you tore pages from a 1950s set of the *Oxford Children's Encyclopædia*. Hunting periodicals lay around the room, featuring gun tests and photographs of hunted deer.

At the bar of the nearby United Services Club I was introduced to Greg Bayliss. He was a short, stocky man, wearing a well-worn nylon bomber jacket. We shook hands.

'He wants to see what top-dressers get up to,' one of pilots said.

Greg shot me an appraising look. He wasn't going to make up his mind straight away. We had some beers. He seemed direct, generous and funny and I took to him at once. Later in the evening he said, 'I don't see any problem there, Martin. But I hope you're not in a hurry. The weather looks pretty shitty.'

For days, it rained. Greg invited me round for a coffee. We sat on the sofa and he opened a large picture book, a history of his profession. I saw a black-and-white picture of a biplane, with a small dark cloud blossoming underneath it.

'They first started talking about top-dressing in the Thirties,' Greg said. 'You've probably noticed we have a fair few hills in New Zealand. And at that time most hill country was non-productive. The land's deficient in certain trace elements, selenium, cobalt and others, which basically meant unhealthy stock. The only way of getting at it was on horseback and spreading the fertilizer by hand. But labour was intensive and costly and the land they could reach was minimal. Then, after the war, the Public Works Department began trial delivery from the air.' He pointed to a photo of a Grumman Avenger, a rotund American carrier-based torpedo bomber nicknamed the Pregnant Beast. A cloud of fertilizer emerged from its vast bomb bay. 'The RNZAF did some of the trials. But in the end it became a commercial operation. And it was a roaring success.'

'What did they want to spray?'

'It wasn't spray. They wanted to dress the pastures with superphosphate, which is a granulated fertilizer. This isn't crop country as in wheat prairies, it's grassland, ideal for meat and wool.

'After the war there were hundreds of cheap Tiger Moths around, so people started taking the front seats out and putting in a hopper with five hundredweight of fertilizer and a door in the bottom the pilot could open and close. Looks archaic, but remember this was 1949—it was revolutionary. And all that land brought into production over the last fifty years still needs top-dressing to keep it going. That's why we're still in business.'

'What does it cost the farmers?'

'The phosphate itself is quite expensive, but the cost of applying it is economical, maybe $2.50 to $4 an acre. Anyway, the industry blossomed. The Tiger Moth was the mainstay through the Fifties. Even though it was a frail, underpowered machine, it was actually very safe, because of its crashability.'

'Its *what*?'

'Crashability. They had a lot of accidents, but the wings and fuselage used to crumple up and absorb the impact and the pilot could walk away. Having said that, there were a fair few pilots killed, simply because there were so many of them out there, in planes that weren't high-powered enough to manœuvre safely in the valleys. A lot were killed. There's a whole bloody list of 'em in the back of this book.

'Later, they started using Dakotas. Then they became uneconomical, with high fuel costs and elderly airframes. Our company had one in the mid-Seventies and the wing came off it when a guy was sowing a load.

'So the plane we use today was born out of a need for a high-performance, large-capacity machine. It's based on a Fifties American design, the Fletcher. The design was bought up by New Zealanders and it resulted in the plane we use today: the Cresco.'

There was ice in the wind the next morning. Greg picked me up before dawn and we drove to his private airfield on the outskirts of town. At the edge of the field, close to a ridge of trees and a stream, were a small building and a fuel tank. Parked beside them was the Cresco, a strapping, single-engine aircraft, not a pretty machine, its fuselage too thick and its nose too short to approach the ethereal harmonies of a Spitfire. Notoriously, pilots couldn't see over the Spit's aristocratic nose, whereas the Cresco's tapered cowling permits excellent visibility. Designed to take on and dump two tons of fertiliser every ten minutes, year in, year out, the Cresco is tough and powerful, a sort of aerial tractor.

Greg fired up the engine. Silver-blue clouds burst from the exhaust pipes. The turbine wound itself up into a scream, the huge propeller scythed, the aeroplane trembled and shook. I climbed under the bubble canopy, into the right-hand seat. There was a harness but no connection for a set of cans. The cabin was sparse and utilitarian. Greg reached over me to rotate a big handle to secure the canopy, murmuring his pre-flights as he turned the nose towards a cinder runway. In moments we were climbing past telegraph wires, the road narrowing beneath us. The take-off run had seemed to me almost as short as the Porter's.

'Yeah, it's basically STOL capability,' Greg yelled over the turbine. 'The wing is very high-lift, which also means a lot of drag, but the turbo compensates—750 horsepower gives pretty startling performance.'

'How does she fly?'

'Superbly. Empty she goes up like a rocket—3000 feet a minute at ninety knots. Even with two tons in the back, the climb rate can be 1000 feet a minute.'

Our view unravelled from a flat field on the edge of a small town to a complex landscape of relief, vegetation, erosions, meanderings. We were heading east. Greg pointed at distant, dark peaks. 'They're the Grampian Mountains over on the right, and on our left is the Dalgety Range. Back in the 1800s the famous Scottish sheep rustler James Mackenzie herded sheep he stole on the east coast through here, into what they call the Mackenzie Basin, where nobody could find them. This is the Mackenzie Pass we're flying through now.'

There was a low ceiling, so we were flying far closer to the deck than I was used to, hugging the landscape, winding through valleys, skimming across steep hillsides bristling with coarse-looking grass.

'We used to be forever struggling to get across ridges; but with this turbine, you just aim where you want to go and it'll take you, clear the ridge by any margin you choose—within reason. Like any aeroplane, you have to respect it, you don't wanna be I say.'

'You don't wanna be *what*?' Over the roar of the engine, I could barely hear him.

'Blasé! Cocky! "I've got a 750 horsepower turbo up front, *watch me*." Cut your margins and get into a confined space with a heavy load, with the wing doing a lot of work—she'll bite yer.'

It was too noisy for conversation. After forty-five minutes we left the mountains and were flying over downs with a view to the teal-blue Pacific Ocean.

Greg turned over a long gulley, which ended in a rolling hill. 'That's where we're landing.'

I peered in vain for an airstrip. '*Where?*'

There was no strip. Greg simply put us down on the hillside, its steep gradient helping us to lose speed.

We taxied up towards a brick shed near the brow. A mound of greenish super-phosphate had already been deposited there, and the farmer and Greg's driver Shane Lancaster were waiting. We climbed out and Greg greeted the farmer, then swung his plane round while Shane manœuvred the truck, scooping up a load of fertilizer and dumping it in an orifice on top of the Cresco's fuselage. At once, the engine roared and the plane trundled forward, the two tons weighing it down. It accelerated down the slope, out of sight. I watched with bated breath; then I saw the plane, halfway along the gulley, climbing. Greg was gone about eight minutes. For his next run, I squatted among the thistles and sheep droppings at the lower end of the 'airstrip'. Resembling a take-off from an aircraft carrier, it made a strong impression on me. If the pilot made a mistake, or the plane experienced an abrupt loss of power, they would both plummet into the depths of the gulley. The Cresco leapt off the steep hillside, seemed to sink slightly over the first half of the gorge, then gained height and climbed out at the far end, banked left and disappeared over the bosomy ridge to dump its cargo.

It took Greg a couple of hours to work his way through the mound of phosphate. Then Shane set off in the loader truck to where they'd be working in the afternoon. We took out our sandwiches and Greg's thermos of coffee. I told him how impressed I had been by his flying.

He deflected the compliment. 'It's a superb plane, because it's designed for our conditions. As you see, we're working off hillside airstrips with very little visibility. Rolling off the top of a hill is like going over a ski jump, you don't want a big nose sticking out in front of you. In this plane the visibility's superb and there's a good safety record for that reason. Mind you, when they built the first Cresco in about 1980, the tail fell off it. They wanted to increase its Vne—its maximum speed—and they kept pushing the envelope, but the all-flying tailplane didn't like high speed too much. It got flutter and came off in flight—the pilot survived, he parachuted out. But the tailplanes didn't like cow manure much, either.'

'*What?*'

'Yeah, I dare say there aren't many forms of aviation activity where getting cow and sheep shit stuck all over your aeroplane is a common eventuality. But up into the dairy provinces it's a major problem— you land and *splat*—round the canopy, all over your wings . . . Anyway, these globs of manure used to put the Cresco's tailplane centre of gravity out a bit, but they sorted it out . . .'

It had been a windy, drizzly morning, but as we ate our sandwiches the sun appeared, transforming the landscape's dull military greens and khakis into rich emeralds and golds. Greg had left enough phosphate aboard to do a last couple of runs with me in the cockpit. We took off, a thrilling catapult into that craggy gorge, then hooked left.

As Greg started his drop run, it seemed to me we were attached to the landscape by rails. He flew with one fist round the stick, his body twisted to the left slightly, eyes under his long-peaked cap fixed on the ground 150 feet below. At the end of each run he turned. 'Turned': he flung the wing down, so that the fields lunged up to try and grab its tip; the plane rotated round the axis of the wing, levelled out again, and Greg began another run. This was low-level aerobatics, and my stomach tightened, my skin tingled. It was flying of consummate skill and confidence, the result of twenty years of experience. But the turns were hair-raising. A hundred feet above the telegraph wires, I felt I could reach out and play cat's cradle with them.

Job done, Greg set out for the next farm, a ten-minute flight away. We flew over the loader, toiling up ghat roads. The farm looked pretty from above, a redstone house perched on a hilltop, among spreading deciduous trees, with a valley falling gently away before it. This valley was the pasture Greg had to sow next.

As we waited for the loader truck to arrive, I asked about our speed in the low turns. Everything I'd been taught about flying emphasised the danger of turning too tightly, leading to a drop in speed and a potential stall.

'Working speed sowing is 140 knots and 95 or 100 in the turn.'

'What's your stall speed?'

'In the turn, fully loaded, around sixty-five knots.'

'And your angle of bank?'

'Not beyond 60 degrees heavily loaded. But once you're under the ton mark, you can start to throw the plane around and the last couple of runs you can do wing-over, tight manœuvres. Which is why people sometimes call top-dressing pilots cowboys.'

'Is that unjustified?'

'Totally. If you're the kind of guy who takes a wide turn at the end of the run when you don't have to, you're costing the farmer money. And it's a competitive industry: for a pilot to succeed he has to be productive. Of course, you don't want to kill yourself, either. When I first started, I used to make the odd mistake, I think most pilots do. Most top-dressing aircraft don't have artificial horizons fitted simply because they don't survive the rough airstrips, the treatment the airframe gets. So it's seat-of-the-pants flying.'

I asked if he'd ever had a near miss.

Like most pilots, he was slow to answer. 'Well, the worst was probably one time when I'd only done a few hundred hours. Funnily enough, I was being supervised by a company senior pilot that day. He took me in his plane for a briefing, warned me there was no natural horizon, keep your speed up. I started sowing the valley, but when I got to the turning place I realised I was way too low and didn't have enough speed to turn. I started dumping the load—we can emergency-jettison, get rid of it in about five seconds. But the aircraft was only just flying. I thought I was gonna squash into the hillside. The wheels were inches off the scrub . . . Yeah, stalling in the turn has been the number one killer in top-dressing. They drum these dangers into you, but the accident rate in past years was pretty horrendous.'

Shane arrived in the loader truck and Greg began the afternoon's work. As the winter sun sank lower, brilliant golden light sliced through the rain-washed air. Every surface dazzled, from blades of grass to the Cresco's bubble canopy, against a curtain of imperial purple hanging, rain-swollen, in the west. Greg made run after run, sowing the gently rolling valley. Slowly the mound of phosphate diminished, but as the sun slipped behind the trees on the ridge, it was obvious that he wasn't going to finish that day.

As we returned to Twizel the way we'd come, low among the

valleys, the light show continued, the sky a table of turquoise-blue with clouds like mountains of buttery mashed potato. It was a matchless evening on which to be up in a small plane.

'I think we've just got time for me to show you something,' Greg said. He turned into a network of gullies running west off the Mackenzie Pass. 'This is what they call Gray's Hills.' He went low over the steep, bleak, straw-coloured slopes. 'See that?'

At first sight it looked like a cartoon fish bone. Then I realised I was looking at the ribs of an aeroplane wing.

'It's an Auster,' Greg went on. 'It was an English pilot, dropping rabbit poison back in 1952. As you can see, the plane's almost complete. It's so remote up here it's kept the souvenir hunters away.'

'What happened?'

'Probably the usual thing, he lost his sense of the horizon, lost speed in the turn, stalled . . . and was killed.'

It rained, it blew.

'What do you think?' I asked.

Greg narrowed his eyes dubiously. 'Fifty–fifty,' he said.

It was the following morning, warmer, but wetter. As we flew east, retracing our route of the previous day, the windscreen swarmed microbially with drizzle. Fast winds eddied through the Mackenzie Pass and the plane leapt around like a March hare. So this, I thought, is what it was like for the postal pilots—only, their planes had barely 20 per cent of the power of ours.

Greg was flying low, skimming over the hills, wrestling with the stick to keep us straight and level. The plane was doing 120 knots, but our ground speed was 165. That meant forty-five knots of tailwind. The gusts were determined to push us into the valley walls. Scraping the bottoms of the clouds, we couldn't go any higher. Beneath our wheels were webs of high-tension cables.

Greg yelled, 'In this weather, you're forced to fly through these passes. And of course, so's the air. It behaves like water; it takes the easiest route and speeds up through the passes. This is like coming down a hydroslide, we get spat out the other end. And, of course, that's where all the turbulence is—out on the leeward side of the gorge.'

At last we emerged from the turbulent valley and reached the farm we'd left the previous evening. The sky was gloomy and it was evident from the way the feathery treetops along the ridge were whipping around that the winds were strong. Greg nonchalantly popped the plane down.

We sat for a while, with Greg closely observing the action of the wind in the trees. 'A windy old day. 'S what you get for living in the Roaring Forties.'

'Personally, I don't mind being back on the ground,' I said. 'Was it as bad back there as it seemed to me?'

He grinned. 'Naw, we get it rougher than that.'

The drizzle was turning into drumming rain. He looked up at the sky. 'This is too heavy for us to work. We'll have a cup of coffee, see what happens.'

'We were pretty damn close to that hillside back there,' I insisted.

'We didn't take any paint off the wing, that's the main thing.' He laughed. 'I mean, I wouldn't encourage a beginner to fly like that. I come through there hundreds of times a year. It's like anything in life, the more you do it, the easier it gets. If you were an aerobatic pilot doing 1000 hours a year it'd be pretty routine after a while. Even boring.'

'You've got to be kidding?'

'Some days I think I'd rather be doing something with less pressure. I'm in my twenty-first year of commercial flying and seventeen of those have been top dressing: 15,000 hours total. I had the chance to move on to the airlines, but I stayed with this. So I s'pose I must be happy . . . A lot of guys gave their lives to get this business going. In the Fifties we were held in high regard. But now we're just a pain in the butt to most people. You start working near populated areas and you're disturbing their Sunday morning cup of coffee. Making a lot of noise and probably poisoning the environment—which we're not, because it's a natural product—but they think you're spraying toxic chemicals that are going to drift in through their kitchen windows and give their kiddies asthma.'

With his telescopic eyes, Greg spotted the speck of a distant plane going in to land on some farm strip. 'He's running for cover—I don't blame him. The wind's getting worse. You know, I don't even think we'll have that cup of coffee.'

He fired up the turbo. As the Cresco trundled forward at the start of its take-off roll, the wind whipped under its wings and suddenly we were slewing sideways. It felt like slipping in mud—not a sensation you want to experience in an accelerating aircraft. For a sickening moment I thought we were going to be flicked over. Greg jerked the plane to the left—into the wind—and put on power. We were no longer heading down the gradual slope of the grass strip, but down a precipitous side slope, barred by a wire fence about 200 feet below.

The moment is perfectly preserved in my memory: the heavy slate sky and matt green grass, and that childhood sensation when you're running too fast down a hill and you realise you can't stop without tumbling headlong. When we seemed certain to hit the fence, Greg pulled back the stick—and we were in the air, buffeted but climbing strongly. He casually turned to me and shouted, 'And that wasn't even on full power.'

Out on the littoral, south of the town of Ashburton, is the Vincent farm. The Vincents own a sort of miniature squadron: three World War II-vintage British Austers, shared between Les Vincent and his two sons. Greg knew Les and knew the airstrip in a broad field beside the Vincents' farmhouse. Seeing as he wasn't going to get any work done today, he offered to take me there.

'We're going to go past the monument to Richard Pearse,' Greg told me. 'Big New Zealand aviation hero, neglected genius. They say he beat the Wright brothers. Flew a plane before they did.'

We dropped low over the fields and circled a monument representing a small aeroplane with stubby, rectangular wings.

A few minutes later we had landed on a cruciform airstrip in a field behind the Vincents' farmhouse, and were sitting in the kitchen, a big, square room with a large range and a long table. Les and Elizabeth Vincent, a couple in their fifties, greeted us like passing wayfarers in the age of settlers.

'They must be cold and thirsty,' said Elizabeth, putting the kettle on the hob.

'Hope you don't mind us dropping in on you?' asked Greg.

'We don't like it much,' joked Elizabeth, 'but I guess you've got no choice, with the weather up in the hills!'

'Rough up there, is it?' asked Les.

'We had a bit of a hairy time,' conceded Greg.

Les nodded sagely. 'There's a lot of people come unstuck over the years.'

It isn't morbidity; everyone who flies knows someone who has died flying, and there but for the grace of God . . . So pilots, like sailors a century ago, incessantly pore over the evidence of *what went wrong*, in an unending effort to insulate themselves from the elements and their own human weaknesses.

The water boiled.

'Greg,' asked Elizabeth, 'are you a tea person or a coffee person?'

'I'm a coffee person.'

'Good one.'

Cakes and biscuits joined the coffee and tea pots on the table, and the men were firmly told to eat. Conversation turned from the weather to top-dressing, and the competition between rival pilots. 'I get on well with my opposition,' said Greg. 'But in some places it's war, the opposition pilots won't even talk to each other . . .'

For an hour and a half they sat around the table and talked aircraft: old friends, old planes, old times; brilliant feats of flying, freak accidents, wondrous escapes from death. Flying visitors who would beat up the Vincents as they worked in the fields, making them throw themselves flat on the ground.

Finally, Greg said it was time for him to go, resisting with difficulty Elizabeth's offer of lunch. I walked with him out to the field (or paddock, in Kiwi parlance), to see him off. With its hopper empty, the powerful Cresco leapt into the air and climbed almost vertically. Instead of heading west, it circled overhead and seemed to hover motionless—until I realised it was growing larger. It was all that talk of beat-ups. Three thousand pounds of aluminium came hurtling out of the pale-blue sky and I threw myself flat in the long grass as the plane roared over my head and looped magnificently back into the sky.

I stayed with the Vincents for several days and heard about the life of a family for whom aircraft are almost a creed. After the war, Les's father had bought some surplus Mosquitos, just for their engines. 'We cut them up with saws to get at the Merlins and made a bonfire with what was left. *Can you imagine*? But there were thousands of surplus aircraft after the war. This lot's flying days were over and they were considered almost worthless . . . Today it brings tears to my eyes to think of it, because there are so few Mozzies left in the world.'

Elizabeth never felt the yen to fly herself, but she loves the old Austers as much as her menfolk. She talked nostalgically of when the boys were young, taking them on picnics in the back of a small plane. Les's brother had gone into commercial aviation and still ran a small cargo airline, Vincent Airlines. Les had been involved with it over the years, but made his living in farming. His own love of aviation took the form of building up this collection of Austers. He passed on to his sons his love of aircraft, in particular the venerable Auster.

Les took me flying in the oldest Auster in New Zealand, the 1944 Mk 5 prototype. It has a cosy cabin of bakelite knobs and big dials with calligraphic white lettering, and a delicious *smell*, like a 1950s automobile—indeed, Les keeps the plane in a garage beside his house and it felt curiously domestic to wheel the maroon and silver-painted machine out on to the lawn. The Auster has a single long, high, strutted wing, a network of finer struts inside the cockpit and a transparent roof. Its four seats are of fine-veined red vinyl, like those of blessed childhood memory in my father's first car, a 1950s Morris Minor.

We taxied round a corner into the paddock and took off. We flew over to Ashburton and landed at the airfield beside a museum run by Les and a bunch of fellow enthusiasts. The collection is impressive: it includes a 1930s German glider, a de Havilland Vampire (the superbly manœuvrable jet fighter that first flew in 1945, three weeks before VE Day) and an enchanting 1930s American biplane, a Porterfield Flyabout.

As we prepared to return, Les asked me if I'd ever done a take-off in a tail-dragger. 'Er, no . . .' I said nervously, hoping I wasn't about to learn. But I was. He told me what to do, I failed to do it and the Auster bounced down the long grass strip like a demented bullfrog.

Les took over, but allowed me to fly us back through an evening of giant velvet clouds fringed with scarlet. When we landed in his field, he told me it was time to try another take-off.

'Do I *have* to?' I asked, like an ungrateful teenager. 'Isn't it getting a bit late?'

'I think there's time for just one. Keep the nose forward, Martin, lots of rudder inputs. At forty-five—stick back.'

I had 2,100 feet of grass available. After what seemed like most of it, at forty-five, I sticked back.

'Not that far back!' Les yelled. Barely off the ground, I was somehow left-banking into a windbreak of fir trees. Les seized control, got us level and over the boundary fence, and aloft. He seemed a little shaken. So was I.

We made a tight circuit. Lights were showing in the crepuscular landscape. 'One more time?' Les said.

'Oh, *Les*,' I whined.

'Fall off the horse, Martin, you've got to get back on.'

'But—it's *dark*!'

He was unbudgeable. 'You'll get it right this time. You were fine till you took off; just stick back more gently, *ease* it back.'

So my third ever tail-dragger take-off took place in virtual darkness. I did, however, get it right. Now the landscape was black, studded with the lights of farmhouses; if Les had not known the landscape and his airstrip intimately, we would not have got down again in one piece.

CHAPTER XX

The Inventors

I SOON LEARNED THAT everyone in New Zealand who is at all interested in aviation knows the legend of Richard Pearse. I was about to discover another facet of the Wright brothers story, a controversy that makes many New Zealanders feel one of their greatest countrymen has been shamefully neglected.

It was cool and damp as Les drove me over to Waitohi, where the Pearse family used to live and some of them still do. We parked beside the monument Greg had flown me round, a full-size mock-up of Pearse's first plane, based on imprecise patent drawings and various acts of palaeography. Its stubby wing is roughly twenty feet by eight, with a vertical fin running all the way from front to back (Pearse called it a 'keel-piece') and a pilot's compartment ('car') with tricycle wheels suspended underneath. The reconstruction is mounted on a pole in such a way that it weathercocks, rather wistfully, on the steady Pacific breeze. 'Richard William Pearse, 1877–1953, New Zealand Pioneer Aviator' a plaque declares. 'This monument commemorates the first powered flight to be made by a British Citizen in a heavier-than-air machine. Most evidence indicates this flight took place on 31st March 1903 and ended by crashing on this site.' The New Zealanders are throwing down a gauntlet: that Pearse achieved a bona fide powered flight as early as March 1903—nine months before the Wrights at Kitty Hawk.

Records show that the Pearse family had been established in Cornwall, south-west England for several hundred years. Richard's father Digory arrived in New Zealand in 1865 and quickly bought some land on South Island. He ran a mixed farm, married Sarah (a migrant from Belfast) and fathered nine children. His success is evident from the family's prominence in the local social scene, playing tennis and golf as well as music—the Pearses had a family orchestra consisting of cello, harp, flute, piano and five violins.

The eldest son was sent to Edinburgh to study medicine; Richard's misfortune was that he was not despatched to engineering college. He and the three other remaining brothers each received a farm of a hundred acres, close to the parental home. Richard was a good-looking young man, sensitive, intense, rather introverted. He was an indifferent farmer—one of his younger brothers remembered him ploughing a field with the horses' reins round his neck, while reading a science textbook! He continued to live with his parents and converted the cottage on his farm into a workshop, using the income from farming to fund his preoccupation with engineering.

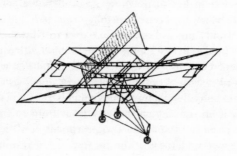

1906 patent drawing of Pearse's aeroplane, showing trapdoor ailerons at the wingtips

He was a fervent proponent of the scientific method, a convinced materialist (he published a fiery letter attacking spiritualism in the local newspaper). By the early 1900s, his experiments had led him to become something of a recluse. The gorse hedges around his farm grew to their fullest extent of twelve feet. Behind them, neighbours would hear strange sounds. He soon became known as 'Mad Pearse'.

At the turn of the twentieth century, Richard Pearse was a sort of hermit of the far-flung cult of would-be flyers. He was a natural inventor, no stranger to the Patent Office. Products of his imagination included a mechanical potato planter and a bicycle whose tyres could be pumped up as the rider cycled along. Like the Wrights, he was caught up in the cycling revolution, but his real obsession was the aeroplane. As a child he had played, like Cayley and the Wrights before him, with a string-pull helicopter. In adulthood he recognized that manned flight was an attainable goal. Someone was going to do it—so why not him?

Pearse's planes were powered by engines he built, like Pilcher and the Wrights, in his own workshop. Four of these engines are still in existence, admirably lightweight, high-powered designs that compare favourably with the heavy, low-powered designs used by most of his aeronautical contemporaries. He had already made a bicycle frame from bamboo, quite a common practice at the time, since in addition to bamboo's lightness, its strength and elasticity can be superior even to steel. He therefore made his aircraft's frames from bamboo, covered with calico coated, like later cloth-skinned aircraft, with 'dope', or varnish.

In 1902–3 Pearse made a number of flights—or hops, it's hard to be sure. Few people showed any interest in him until the 1950s, when a string of researchers made attempts to obtain reliable accounts of possible flights and accurate dates. Finally, twenty living people were tracked down who could provide first-hand accounts. They recalled that small crowds would gather on the high ground behind Pearse's farm to watch his experiments, curious children clambering on haystacks to peer over the untrimmed hedges. A few favoured friends were allowed to visit and even assist in the work in progress. Despite his reticence, Pearse sometimes needed help, since it took two men to hold the plane back when the propeller was turning.

Next, he appears to have made use of a stretch of the nearby road, which was straight and flat. One flight apparently took place on 31 March, the eve of April Fool's Day, since one neighbour commented, 'Had Dick Pearse waited another day he would have been a proper fool instead of just a bloody fool.' Indeed, reports of the flight were taken by some people to be April Fool's jokes. As to the *year*, no one is sure if it was 1902 or 1903.

Eyewitnesses remembered a plane with a wingspan of roughly twenty by eight feet taking off, pitching around as Pearse sought to control it, and flying for well over a hundred feet, before it swerved into the tall gorse hedge. Pearse was carried to hospital in nearby

Temuka, in a dazed condition. The plane apparently remained perched on the hedge for several days. Some time later Pearse made a longer flight from a large flat area called the Terraces, which overlooked a river a mile or so from his farm.

In Waitohi there's a folk memory that Pearse flew long before the Wrights; of course, it wasn't until 1908 that Wilbur Wright's demonstration at Reims made headlines all around the world. But Pearse, a subscriber to the *Scientific American*, read in January 1904 that the Wright brothers had flown three miles. This was utterly wrong, the true distance having been 852 feet. But Pearse lost heart. He didn't register his patents for two more years—a delay that might have changed the course of his life and aviation history.

Les and I looked for the river bank where Pearse had made his longest flight. A farmer working on a cattle dip confirmed that we were at the right spot. I climbed over a fence and walked around the edge of a broad, flattish ploughed field. It ended in a cliff about twenty feet high. A hundred years ago this cliff looked down on the river, a broad expanse of gravelly mud with fingers of water winding through it. Around half of the river has now been reclaimed, and it flows beyond a broad bank with a screen of trees. Still we could get enough of a sense of the lie of the land to see where Pearse had begun his flight and where it ended—on the far bank of the river, close to a modern road bridge.

Standing among the poplars I became rather excited, but Les pointed out that since Pearse had taken off higher than where he landed, he had probably achieved only a *powered glide*, not a self-sustaining flight. And anyway, the evidence was too sketchy to prove anything.

In 1910 Pearse contracted the disease that was to kill Wilbur Wright the following year: typhoid fever. His sisters nursed him back to health, but he seems to have reached a watershed in his life. He abandoned the suffocating atmosphere of Waitohi, the nosy neighbours and the disapproving paterfamilias, and moved south to Milton, buying a farm on a quiet road completely screened by hills. Here he continued to build aeroplanes, as well as a home-manufactured motorbicycle. Perhaps because aviation was now known and accepted by the general public, he entered a happier phase of his life. He became a pillar of the local community and even a popular dancing and tennis partner—though understood by all to be a confirmed bachelor.

In 1917 he was called up. He trained with a New Zealand regiment in England before being found unfit for active service. Returning home, he found that his farmhouse had been vandalized. The post-war depression soon started and Pearse was able to make little money from his few sheep and pigs. He sold the farm and moved north, to Christchurch, where he built three houses, living in the third on the rental from the first two. Now he devoted himself to a new vision: an aeroplane for the masses, one that could take off vertically and fly in and out of confined spaces—an aerial motorcar.

It absorbed Pearse totally for more than two decades, which included five years of wrangling with the Patent Office. He showed the obsessive, furtive behaviour of the authentic recluse. But even as Pearse laboured on his vertical take-off plane, it was completely superseded by the invention of the helicopter.

Through the Forties, Pearse's eccentricity and remoteness increased. The tragic history of his life ended in 1953, at the age of seventy-five, in a sanatorium where he had been for two years. He only came to public attention when his vertical lift-off plane happened to be seen by some aviation enthusiasts after his death. Today it hangs in the transport museum in Auckland, an ungainly and poignantly comic contraption. Most of Pearse's papers, which could have answered so many questions about him, had been burned.

It is hardly surprising that Richard Pearse, living in rural isolation, failed to achieve his goals. But in 1903 he may have been closer to the goal of a powered aircraft than anyone else in the world, except the Wrights. Even here, there is an extraordinary twist. Registered patents prove that Pearse independently invented the aileron. His patent drawings of 1906 show movable flaps in the wings, much more like modern ailerons than the Wrights' 'warping' wings. The Wrights' entire legal case for their ownership of aviation was based on the control systems in their 1906 patents; it is interesting to note that if Pearse had registered his patent just *three months* earlier, the bicycle manufacturers from Dayton might have had to concede some of the high ground—and even some of their earnings—to a farmer in a remote corner of New Zealand.

Winter now offered a few days of high winds and, in the mountains, the season's first heavy snows. Les, who had hoped to fly me to the next stage in my journey, was grounded. So he dropped me at the coach station and I headed into the Southern Highlands by road.

The ski resort of Wanaka is where New Zealand's greatest annual airshow is held, the home of a collection of vintage aircraft assembled by one man, a plane-obsessed millionaire called Sir Tim Wallis. I had hoped to meet him, but he was still recovering from a bad accident two years earlier when he had crashed a plane from his collection— one of his two Spitfires.

The collection's curator, Ian Brodie, showed me around the museum, inviting me to climb into any of the planes. I approached the Spitfire with particular awe, feeling a frisson when I slid down into its seat. The Spitfire pilot occupied a cockpit in which every control was within a finger's length. One's soft, humid, human body is hard up against surfaces of brass and steel—except for the head which, domed in the Plexiglas bubble, has a remarkable view past the wing's leading edges to the ground beneath. Sitting in a Spitfire is an extraordinary experience of man-machine intimacy.

Yet in some ways the Wallis Collection's Hurricane made an even stronger impression on me. It has been the Hurricane's fate to live in the shadow of her more glamorous and technologically evolved sister. The Hurricane preceded the Spitfire into service by ten months and bore the brunt of the initial fight with the *Luftwaffe*. During the Battle of Britain Hurricanes outnumbered Spitfires by three to two, and accounted for 70 per cent of enemy aircraft destroyed (though the Spitfire's technical superiority over the Bf 109 gave the RAF the edge). The irony is that today there are hundreds of the highly prized Spitfires still flying, but of the 14,533 Hurricanes built, only a handful survive. When Wallis wanted to acquire one, he had to buy a pile of junk—literally. The tangle of a shot-down, crash-mangled Hurricane was pulled from the tundra near Murmansk, in Russia. Although some of the plane was salvageable and some original spare parts were sourced in various parts of the world—including an unused Merlin engine located in England—most of Hurricane Mark I serial no. P3351 had to be built from scratch, from the thousands of design drawings the reconstruction team painstakingly assembled. The complexity of this act of archaeological engineering exceeded the team's worst fears. It meant forging special grades of steel that are no longer in use, re-creating jigs and tooling machines working to tolerances of three-thousandths of an inch, and building complex devices like radiators, oil coolers and retractable wheels from scratch. It took five and a half years, the labour of a large group of volunteers and the expenditure of several million pounds, much of it injected by Air New Zealand. The plane's control column, a leather-bound ring with a brass gun-firing button built into it, was a war souvenir donated by Bill Kain, a World War II veteran who had flown in 73 Squadron, the same squadron in which P3351 had served.

What I found so extraordinary about this aeroplane was that it has not been merely restored, as many aircraft have been in museums the world over, but *reincarnated*. Its skin is as smooth as a newborn's, its paintwork is unscratched, unscuffed, unstained by grease or exhaust fumes. P3351 is in showroom condition. Such surface perfection plays tricks on the mind; having expected to see a machine sixty years old, I encountered one supernaturally new. It had somehow transcended time.

Heavy snows had closed the high road from Wanaka to Queenstown. But after a couple of bright, cold days, it was possible for buses with snow chains on their wheels to get through.

I had heard of a man living in Queenstown called Bill Barber, who, people said, had built a plane. Many pilots have toyed at some point with building a kit plane—like Jo-Jo Alfonsi's Europa—but Bill Barber's planes weren't assembled from kits: this retired farmer had *designed and manufactured* a new type of aeroplane from scratch.

When I met Bill and Bridget Barber, they invited me to stay with them. After a life of farming in the wetter lowlands south-east of Queenstown, they now live in a large house above New Zealand's most exclusive winter resort. They find Queenstown sympathetic, but Bridget dislikes its icy winters.

Below the house, Bill has the workshop where he builds the plane he calls the Barber Snark. 'After Lewis Carroll, that is. Not, as someone asked, "Has a bit of the 'h' fallen off?"—it is *not* a "Shark".'

He is as methodical and practical a man, I suspect, as his predecessor Richard Pearse. He is slightly built, very slim, with regular features and a full head of hair. He is quiet and self-deprecating, drily humorous, very intelligent. Comparisons with Pearse are inevitable, if for no other reason than that it's so hard to imagine Bill Barber as a farmer.

I am standing in his large workshop. Scattered around are Snarks in various stages of construction. There is also an early one that he's rebuilding, somewhat grumpily. Someone had crashed it into the ground from a height of fifteen feet. The pilot's survival, and the fact that the plane is reparable are obvious marks in favour of the Snark, but Bill is bored by the rebuild—his ideas and his methods have moved on. The model currently under construction is similar externally, but the *structure* has changed.

The Snark is a highly original design. At first sight, it looks more like a helicopter than an aeroplane. It has a sleek, dart-shaped fuselage with a forward-sloping perspex canopy. The pilot sits near the nose, the passenger behind and above him. Behind the passenger is the engine, with its 'pusher' propeller. A high, helicopterish boom juts aft, evolving into a sharply aerodynamic vertical tail section.

As he talks, Bill frequently laughs at himself, as though, after all these years, it still surprises him that he achieved anything at all.

'Because, for a start, no one ever taught me any maths. They didn't think farm boys needed maths. I worked for my two years of secondary school out of a little wee thin book and the most complicated sum in it was how many cubic feet of hay in a haystack—and I'm not joking. It was bloody awful! Because I wanted to know how things *worked*, I wanted to *make* things. I'd constantly run aground through lack of maths. Way back, I sent for a book from the Wellington Technical Book Company on aeroplane design. There it is.'

I lifted the dark, heavy, hardbound 1950s book from his shelf and opened it: a mass of equations.

'Wall-to-wall algebra!' Bill laughed. 'It could just as well have been in Swahili. I learned later that it was one of the standard references on the subject, so eventually I took it out again and . . . got what I needed.'

'But why did you want to build a plane?' I said.

'I dunno . . . It was just there, in me. I could have built any number of kit planes, but that didn't interest me—it had to be *mine*. I woke up one morning—and I can remember this clearly—saying to myself, "Jeez, I'm gonna do this, 'cause if I don't do it soon, I never will." And I got out of bed and started work on it.'

This gave me a vision of Bill at the drawing board wearing his pyjamas. In fact, designing the plane had taken him almost twenty years—'two years on the design, and eighteen mucking around with the bloody thing!

'I started by drawing little pictures . . . Then I got the maths—that took a while . . . The plane had to be totally modern, not another high-wing job, the world's got enough Cessnas. I went back to basics. Putting a propeller at the back is supposedly 15 per cent more efficient. The tail went over the top. And the pilot ahead of the wing, for visibility. That's how it evolved.

'What I envisaged wasn't really possible at first, because of regulations. Then microlights came along and changed everything. I bought an early microlight, a Pterodactyl. I did a lot of crop-spraying with that. Very effective and fun. But they were slow, they only did about 45 mph, which gets boring after a while. My idea was for a 100 mph microlight. Then along came modern lightweight materials like carbon fibre and kevlar and suddenly it looked possible. I finally started work in about 1986. Like all first-time designers, I tried to put too much in. It was really a process of elimination. It would have been so much easier, oh God, vastly easier, to make a conventional plane.'

To fly the Snark, we had to leave Queenstown and drive north-east, down the steep-sided Kawarau gorge. As we descended the valley, the air became noticeably warmer. After half an hour the ground flattened out on either side of us and we began to pass vineyards. Bill pulled off the road and drove up to a silver hangar. He opened the doors, and there was his baby.

Bill Barber has created an uncompromisingly modern aircraft, with better visibility than almost anything else you could buy and astonishing aerodynamics—the Snark only has a 1300 cc motor, but we cruised over the vineyards at 130 mph, and the top speed is 150. This is an aeroplane with the weight and speed of a motorcycle. When I flew the Snark, I found it swift and well-balanced, but at the same time it felt very sure, very safe. It is an impressive achievement, since nothing like it exists in Europe or America. But only a handful of Snarks have been built. Will Bill ever find someone who wants to manufacture it?

I believe that a generation of new planes will soon change the way we think about small aircraft. The Snark's construction is immensely simple, the plastic mouldings far easier to produce than the riveted panels or complex ribs of a Cessna or Auster. Fitted with an autopilot and GPS navigation, the Snark could be the shape of twenty-first-century aviation, the spearhead of a flying revolution.

(As this book goes to press, I learn that an Englishman, Tim Cripps, has bought the manufacturing rights to the Snark. It will be built at a factory in Haverfordwest, in Pembrokeshire. Bill Barber's baby has a future, it seems.)

Barber and Snark

Jules Tapper had said he would pick me up some time that afternoon. Around 3 p.m. there was a whining, clattering noise and a tiny Robinson helicopter appeared over the fir trees and made a delicate but assured descent, settling finally on the Barbers' snow-covered lawn. Bill and Bridget were suitably impressed. Feeling like James Bond, I trotted towards the chopper, Jules gesturing for me to keep my head below rotor range. The helicopter's door was a flimsy concave of Plexiglas, fastened with a lightweight catch. Everything about the machine seemed insubstantial. I found myself in the delicate head of a dragonfly. Such impressions were countered by the presence of Jules Tapper—a man with a brisk brush of a moustache and a no-nonsense, decisive air. He rattled through a couple of take-off checks while I pulled on harness and headphones. There was a roar from the engine and the helicopter settled itself forward—the image that came to mind was the crouch runners adopt at the start of a race: it was as though the 'copter was poised on its fingertips and toes. Then, decisively, it parted from the earth and slowly rose. At forty feet it hovered for a moment or two, rotated a few degrees north, then darted forward.

Mounted like a trophy over Jules Tapper's mantelpiece is a propeller. It fell off a Tiger Moth he was flying when all the attachment bolts sheared, but somehow he managed to land the plane— slipping under some power lines to do so. A few years later, someone working in the hills above Queenstown discovered the prop and it made its way eventually to the wall of the Tapper living room. Jules took up flying as a teenager. For years he ran a lodge at Martins Bay, on the coast west of Queenstown. It could only be reached by a two-day trek—or by air. He still is a fanatical pilot, the owner of two aircraft.

The Queenstown ski slopes slid under us. Snow-making machines plumed and a few Day-Glo figures leaning on their skis looked up and waved. We climbed on, until we reached the height of a great butte overlooking Queenstown. The slab sides were too steep to collect snow, so, sandwiched between the cap of snow and the snow-covered shelves below, there was a vertical band of rock.

'Mountain goats live in caves in the rock,' Jules told me. 'Let's see if we can find some.'

He flew parallel to the wall—so close that it seemed the chopper blades must bite the rock. From this proximity I could see that the cliffs were not, in fact, vertical but very gradually shelved, pocked with chinks and hollows, a filigree of narrow paths etched into them. At a prow-like spur, Jules made a vertiginous turn. He was a man, I realised, with complete mastery of his machine, who flew for the sheer joy of it.

As we roared along the far flank of the bluff, a dozen long-horned goats broke from some invisible cave and stumbled along the cliff-face. Jules made a sort of vertical handbrake turn, pirouetting back down to pursue them. Beyond the Plexiglas the white landscape pitched wildly around us. It was consummate flying, exhilarating and hair-raising.

A decade back, when venison herds were being built up for commercial exploitation, hunters leapt from choppers like this one to wrestle wild deer to the ground—one of the most testosterone-fuelled episodes in a country of hairy-chested aviation. Fatality rates among both hunters and pilots were high.

The goats scattered beneath our landing skids. 'Used to shoot them, once,' Jules said, sounding nostalgic.

I felt like a hunter, but not a human one: a mountain eagle, effortlessly in its element, of the mountains, yet free of them.

We left the startled goats to their wintry fastness and headed higher into the range. The landscape was chilly, monochrome, deserted—though now I knew that life was there, hidden. Dense snow had swallowed the lower branches of the pines. Occasionally we glimpsed the ruins of a hut. 'Gold prospectors,' said Jules. As we over-flew the 300-foot gorge carved by the Shotover river, he told me that in the 1860s this was the world's richest goldfield, attracting frantic prospectors from all over the world. By 1900 a tough mining town of 5000 had stood on a bluff high over the gorge, complete with saloons and whorehouses. But the bluff itself was found to contain gold; today, nothing remains.

Jules took the chopper out into the middle of a broad valley, its flanking walls white as bed sheets, the floor perhaps 2000 feet beneath us. Without warning, he said, 'Here, you have a go.'

'But—I can't fly helicopters.'

'S'all right, you just keep her straight, I'll do everything else.' He set my hands on the controls. 'This is your cyclic or altitude control lever, this is your collective-pitch power lever.'

Strong mutual prejudices exist between the pilots of fixed-wing and rotary aircraft, chopper pilots cocky over their larksome manoeuvrability, fixed-wing pilots holding that the helicopter is inherently unsafe. Given engine failure, a fixed wing aircraft can glide, but a helicopter's wings *are its rotor blades*—any mechanical failure in main or aft rotors is catastrophic. Perhaps there is an element of envy in the way fixed-wing pilots view their whirling cousins: the

Tapper and chopper

family man's loathing of the sports car driver's slick overtaking and sexy companion. As it happens, Jules Tapper is one of that rarest of hybrids, a pilot with *both* licences. His view is pragmatic: 'Properly maintained, a helicopter is safe. Of course things can go wrong; but if you're afraid of risk, you stay away from planes. Aviation has inherent dangers, but it's more fun than sitting at home waiting to die of overeating or boredom.'

I clutched the controls in uncertain hands and the chopper made an unpleasant rolling yaw. Free fall! my nerves screamed, wrongly.

'Relax,' said Jules. 'Remember, *very* subtle movements with a helicopter. But don't trust anyone who tells you that flying a 'copter's difficult. They're lying bastards.'

Several days later, I flew with Jules again. He wanted to take me for a jaunt in his other plane, a Cessna 185. As we climbed over Lake Wakatipu he handed me the controls and made a call on his cellphone. He directed me to fly south-east. Jules also flies a vintage de Havilland Dominie, an airforce version of the sleek, art deco Rapide (Stornoway's first shuttle plane). It was currently being refitted at Colin Smith's workshops, one of New Zealand aviation's most hallowed grounds.

For enthusiasts, the name de Havilland has more mystique than almost any other. Its Gipsy Moth biplane has passed into legend. Intended as a mass-produced aircraft for the man in the street, its reliability led to it being chosen for long-distance flights all over the world. It revolutionized flying in Britain and its colonies during the 1920s and 1930s. The Tiger Moth military trainer followed. Then came the Rapide, the legendary Mosquito, the ill-fated Comet (the world's first jet airliner, the fuselage of which had a nasty tendency to peel apart like an orange skin in mid-flight) and rugged STOL aircraft like the Beaver and the Dash 7. But it's the Gipsy and Tiger Moth that still arouse the most love.

Colin Smith is a quiet, almost painfully shy man. His grey cotton foreman's coat is the mantle of a high priest and he oversees his force of workers, filing engine blocks or repairing the complex wooden rib structures of wings, with a sort of benign severity. There is no noisy pop music in this factory, no gossip. An almost worshipful hush prevails. The workshops hold many examples of de Havilland engineering, painstakingly restored. As Colin Smith showed me some of these aeroplanes' secrets, allowed me to touch fractured struts or rebored cylinders, I seemed to be present at something as mysterious as the dissection of a human body.

Smith seems to live in a sort of eternal present, a custodianship of the de Havilland legacy. His humility and obvious love of these machines evoke an immediate sympathy. I began to see the planes through his eyes.

The aircraft yet to be restored include one of extreme rarity, the *first* de Havilland Comet, the predecessor of the Mosquito, a fast twin-engine monoplane designed for the 1934 England–Australia air race. Only five were built. Many people think it one of the most beautiful and glamorous planes ever made. Currently it is a pile of wood up against a wall in the workshop; its reconstitution as an aeroplane will be a sort of Communion, the Idea made Flesh.

A couple of weeks later I visited New Zealand's other de Havilland shrine, at the opposite end of the country, North Shore Airfield in Auckland. When I walked into Stan Smith's workshop, he looked up and, studiously avoiding all civilities, asked, 'Now what can I sell you? Have a new and unused Tiger Moth. This one here is 99.3 per cent new. Rebuilt from the original plans. Better than it was when it was new, as a matter of fact.'

The air around Stan Smith is generally blue from a string of inventive obscenities. As I arrived, he was struggling with a Continental Stearman engine. 'C for Continental and C for c★★t. The owner wants the fucking cylinders repainted. *WHY*? They're impossible to get at! He'll get a big bill, plus the special tool I had to make for going round corners. Well, if people will buy these abortionate bloody aeroplanes. Terrible fucking aeroplanes!'

Stan's workshop makes a sharp contrast with Colin Smith's, being less a hushed shrine than an Aladdin's Cave of a million spare parts. 'I've got the bloody thing in here somewhere' is a phrase he uses every few minutes. But this is Stan Smith's sacrament: each of these objects is touched with magic—is the seed from which some ancient aircraft might be reconstituted, reborn.

Stan Smith is as much a flyer as an engineer. He has cherished and possessed countless planes. While an expert on de Havillands, he currently lavishes an indulgent love on a relative of the Auster, an American Army Piper L-4 A, an artillery spotter. 'With fifteen 5½-inch Howitzers at its disposal, it was the most heavily-armed aircraft of World War II,' he joked. 'But it's probably the smallest, lightest warbird [military aircraft] in existence.' In the days before helicopters, the Piper was designed to hover over a target, a precursor of counter-insurgency aircraft. We took the Piper up, and he had me cut the power back, put a wing down and trim; at 42 mph, the plane gently waltzed round its own wing-tip. 'Turns on a sixpence,' said Stan complacently. 'Try stalling her.' I dropped the speed to 40 and the Piper stalled, a sort of friendly, cosy little shuffle.

Aircraft designers always have to find a compromise between safety, predictability and 'performance'. Part of one is grateful for security. But another part lusts after power, that fantasy again, the desire for the freedom of the skies, the dream of twisting through the air like a lark.

CHAPTER XXI

Absent Friends

I STAYED IN NEW ZEALAND longer than I had expected to. Aviation there is truly a kind of brotherhood. Generous men like Jules Tapper and John King, the editor of *Sport Flying* magazine, took me under their wings and at every turn I was offered a flight in some ultra-modern, ancient, or otherwise exotic aeroplane.

When Ken Walker took me up for the aerobatic display I described at the beginning of this book, it was the most ridiculously enjoyable rush I'd ever had in a plane. 'You can feel it between your legs,' he had told me. He was right. Eros and *thanatos*. Aerobatics is a powerful drug; addiction is expensive and potentially fatal.

After we got back, Ken talked about some of his heroes in New Zealand aviation. There was Sir Tim Wallis, millionaire pilot and resurrector of Hurricanes. There was Doug 'Dougall' Dallison, the first owner of the Magister we'd flown (now owned by the syndicate Ken belongs to). 'He flew in both the RAF and the bloody French air force. Died in 1999, aged seventy-five. He had one of the best wine cellars I've ever seen, and at his wake his wife Shirley opened it up. Out of respect for him we painted the Magister in the colours of the *Patrouille de France*, the French national aerobatic team.' Thirdly, there was Sir Ken Hayr. 'He was knighted twice, the first time for the Falklands, the second for the Gulf War. Nowadays he flies for fun, aerobatics in warbirds. Hunters and Yaks here, and he's over in England at the moment, doing a display at Biggin Hill.'

It had been a hot day, the sticky heat of Auckland in stark contrast to the snows in South Island. We didn't need much persuading to go for a beer that evening.

Someone in the club bar had put the TV news on. Suddenly the room was stunned into silence. Sir Kenneth Hayr had been killed earlier that day at Biggin Hill, flying a de Havilland Vampire in a mock dogfight.

Ken Walker was visibly shaken. 'I was only just telling you—' he said. He stared hard at his glass. 'Ken was a real gentleman and a real aviator. He was probably the most distinguished pilot in New Zealand. And he flew the flag for this country. It's a terrible bloody loss.'

'That makes three dead in the last couple of years,' I overheard another voice say.

'Too bloody many,' someone replied.

If I felt hooked by the phallic, testosteronal thrills of aerobatics, I was also seduced by its exact opposite. Because I met Frank Gatland, who at eighty-five is still an active instructor—perhaps the world's oldest. Frank teaches people to glide. A stocky man with a cowlick of snowy hair and an almost permanent grin, he took me for a long flight in one of Auckland Gliding Club's sleek high-tech gliders. The Club's success is partly attributable to the fact that New Zealand has sublimely good gliding weather. Devotees can take off and fly vast distances around the islands, soaring over turquoise seas and snow-covered peaks in a single day.

My previous experience of gliding had been, I think, only the second time I'd ever sat at the controls of a plane. Now allegedly a trained pilot, I was able to worry less about how to control the thing and to enjoy the apparent weightlessness of a sailplane. We were towed to 5,000 feet and when released into the sky, we stayed there. A Cessna has a glide ratio of something like 7:1—it will drop one foot for every seven feet it goes forward; but a glider's ratio can be over 65:1, a rate of descent so mild as to be imperceptible either to the pilot or a spectator's naked eye. Hence the hypnotic grace of gliders as they perform their aerial ballet. The absence of a motor, the way a glider pilot must learn like a sailor to harness invisible currents, make it one of the most natural and serene forms of flight. An aerial meditation.

Frank invited me to stay with him for a few days. During our conversations I learned about his past. He had flown with the RAF in the war and survived being shot down over France in 1942.

Imprisoned in Germany, he made several escape attempts—one time getting as far as the Baltic.

After breakfast one morning we sat down in a sun lounge full of light and he told me about his war. He was oddly hesitant when it came to the flying. I realised it had left a painful mark on him.

'We trained at Whenuapai, north of Auckland. I was considered an average pilot, I think. But time was fairly short; we flew Tiger Moths every day for about three weeks, twenty-five hours dual and twenty-five solo. Then twin-engine training aircraft called Oxfords.

'When we got to the UK we converted to Wellingtons, the RAF's main bomber of the time. We chose our crews ourselves. We all went into the mess and talked to our mates, and gradually teamed up. After that, we were the plane's only crew—every time it took off, we'd be in it. We trained at Lossiemouth in Scotland, doing navigation at sea, flying all over Scotland by night, dropping live bombs. The idea was that the first mission you did wouldn't be any different from training—it would just be over Germany instead of Scotland.

'Then the Stirling came on line and they asked for crews for it. We were lucky enough to be put on them. Lucky because it was the first four-engine bomber, and to us it was *the* aircraft, we all wanted to get into it—there were two more engines, it was twenty-three feet high, it looked wonderful. We had to retrain to fly the Stirling and by the time I got on to a squadron, most of the friends I'd trained with had already been shot down—one on his second operation. One chap, Anne's (his wife) fifth cousin, I think it was, had done three ops. I asked him how was it and he said, "The first one was hell and the other two were worse." And he said, "They're gonna get me." I said, "Hey, don't talk like that." It wasn't the attitude most of us had—but we didn't think about it much. We had to go out to our aircraft an hour before take-off. That's when you started to get nervous, wondering what it'll be like . . . But as soon as you opened the throttle it was just a job. You never thought about trouble until something actually happened.

'For a raid, lots of different squadrons would converge. We'd generally go to Cromer in East Anglia and set off from there, finishing up as a "stream". Our first night was a raid on Düsseldorf. When we got there the whole city was on fire, it was a beautiful sight . . . A strange thing to say? Well, as somebody said, we dropped the phosphorus bombs, but we didn't see the baby catch fire . . . But war's like that. If you shoot down an aircraft, you're shooting down an aircraft, not a person. You've got a job to do, and that's that . . .

'So there we were, and this amazing display of fire and light. I said to the navigator, "What a wonderful sight, Pat, come and look at this!" And he said, "If I came out there I might get scared." As long as he was in his little cubbyhole, he was happy! Then there was a *whoomf-whoomf* and he said, "What was that?" I said, "Oh, er, flak, I *think*—I'm not sure!" That was our introduction. There'd be a mighty *Whoomf!* and a black cloud would appear—you could see the smoke, because we usually flew on moonlit nights. Over the Alps, full moon, 16,000 feet to get over the peaks . . . Lovely. And the navigator said, "Ooh, the Matterhorn, I've climbed that!" This sort of chat went on, because it might be eight hours there and back, there was plenty of time to fill in. The rear gunner was a Welshman and we'd say, 'Give us a song, Taffy!' and he'd burst into song . . .

'The chop rate was about 10 per cent per sortie. So you had a 90 per cent chance of getting back—and of course we always included ourselves in the 90 per cent, you were never the one that was gonna get shot down. Those are averages, of course. The first raid I went on was a big one, we lost thirty-three planes. But the night I was shot down I was the only one lost . . . Opposition varied, it was largely a matter of luck. We certainly didn't realize at the time that the numbers who'd get shot down would be so enormous. About a one-in-three chance of survival, I think they had, by the end of the bombing campaign in Europe . . .

'It happened to me on my fourteenth sortie. We were coming back from Italy, from Turin, I think, back over the Alps. A night fighter, it must have been. I'm not sure how they honed in, a mixture of being guided in and personal radar, I think. You wouldn't see him coming. All you'd know was that suddenly there's all sorts of stuff flying about, and just try and get out of it. Roll over and get out of it. Then you find you haven't got an aeroplane any more to fly . . .

'All the control surfaces were shot away, I think . . . The stick was disconnected, everything had gone. The elevator didn't seem to work, trim didn't seem to work, the flaps . . . I was trying to get back some kind of control, to get back home. But that wasn't to be.

'I'd rolled over—we usually got away from flak or a searchlight by just rolling over and pulling out at 90 degrees to our previous track. That was the initial manœuvre and it was more or less instinctive. But we'd rolled over and it wouldn't come out again. It was dark, no horizon to speak of. And no control.

'I ordered a bail-out. The rear gunner didn't have his parachute with him, he had to get out of his turret to put it on. We had to get parachutes, too. We're sitting up on the flight deck and the hatch is below us and forward. My front gunner helped me clip my parachute on while I was still in the seat, then he got in the second pilot's seat to try and give me a hand, but . . . I punched him out of it and said, get the hell out of here—or words to that effect. So he jumped.

'There were three guys killed. There were four at the back, we never found out if they were all able to get out . . . I landed quite close to the aircraft, I was actually able to walk over to the aircraft, so we must have been extremely low. One guy died in hospital, one guy actually evaded capture, got through to Gibraltar and got home. I was on the loose for eight or ten days heading for Switzerland. The others were caught immediately. The crew of a Stirling was seven men. Four of us survived.'

CHAPTER XXII

The Coral Route

FROM NEW ZEALAND, I had to cross the vast Pacific Ocean, to America. But I had no intention of flying straight there; I hoped to island-hop with some of the small operations that provide aerial communications between the many thousands of Pacific islands.

The South Pacific was opened up by Air New Zealand's predecessor, TEAL—Tasman Empire Airways Ltd. The airline was first set up by imperial Britain to forge an air link between New Zealand and Australia across the 1000 miles of the Tasman Sea. In 1949, TEAL created the most glamorous air route in the world: the Coral Route. From 1949 to 1960, immense Shorts Solent flying boats island-hopped from Auckland to Tahiti, a twenty-two-hour flight made in daylight over four days.

But I left Auckland in a Boeing . . .

The 767 took off from Auckland at 1 a.m. to fly east across the international time zone and into Rarotonga, 2000 miles distant, at 6 a.m. *the previous day.* This was as confusing as it sounds. Rarotonga is an island so small the airport's runway extends a third of the way across it. We arrived in a low drizzle that was almost fog. In the days when they used sextant fixes to navigate the Pacific, finding a speck like Rarotonga was the product of intensive calculations at the best of times. But on a day like this—what hope would a pilot have had?

Our knot of sleepy passengers wandered into the tiny terminal, where a man in a floral shirt twanged a welcome on a ukulele. I checked into a hotel. As I reached my room, pink lightning lit up the sky, violent winds shook the palms and sheets of rain strafed the gardens. I trudged, drenched, back to the airport. I wanted to explore the remote atolls around Rarotonga and there was only one man who could help me do so—Ewan Smith, the owner of Air Rarotonga.

He's something of a legend on the island, a man of immense influence. A Kiwi, he first came here in 1973, recruited by Air New Zealand to fly and maintain Britten Norman Islanders, a bush aircraft found on rough airstrips the world over. 'In 1978 I set up my own company, hoping to get rich—I'm still hoping.'

In fact, 'Air Raro' has flourished. Smith is a compact, wiry man who exudes wariness and impatience. Clearly he has whatever it takes to make a success of a small airline. He told me that the isolation of somewhere like Rarotonga favours an indigenous operator. Air New Zealand flies in and out, but Air Raro dominates the network of outlying islands.

He proudly pointed at the airport's compact apron, where all three parked planes wore the pink blossoms of the company logo, including a Cessna 172, Smith's personal plane. He offered to take me up in it as soon as the weather cleared.

Unfortunately, it didn't.

Instead, two days later, Smith put me on the jump seat of a Saab 340. Captain Sean Willis took us up, over an impenetrable, many-layered blanket of cloud that stretched over 1000 miles from Raro to Fiji. An hour later we descended over Aitutaki, the flat, white, sand-fringed lagoon where the Shorts flying boats had once landed to refuel.

Days earlier in Auckland I'd visited the museum where one of Tasman Empire Airways Ltd's four Shorts Solents is displayed. John Van Duyvenboden, a Flight Clerk on Shorts in the 1950s, took me aboard. The Mk IV Solent is an immense beast, with its deep hull and purposefully scalloped lines, 113-foot wingspan and an empty weight of 81,000 lbs. It has been restored by volunteers, mostly retired engineers—'not bad for a bunch of old buggers', as one of them said to me. This flying boat is one of the genuine wonders of the aviation world and one of only two Solents still in existence today. It is immaculate. You go aboard through an imposing lower deck hatch that wouldn't disgrace a nuclear sub, stepping into a restaurant out of the Orient Express. No microwaves and instant tray meals in those days: the galley (complete with dumb waiter) would prepare fresh meals to order, famously offering breakfasting passengers a choice of eggs boiled, scrambled, poached or fried. A circular staircase leads to the upper deck cabin and bar where a mere forty-five passengers cruised at 200 mph, in considerable comfort. During the restoration an appeal was made for anyone who might have 'borrowed' souvenirs from TEAL flights. The response was enough TEAL-logo'd travel rugs, ashtrays, plates and *silver* cutlery to equip the entire plane!

TASMAN EMPIRE AIRWAYS LIMITED

COMMANDER   CAPT. O. GARDEN

ZK-AMC   "AWARUA"

Menu

LUNCHEON

Oysters on Shell

Tomato Soup

COLD BUFFET

Roast Chicken

Pineapple Ham

Lettuce   Tomato

Cucumber   Beetroot

Assorted Pickles and Sauces

Fruit Salad

Fresh C

Assorted C

Up for'ard, the flight deck had an acre of desk for the person who was probably, on Pacific crossings, the most important member of the crew: the navigator. Above, an astrodome allowed him to take astro fixes with a hand-held sextant, shooting sunlines by day and stars by night. Great Plexiglas windscreens gave the pilots good views of the engines, four brutal, 2040 horsepower Bristol Hercules radials. The beefy throttles are painted red and green—port and starboard.

John Van Duyvenboden explained how a fuel dump for the Solents (300 gallons a wing, pumped by hand) had been located on a tiny crescent-shaped island in the middle of the Aitutaki lagoon. Legend has it that the islanders provided labour on a grass hut and jetty, in return not for wages, but for TEAL re-equipping their brass band with new instruments.

Ewan Smith had arranged for a boat to take me to the old Solent landing jetty. Andrea Katu motored me out into the lagoon. It was easy to see why a phrase like 'paradise on earth' comes so readily to anyone seeking to describe these Pacific atolls—the air was balmy, the minute islets were darkly green with coconut trees, fringed with delicately yellow sand, the coral waters pale turquoise and invitingly warm. Lest I succumb entirely to the sensory delights, Andrea recited the varieties of dangerous and deadly fish found in the waters.

In a few minutes we reached a tiny jetty on an uninhabited island. Little remains of the original TEAL pontoons. But this islet was the scene of one of the most beguiling episodes in the history of civil aviation. One day in the late 1950s, an engine developed problems on approach to Aitutaki. The captain landed safely, but announced that it was not possible to continue on three engines alone. He would off-load the passengers and cabin staff, fly on to Auckland and come back when everything had been sorted out.

The habitually pampered passengers found themselves marooned. One of the stewards, Dennis Marshall, recalled, 'At first they wanted to lynch me and the stewardesses. But by the second day they'd calmed down. It was eight days before a plane arrived, and by then they were so in love with the place it was hard to get them to leave! I think it was probably the holiday they'd been dreaming of all their lives.'

Two days later I hitched with one of Air Raro's smaller planes, a Brazilian-built Embraer Bandeirante, around some of the smaller islands in the Cook Island group. We were dropping in on emerald islets with runways that start and end on cliff-tops. Air Raro keeps their small populations in touch with the outside world in a way that was once unimaginable. These isolated communities have a tough existence, living off the fish they catch and the vegetables they grow. Social life is in the grip of a conservative brand of Christianity imported by missionaries 200 years ago. There are few tourists, and these routes do not make Air Rarotonga much money. Several of the travellers I met were young islanders, visiting from the far-off places—New Zealand, Australia, even the US—where they've gone to seek work. They are still greeted and sent off with great garlands of flowers hung around their necks.

From Rarotonga I was offered an Air New Zealand flight not east, towards America, but back to the west. And so I found myself in another island paradise—Fiji. A paradise still recovering from a coup.

The Nadi Aero Club is built on an inclined airport runway. The Club may have seen better times—the two evenings I went, there were only two other drinkers. One of them was Don Collingwood, who turns up every night without fail to watch the BBC news on the telly. Collingwood is a rubicund chain smoker with a grey moustache, a sceptical eye and a gruff manner. His lifetime has been spent in aviation. Today he owns Sun Air, Fiji's largest independent airline.

He was born in Christchurch, New Zealand, 'For my sins. My arrival stopped the war. My dad had a hotel called the Clarendon, next door to the Wigram RNZAF base. Planes fascinated me as a kid, as soon as I could, I learned to fly. Took a job in a mutton-freezing works to finance my training. In those days the mortality rates in top-dressing were appalling; the planes used to be overloaded to hell. Jobs were relatively easy to get, even though I had bugger all hours.

'When I was twenty, with 1500 hours of top-dressing behind me, I charged across the Tasman and flew 'ag' planes in Australia. You worked whatever hours you could get, and they were bloody long days, believe me.

'At twenty-two I went to the UK and got contract spraying work for the Sudan season. It was the "Ghazira Scheme", between the Blue and the White Nile. They put tenders out all over the world. There were Swedish pilots, a bunch of American hooligans . . . A Russian team that came out in Antonov A-2s—their redeeming feature was that they used to bring a forty-five-gallon drum of vodka with them. We used to drink a lot in those days; I think ag pilots still do. Our lot flew from Southend, via Lyons, Cannes, Sardinia, Libya, Egypt. We flew over tank traps in the desert that hadn't been disturbed since World War II. Our maps had been made in the Thirties—amazing bloody mappers in those days. The dunes were all exactly as depicted, and an occasional isolated tree. We'd fly over hundreds of miles of sand and sure enough, there it'd be, this lonely bloody tree!

'Anyway, we ended up 200 to 300 miles south of Khartoum. It was dead flat. We used to start at daybreak—all ag work does. Knock off when it was too windy or too hot. Bloody big money for a young man—and tax free. Every now and then, up to Khartoum for a break. There was a nightclub called the Gordon, I recall.

'After that season I went back to London and got married, and still am—amazing in aviation. Then I went to Kenya, spraying again. I got offered a job with Desert Locust, a UN mob. Right out into the bush in Somalia, Eritrea. A lot of ex-Long Range Desert Group guys, they'd been there for fifteen years, since the end of the war, and couldn't bear to leave the desert—sand-happy. We had absolute freedom to cross borders, we did what we wanted, when we wanted, nobody stopped you. It had its hairy moments; there was a lot of scrapping going on. We had one chap killed as he sat under a tree next to his de Havilland Beaver—they found him sitting there with a bullet in his head.

'The wife and I decided to go back to NZ to have young Ian [who now jointly runs the airline]. I did some top-dressing in a DC-3—it was like trying to fly a ketch. And bloody hard work, up at four, back at nine, a lot of hours. Every top-dressing pilot keeps two logbooks, y'know, always have done—the hours they've flown and the hours they'll *admit* to having flown. But boring, all those endless bloody lines. *Bloody* boring. There was always a stack of books in the plane, everyone used to fly reading a book or doing a crossword.

'I tried to settle down in civilization, but the over-regulation got to me. New Zealanders are wonderful people, but they do love making laws, bless 'em. I couldn't adjust to a place where you had to get a permit to change the colour of your roof tiles. And evenings in front of the TV—how many bloody times can you watch *Coronation Street*? I was too used to the freedom of Africa. So I came here.

'Flying commercially here looks easy, but it's hard work—you have to do it a lot to get good at it. I've been a Fijian for twenty years now. And in the South Pacific I'll stay. It's a fucking big puddle, y'know.'

I was sitting in the right seat of a Sun Air Twin Otter en route to a hotel that can only be reached by small plane. 'You'll enjoy this landing,' the pilot told me. 'Does anything about the runway look strange to you?'

'Apart from the fact that it's very short and ends at a cliff edge?'

'Yes—also, we land on a hillside. We have to touch down on the threshold every time and the first part of the runway is downhill; it's quite steep. *Bloody* steep, actually.'

But we came down to earth without a bump, to be greeted by

hotel staff bearing fruit cocktails with little umbrellas in them! The Yasawa Resort was the most luxurious hotel I had ever visited, and the most isolated. Visitors do not always use the dirt strip; Yasawa is also served by a de Havilland Beaver floatplane, operated by Turtle Airways. When I left, a speedboat took me out to meet the tubby Beaver. From the right-hand seat I peered down at waters that turned a hallucinogenic shade of turquoise as we crossed coral reefs.

Back in Nadi that night, the Aero Club was spectacularly empty, with just one man drinking at the bar. His name was Marc Keller. He bought me a beer and threw himself into an enraptured account of flying over these turquoise waters. From a sports clothing outlet in Switzerland, he had dreamed of selling up and moving to the South Pacific. 'I decided to make my dream come true.

'Landing a small seaplane beside a coral island is like nothing else on earth. The best flying in the world. The plane is a four-seater, so I can fly three passengers. I go out to the remote subterranean caves where the movie *The Blue Lagoon* was filmed. I land on the waters, provide snorkels for the swim, then a five-star packed lunch including champagne. In the afternoon they wander off and do whatever they like.' He gave a wink. 'It's none of my business. My only aim is to give them a day they will never forget. And to keep flying. But . . .'

We finished our beers and went to see his plane. It was a Lake Buccaneer, a tiny seaplane with its engine mounted on a stalk above the fuselage. It was in store at a car-spray workshop, stripped of its engine. With a mixture of pride and frustration, Marc showed me over it.

'After a few months of operation, it needed some maintenance. The mechanics found extensive corrosion. Suddenly I was looking at a bare-paint rebuild. It's been a nightmare. The engine parts all had to come from the US. There were the usual delays, and it's hard to get work done on Fiji. I realised I was going to miss a whole year's income. Now, I'm working flat out to try and get it airworthy so I don't miss the *next* tourist season.'

We went to find some dinner. The restaurant, run by a friend of Marc's, had an open terrace on the roof, where they barbecued giant prawns with handfuls of chopped chilli and garam masala.

'In 1995, I lost the love of my life. When she died, I sat in front of a map . . . I saw an ad in an Aussie magazine called *Aviation Trader*.

"Small Seaplane Company with Lots of Potential for Sale." I looked at the books, I looked at Fiji—it was stable then. I made the leap. I had loads of customers, everything went fantastically. Then the mechanics found the corrosion . . .

'I didn't give up. I'm hanging in there. There's enough business for two aircraft, but I can't get into the air. I'm getting close to despair . . .'

More beers. 'You see, it's a dream!' Marc told me. 'And it's also reality! You *dream* of those waters, those skies—and you know that it *is* possible to fly out here. But not easy. I was pre-flighting the plane at 5 a.m. with a torch in my mouth. Up at five and landing at dark. Then an hour and a half to hose the plane down. Often I'd drive the Customs boys home at night! But you're in this because you love it, you're never gonna make big money. If you want that, you go and work in the stock markets. You know how to make a small fortune in aviation? Start with a large one.'

As the 747 ploughed across that great puddle, I was invited into the cockpit. I walked past Business Class passengers as they slumbered in artificial darkness under their New Zealand wool blankets. In the cockpit, all was daylit brightness and clarity, the crew wakeful in their crisp white short-sleeves, the hazy-blue ocean outstretched below us. The passengers might be snoring, or staring at movies, but here all was discipline and calm, the nobility of the professional pilot. A hundred years ago it was the bridge of the *Mauritania* or *Lusitania*, a glamour transferred to the captains of the great transatlantic airships until the catastrophe of the *Hindenburg* in 1937 brought the age of the airship to a premature close. (Though airships are currently being reborn in Germany, immense cigars we shall grow familiar with in the next decades, as they hover motionless over our cities working as aerial cranes.) Now, the 747 captain is the emblem of the professional who makes possible our busy bustling round the globe, en route to beaches and business hotels.

New Zealand is a small country, but a big boy on the South Pacific block. The rôle of the national airline is critical. Air New Zealand is still small enough to have a family feeling and a strong sense of its heritage. It is a global airline—though a small one. In an increasingly cut-throat environment, it struggles to stay independent of the big fish who'd like to gobble it up and plunder its more profitable routes. It was privatized in 1989 and, seeking to expand, it bought Ansett, a major Australian airline, in 2000. Ansett promptly collapsed, threatening to suck down Air New Zealand with it, and the New Zealand government was forced to bail out its national airline at a hair-raising cost of NZD$850 million. The politicians have since talked darkly of selling off much of Air New Zealand to another airline.

Every nation, however small, likes to have a national flag carrier. All around the world taxpayers' millions have been spent propping up obscure airlines. In many cases it's a vanity thing: when the President flies, he doesn't want the humiliation of climbing into a 747 with his next-door neighbour's flag on its tail. But in recent years there has been a shake-out in aviation; higher costs, reduced subsidies, anti-monopoly legislation and the shock of '9–11', have exposed airlines to harsh economic winds. The unthinkable has been thought more than once. Pan American, for decades the confident face of expanding US influence, collapsed; United filed for bankruptcy; Swissair, one of the world's most prestigious airlines, folded; Belgium's Sabena teetered; other national airlines have disappeared or had their foundations rocked, while many smaller companies have vanished. 'Budget airlines' have prospered, but deregulation in the name of competition must, in the end, have much the same effect on aviation as it has had in the car industry: fewer, bigger, players. The days of the national airline may be numbered.

CHAPTER XXIII

High Ways

W E WERE FLYING to the greatest air show on, or above, the earth. For a pilot, the *only* way to visit Oshkosh is in your own plane, and 14,000 of them turn up every year. Hundreds of acres of airfield (and agricultural field) fill with aircraft of every conceivable description, from World War II bombers to jet-powered microlights. It is the private pilot's Mecca.

I had arranged to reach Canada in August and fly to Oshkosh in Linvic's twin-engine Cessna 310. It was the plane in which, less than a year earlier, I had sat in the back seat and watched Alastair make his first landings. A twin is an expensive plane to charter for four days, so six of us were sharing the costs. I was going to be reunited with Tim Coombs, my first instructor at Linvic, and Tim Pattinson, the young English instructor with whom I had done my mock flight tests.

They had arranged to pick me up at Toronto's Island Airport. It's a small training airfield and executive terminal, built on a sliver of land in Lake Ontario, a few hundred feet from downtown Toronto. At dawn I took a taxi through the sleeping city. In front of the glittering new towers along the shoreline is a small, old-fashioned car ferry, with room for three or four cars nose to tail. One other passenger was waiting, a sleek businessman driving a BMW. The crossing took barely a minute. In the executive lounge, we helped ourselves to the obligatory free coffee and, this being Canada, doughnuts. After some time, the white-and-orange Cessna settled on the runway and taxied to the terminal, the two Tims at the controls. I threw my bags in the back and climbed aboard.

Few urban airports can have a location more spectacular than Island. As we climbed away from the runway, Toronto was a solid wall of sun-bright steel and glass off our starboard wing-tip. We headed west, along the lake shore, then inland across the rich farmed plains of the Midwest, across Lakes Huron and Michigan. There was a faint haze at ground level, but visibility was good. The flight south took three hours, including a landing en route to go through American customs.

As we approached our destination, an air of intense concentration settled over the cabin. For ten days every August, 14,000 arriving and departing aircraft make Oshkosh the busiest airport in the world. Modern jets and Thirties airliners, Spitfires and Mustangs, helicopters, 'homebuilts' and many hundreds of Cessnas converge on what is for 355 days of the year a quiet rural airport. In a triumph of still very old-fashioned logistics, the planes are guided in by the voices of the Oshkosh air traffic controllers. They form into two streams, landing on two parallel runways around 400 feet apart, with fore-and-aft separations of about 2,000 feet. Eight landings a minute.

Pilots are generally taught to keep as far away from each other as possible, so to find oneself in the midst of a swarm of aircraft concentrates the mind wonderfully. It is an *orderly* swarm, of course, but only an experienced and self-confident pilot submits his skills to such a test. It would be miraculous if no one became disorientated, and deaths at Oshkosh are not unusual. On our first day, one arriving pilot apparently became confused about his position, slowed, stalled and crashed. There were other deaths that year, too. But the show must go on—general aviation is bigger than a few individual deaths. Or are they sacrifices to the great Aviation God? The Oshkosh extravaganza (officially the annual shindig of the Experimental Aircraft Association) seemed to me to express America's schizo-phrenic attitude to risk. It is a country obsessed with preserving human life, where automobile speeding limits are obsessively policed and people litigate against fast food restaurants because their coffee is too hot. On the other hand, people can, in the name of freedom, walk the streets with assault rifles up their jumpers, there's an admirable lack of safety rails round the Grand Canyon (people are always falling in), and they allow Oshkosh.

We landed and taxied—guided by scores of Day-Glo-clad marshals—through dense mazes of aircraft to our parking spot. It was an astounding spectacle—you would see not one example of a World

War II military plane, but ten, all with different markings, but parked wing-tip to wing-tip like a squadron. We pitched our tents, or, in time-honoured style, unrolled our sleeping bags under the fuselage or a wing.

Recently I was entertained to find in the periodical *The Aeroplane*, published in London on 4 October 1957, the following entry:

> The 1957 Fly-In of the Experimental Aircraft Association was held on the weekend of August 30–September 1. The E.A.A. was founded by a small group of Milwaukee enthusiasts in 1953 and at present has some 3000 members . . . Fog and haze kept many aircraft from arriving, however, a score of homebuilts eventually managed to [do so] . . . along with nine vintage aircraft and over 200 civil machines. The Fly-In officially got under way on Friday evening with a delicious and varied buffet . . . [later] the E.A.A.'s president, Paul Poberezny, gave the signal for the lights to be put out for the showing of a motion picture, narrated by Ray Stits, builder of several unusual aircraft. So interested was the crowd in this movie that Mr. Stits was obliged to run it through four times.
>
> Saturday dawned hot and hazy, but by mid-morning . . . more aircraft began to appear . . . the common interest in aircraft and the complete lack of concern over the matter of social position brought everyone together.
>
> On Sunday a television camera was set up and an announcer interviewed the builders of several of the most interesting aircraft. The E.A.A. has organised a design competition for the best two-seater for amateur construction, having wings arranged so that the craft can be stored in the average garage. The winner will receive $5000, along with a trophy. The thing is 4 ft. tall . . .

About the only thing that has declined since 1957 is, evidently, the quality of the food (one of today's 'proud sponsors' is Nestlé, 'bringing you the brands that make life richer', including Coffee-mate, Wonka, Juicy Juice and something called Friskies, which I had thought was a cat food). There's still a focus on 'homebuilts', whose attendance by the thousand demonstrates how the US leads the world in recreational aviation. Informality is still rigorously enforced (its uniform is the baseball cap). But gigantism has become the order of the day. The annual fly-in has become a gargantuan, revenue-generating air show, rechristened 'AirVenture' by the PR men and aimed at the general public. Several days are needed to take it all in, for not only is almost every plane and accessory manufacturer in America (and much of the rest of the world) exhibiting, there are also a museum, static displays of military and commercial aircraft (the world's biggest freighter, its heaviest bomber . . .), low-level aerobatic displays of hair-raising brilliance, and fly-bys of some of the world's most exotic aircraft—I saw a replica of the Vickers Vimy biplane, in which John Alcock and Arthur Whitten Brown made the first transatlantic flight in 1919, and a stunning low pass by a Rockwell B-1B, the USAF's semi-stealth low-altitude penetration bomber, which made the very earth quake. For enthusiasts there are thousands of lectures, forums and workshops, pavilions for homebuilts (plans and kits), microlights, ultralights and gyrocopters, a vast array of markets, an Authors' Corner, and marquees for every federal body connected with aviation from the meteorological service to the Air Force and NASA.

Prominent among the displays in the NASA tent were not satellites or Space Shuttle mock-ups, but two small, four-seater planes. Utterly modern, these plastic (composite) planes suggest the future of aviation. Small-plane manufacturers are at last installing the crash cages associated with more expensive cars. Video screens showed the results. Black-and-yellow dummies wobbled traumatically in slow motion, but the passenger cells held together. The message: death no longer needs to follow almost inevitably from a serious air crash.

The NASA marquee was also full of computer technology. In the wake of the 11 September 2001 terrorist attacks, the US government asked NASA if there was a way to secure the airways of America. As it happened, NASA had been working for a decade on technologies that do have the potential to deliver greatly heightened security. In fact, NASA has been looking even further than the future of civil aviation. For a decade it has been developing the extraordinary concept of a 'flying car'.

I had the opportunity to speak to a senior NASA official, Bruce Holmes. A relaxed, bright, easygoing man in his mid-forties, he is responsible for the research and development NASA has devoted to its SATS programme—Small Aircraft Transportation System. (NASA is not exclusively concerned with space—it is the National *Aeronautic* and Space Administration, the government body concerned with all non-administrative aviation. The Federal Aviation Authority worries about regulation and safety, leaving NASA to do the blue skies thinking.) Holmes quite simply believes that the small plane is the car of the future. It will be a personal vehicle that goes automatically wherever you tell it, discreetly avoiding all other traffic. Holmes told me the planes on display in the NASA marquee could be the precursors of Henry Fordish aero-cars for the masses.

His vocabulary is steeped in the rhetoric of consumer capitalism, studded with quotations from Aristotle, Hobbes and Rousseau. 'We're gonna put wings on America,' he says with evangelic fervour. 'You know, for many Americans, the "American Dream" of freedom is inextricably bound up with the notion of mobility. People love to climb into recreational vehicles and spend their vacations, their whole retirements, exploring this vast land. The dream of the West— "Go West, young man"—the possibility of self-improvement, of reinventing yourself—it was all bound up with *freedom of movement.*' He believes that today's citizen-consumers demand the right to unimpeded travel and that NASA will help make that dream (or God-given right) a reality. NASA will liberate us, finally, from the earth itself.

Behind the free-market rhetoric lies hard-headed industrial ambition. NASA believes it is laying the foundations of a transport revolution, with American industry as the leader and principal beneficiary.

Holmes told me his vision of a flying family car began at a gridlocked airport a decade ago. In the early Nineties, it was already becoming obvious that civil aviation was approaching saturation. While cheap flights were attracting ever larger passenger numbers, journey times were getting *longer*. Almost a quarter of *all* annual flights are late, and during the annual ritual of holiday flights, nearly *50 per cent* are late. Then there are the subsidiary delays—travel to and from airports, eternities in passport and security queues, miles of corridors and more queues at the gate. For most flights, getting to and from the aeroplane takes longer than the flight itself. In America, journeys up to 500 miles are quicker by car than by plane!

Airlines use a 'hub-and-spoke' system, where big jets fly between major 'hub' airports (Frankfurt, Paris, Chicago, etc.) and feed passengers along 'spokes' to regional airports (Bristol, Bologna, Buffalo, etc.). Aircraft use take-off 'slots' and air traffic-controlled 'corridors', and follow radio-navigation beacons to the hubs. The system resembles a railway line, with finite sets of tracks and platforms—and gives aircraft even less autonomy than cars on a motorway. Developed half a century ago, it is now under severe pressure.

Britain has calculated that in order to cope with the projected 40 per cent increase in passenger flights over the next decade, it needs at the very least several new runways. But even if all environmental objections to new airports were dismissed, if runways proliferated, there are limits to the numbers of large planes that can be landed on a given runway or fitted into existing air corridors. Something has to give.

A measure of temporary relief on the big hubs has come in the form of 'no-frills' airlines exploiting spare capacity in regional airports. But low-cost flights *create* demand. They temporarily relieve pressure on the big hubs, but increase the overcrowding of the air corridors.

This is where NASA comes in. It believes that new technologies will allow the numbers of flights to increase many times over, at the same time making aviation safer than it has ever been. The basic idea is a sort of computerised communication web interconnecting every object in the sky. NASA wants to combine GPS (satellite-based position-finding) with plane-based transponders that feed information to and from a central navigation computer. The result will be an utterly precise three-dimensional computer image of all air traffic, from the jumbo jet down to—literally—a parachutist. The information will be available on-screen to controllers and pilots alike. Automation will control traffic flow, computers ensuring that any 'conflict' (potential collision) is avoided. Planes will be able to navigate more safely, yet in far greater density than is possible today.

To eliminate danger, it is necessary to eliminate human error—i.e., human beings. NASA's navigation systems will interface with on-board autopilots to remove human decision-making from the situations that lead to most accidents. The other most common danger involves adverse weather conditions. In the future, thousands of miniature weather stations will transmit to aeroplanes' on-board computers a total picture of prevailing weather conditions.

These technologies promise a high degree of centralized control—the ability to *prevent* a pilot, for example, from accidentally landing on an icy runway. The potential for security is obvious. Everything in the sky can be satellite-monitored, with on-board computers programmed to keep aircraft out of forbidden airspace. Hijackers might still threaten passengers, but no longer would they be able to seize control of a plane and turn it into a guided missile. The computers could also be linked to national air defences. Military watchers could be alerted to any aircraft that did deviate from its flight plan. Ground-to-air missiles could attack any object that penetrated forbidden airspace.

At present, buying the smallest Learjet will set you back round £6.5 million. Nor is chartering cheap—executive jets spend barely 5 per cent of their lives actually flying, which translates into charter costs of around £1400 per hour. In America, however, a new generation of business aircraft are starting to appear with price tickets of under $1 million. In Britain, Richard Noble is developing a fast and quiet turbo-prop 'air taxi', intended to bring the glamour of the private plane to that most aspirational of classes, middle management.

These innovations look quite likely to stimulate a boom in small plane construction. It seems worth asking, at this point, why there was never a small-plane revolution. In the century since 1903, when man first took flight in a powered aircraft, the private aeroplane has not *taken off*. Sci-fi movies have imagined bustling personal capsules, while the two images of small aircraft that have most penetrated the public consciousness seem to have been James Bond's gyrocopter and personal rocket suit. But despite the heady predictions, it has all remained pie in the sky. Military and commercial aviation have accounted for almost all aviation development and sales. Private aviation has languished.

There are several reasons for the stagnant state of private aviation. Heavier-than-air machines require thorough training to fly and need continuous costly maintenance; they have to be regulated with expensive, labour-intensive air traffic control systems; and they are inherently dangerous—prey to poor weather and pilot error. As a result, small planes are today as much the preserve of a moneyed elite and a few gung-ho hobbyists as half a century ago. From the Seventies to the mid-Nineties, the numbers of people learning to be private pilots *halved*. Many airports and aerodromes were turned into housing estates, a process that continues. Cessna—the closest general aviation has ever come to a mass manufacturer—*suspended the manufacture of small planes* between 1986 and 1996. Imagine if no one had made cars during that decade, a period in which global car sales exploded and many roads approached saturation!

Manufacturing cost has severely inhibited small-plane aviation. Regulators have awarded manufacturing licences to companies like Cessna that used traditional building techniques, i.e. riveted aluminium, known to be strong and reliable. But it is also extremely labour intensive—a 1930s technology pioneered by the Spitfire. Now, composite plastics mean that aircraft fuselages can be popped out of moulds like shampoo bottles. And a new generation of lightweight jet and piston engines using alternative fuels like diesel and electricity will make planes more fuel-efficient than ever before.

Unlike the present generation of Cessnas (the company's current best-selling small plane, the 172 Skyhawk, started life in *1948!*), these new small planes present themselves as 'Flying BMWs', sleek and luxurious vehicles with leather seating and walnut dashboards, extensive automation, quiet cabins, crash cages, airbags—even rocket-launched parachutes that can be deployed if the pilot loses control of the plane, to lower it gently to earth. They currently sell at £200,000, but mass production could cut those prices by two thirds. Two-seaters currently cost around £75,000, but mass production could bring their prices to *under £20,000*.

Breaking the 20K barrier is seen as the take-off point for a small-plane revolution. NASA believes it will take fifteen to twenty years for a full range of cheap, practical, mass-produced products to be competing for most consumers' pockets. By 2025, plane ownership will be a practical proposition for most middle-class people.

So in the future we will all be pilots—or drivers of flying cars. The driver will choose from a vast network of 'Highways in the Sky', 3-D computer representations of virtual roads. It will be far easier to fly than it is now to drive a car. The system will be so 'intelligent'—so highly automated, with so many fail-safes built in—as to make today's road journeys seem barbarically slow and risk-fraught. Automation will prevent individual planes from getting lost, exceeding speed limits, landing in poor conditions, entering forbidden airspace or flying too low. Customers will climb into pilotless air taxis, announce a destination and be taken there automatically. Families will go on holiday in Lifestyle Aircraft. Reminding me that just fifty years ago private car ownership was still far from universal, a NASA engineer told me he expects to see flying 'cars' with vertical take-off and a cruise speed of 250 mph parked outside every house in America by 2040.

Is all this what the philosophers call a 'good'? At present, living in remote countryside or under a flight path is a personal choice and anyone is free to fly a plane over the home of even the wealthiest reclusive millionaire. But if NASA's vision is realised, the skies, as yet relatively free of aeroplanes and their associated noise and pollution, could become as crowded as motorways. Will the rights of some people to commune with unspoilt nature be infringed by the others who whirr round the sky above their heads?

Bruce Holmes told me it is 'democratic' to give everyone his own plane. Environmentalists will put a different argument. They will talk in terms of overall 'environmental footprints', i.e. the net impact on the environment of a given consumer's lifestyle—for example, the process of manufacturing a car produces more greenhouse gases than the engine will emit through fuel burn in its entire lifetime. The impact on the environment of millions of small-aeroplane engines would, in terms of both manufacture and use, be immense. At present, 200 people are carried by one plane with two jet engines; if they were carried by 200 private planes with 200 jet engines, the increase in pollution would be incalculable. Currently, democracy and the free market allow Western private car ownership to outweigh Third World car ownership by 750:1; 25 per cent of global carbon emissions are produced in the US alone. Whom would the flying revolution benefit?

One of Holmes's colleagues shrugged and told me that just as people have put up with the noise and pollution of freeways in return for the convenience of the car, they will put up with the negatives of flying cars. He also claimed that legions of small planes would realise the 'small is beautiful' ideal of the environmentalists—clearly he didn't understand that the notion of 'small is beautiful' argues for an *overall reduction in environmental impact*. He asserted that universal plane ownership would eliminate the need for large airports, with a concomitant improvement in the environment for everyone. This seems highly unlikely: big planes would continue to proliferate for decades, both for long-haul flights and, at the bottom end of the domestic market, for those who cannot afford to own personal transport—aviation's Greyhound bus.

In fact, little cost-benefit analysis has yet been undertaken by NASA into the implications of their 'flying car' ideal. The agency has not pondered the social and environmental dimensions of the technologies it is pioneering.

It is easy to see a flying car triumphing in the USA: America is vast, Americans love recreational vehicles and business tends to get what it wants. But in crowded Western Europe, with its medieval urban patterns and vigorous environmental lobby, there would be more resistance. In Europe there is now approximately one flight per year for every hundred people, expected roughly to double by 2015. But imagine that half the people in Europe were using private aircraft for all their travel over 250 miles: the numbers of annual aircraft movements would increase by *millions*.

There would be many other consequences. As plane ownership soared, there would be bottlenecks around large cities, with small planes 'stacking up' as they waited to land. The skies must, like the roads, approach gridlock. The impact on bird populations could be catastrophic. The rail system might collapse. There would be real divisions between the aviation 'haves' and 'have-nots'. No one with money would travel long distances by car and roads would be increasingly relegated to the poor. Man would inhabit the sky, or perhaps concrete eyries with vast plane parks built into their upper storeys. The disadvantaged of the late twenty-first century may not be the itinerant, as they traditionally have been—like gypsies and nomads—but the immobile. Society will be freer, but more fragmented, than ever before.

Will endless extensions of the consumer dream—a house, a holiday, a car, two cars, two foreign holidays, a personal plane—unequivocally increase the sum of human happiness? To quote the ugly slogan used by Cessna to market their Citation bizjet, '100% of the earth is covered with sky. Own it all.' If 'freedom of the sky' becomes a euphemism for the commoditization of the sky, is it a price we are prepared to pay? And will anyone give us a choice?

Only costs might hold back a small-plane revolution, but once mass production begins, prices will tumble. Consider the sales pitch: no more extensive preplanning and price-juggling for airline flights, slow trips to the airport, check-ins, queues, overpriced airport food, late departures and arrivals, cramped knees in airliners smelling of baby sick. For domestic journeys, no more sitting in motorway traffic jams. No fear of dying in a terrorist attack on a crowded airliner. And travel times cut by two-thirds. The public will be quickly seduced. Aeroplanes will become universal, even boring. New models will fill the pages of the colour supplements and have TV magazine shows devoted to them. Old planes will be bought and sold in second-hand lots. A few fanatics will spend their weekends gliding or ballooning, like those vintage car enthusiasts who pootle round the lanes on summer weekends, reminding us of a time when the automobile was romantic.

Who could have stood beside the inventors of the first unreliable internal combustion engines and predicted that within a century hundreds of millions of cars would carry people to the remotest corners of the planet? Now we know the awesome power of technology, the speed with which Man can introduce change, transform this planet. No one should doubt it: we will move into the air. The realisation for the masses of this ancient dream will cause us to rethink fundamental notions of society, landscape, space, movement, ownership, trespass. Governments, aviation administrators and environmentalists have yet to ponder the implications of highways in the sky. But they may soon have to.

CHAPTER XXIV

Bizjet

I HAVE MENTIONED the difficulties in crossing oceans without involving a commercial airline. Of course, for the very rich, there *is* an alternative: the private, or executive, or 'biz', jet. I had heard that the British charter company Gold Air was taking delivery of new Learjets from the factory in America. I contacted the company's chief pilot and chairman Will Curtis, and metaphorically stuck out my thumb. He said yes, I could go along for the ride, but he wasn't sure when the next collection would be. When his phone call came, I had seventy-two hours to get to Tucson, Arizona.

Will and his team were putting up at the Sheraton; I checked into the Hotel Congress, an art deco heap that had its heyday before anyone now under the age of seventy was born. It has provided a roof in its time to the Chicago gangster John Dillinger and the infamous cross-dressing FBI chief J. Edgar Hoover. As I made my way to my room, I witnessed an act of congress in progress on two armchairs in the corridor. I'd arrived on a Friday night and the Congress turned out to be Tucson's 'premier nightspot': the Richter Scale bass notes shook the ageing foundations and sleep was a long time coming. My room was above the kitchens, too, and when the chefs arrived at 5 a.m. to warm up the ovens, they turned on the kitchen stereo full blast. I rose, showered, staggered downstairs and breakfasted on black coffee.

When Learjet had learned that Will Curtis would have a writer in tow, they felt it was very important that I should have no misunderstandings about the Learjet Corporation. So I was met at the Congress by Leon Rossow, an alert and elegant man who is the public face of a company providing personal aerial transportation to the wealthiest people in the world.

'How was the hotel?' he asked, with polite scepticism, as we drove off in his brand-new 4x4.

'Not bad at all,' I lied.

At the factory, it quickly became apparent that no one was having a good day. Will Curtis told me angrily that he didn't quite own the Lear 45 (the second of five he had ordered) yet; a hapless accountant had somehow omitted to cash his $10 million cheque and a Bank Holiday was upon us. Will looked like being stranded in Tucson for the three days. 'So *this* is the service you get when you spend 10 million dollars . . .' he muttered darkly.

Leon looked embarrassed and pretended not to hear. 'Martin,' he said, 'while our accountants try to sort this out, why don't I show you around?'

The Lear plant in Tucson is a 'finishing facility'. New jets are flown in naked from the production line in Wichita, Kansas, to be fitted out—Will estimated that about a million of his ten million bucks went on the 45's interior. A room at the Tucson facility is dedicated to swatches of cowhide and mahogany. According to Rossow, in the case of wealthy private clients, the planes are not so much fitted out as 'personalized'. 'We have literally millions of available trim combinations, but some customers do like to provide their own fittings. I guess the wildest ones have included gold taps and zebra-skin upholstery. And certain Brazilian clients have gone so far as to go into the Amazon forest, select a tree and have it felled, sawed and brought to us to make the veneers.' Obviously not millionaire environmentalists, then. But the solid, clubby looks of the Learjet interior are illusory: the wood veneers are microns thick and beneath them are super-lightweight composites. The components of a modern high-performance aircraft are calculated with fantastic precision, right down to the weights of the paints and varnishes.

Tucson also test-flies the Lears after their personalizations. Rossow introduced me to one of the company's test pilots, Gary Sanders. After twenty years flying F100s, F15s and F117 Stealths in the USAF, he now flies the Lears through their 'post-modification cycle' ('making sure the leather bits don't squeak,' said Will). I asked Sanders if the 45 had any of the exhilaration of a fighter. It was a silly question. 'No,' he replied frostily, 'the 45 is really the opposite of a fighter—it's *extremely* stable, whereas a fighter can't be manœuvred if it's too stable.'

I felt he was being rather disingenuous. The Lear came into existence when 'Bill' Lear, the Motorola magnate, saw the potential to turn the cancelled Swiss P-16 fighter into an unprecedentedly fast bizjet. It sold on its speed. Famously, it takes off like a rocket and flies at just under the speed of sound.

But Gary Sanders played a straight corporate bat: 'Basically the Lear is designed to fly eight people in comfort, at 0.8 Mach and above most of the weather, as safely and predictably as possible. The 45 also has a lot of systems integration—for want of a better term, it's been idiot-proofed. It's actually very difficult to make it do anything wrong, which makes it much safer than the jets of a generation ago.' I had met dour pilots before, but no one with this man's ability to make planes sound as though they were built by Otis. No doubt the big flight corporations run courses for their staff along the lines of 'How to Reassure the Nervous Customer by Making Our Product Seem as Dull as Possible'. Don't think Ferrari, think Volvo. If they feel bored, they feel safe!

The bad news came: the banks were closed, *period*. Will's brow became darker still. 'So, the delights of the Tucson Sheraton for three more days,' he said.

'Be grateful it's not the Congress,' I told him.

Seeing that I now had a few days to kill, I decided to visit my sister and brother-in-law in Los Angeles. I asked Will when I needed to be back in Tucson.

'Oh, don't worry,' he replied. 'We'll pop down and pick you up. We have to do a proving flight somewhere, so we might as well do it to LA.' He was going to 'pop' 500 miles to get me—but then, the Learjet does do 550 miles an hour.

Susan and Bill live in Santa Monica, on the shores of the Pacific Ocean. Bill is a film editor, a high-octane Noo Yoiker so speedy he makes the laid-back Californians appear frozen. The following Tuesday he drove me in his Jag-wah to Santa Monica airport and we watched as the Lear 45, with its newly applied UK registration G-OLDL, came in to land. As it taxied towards us, the Californian sun slid over the Union Jack on its tail. Bill gave a whistle. 'This is like something out of a goddam James Bond movie!' Maybe cable TV's *Lives of the Rich and Famous* would be closer. At Santa Monica

Executive Terminal you could almost smell the dollars. A tanned executive (laundered white shirt, silk slacks, Gucci loafers) walked past us from a Cessna Citation (Lear's corporate competition) to a waiting convertible and said into his cellphone, 'Are we still paying four hundred million?'

The Lear's turbines whined down and the pilot, Will's First Officer Tom Burke, gave me a thumbs-up. I had to pinch myself: this $2000-an-hour miracle of modern technology really had been flown to Los Angeles to pick *me* up! And now it would whisk me to London at close to the speed of sound, in the privileged stratosphere, far above turbulence and holiday-maker jumbos.

A police car pulled up and a cop went over to have a word with the pilots.

'Givin' him a speeding ticket,' quipped Bill. His humour turned to outrage when he learned the true purpose of the officer's intervention. '*Would you believe it*? He's tellin' them about noise abatement! I mean, don't they have *civilians* to do that? We pay the cops to keep the scum off the streets and they're wastin' their time drivin' round the friggin' airport warning pilots to keep a lid on it! *Cheesus!*'

I said farewell and climbed aboard. The Lear rocketed away from Santa Monica airport (and this was slower than the usual 140 knots—those noise regulations). We banked over the Pacific shore and began to climb. I sat, surrounded by painstakingly achieved, pressurised and air-conditioned—silence. I had chosen the first forward-facing passenger seat, on the left. I later learned that captains of industry and the Rich and Famous invariably, for complex but ascertainable psychological reasons, make for the *right-hand* seat. Which may explain why they are rich and famous and I have an overdraft.

Incidentally, who *does* hire or buy these Lears? The tight-lipped corporate response goes along the lines of 'Our customers value discretion as much as state-of-the-art personal flying transport . . .' Well, an aviation-obsessed friend of mine had seen a picture of Paul McCartney taken on a plane and claimed to be able to identify the rear bulkhead behind the great man's head as belonging to a Lear 60. But it's safe to say that if this year's Hollywood superstar wanted to cross the Atlantic and wanted, like Greta Garbo, to be 'a lawn', she might well charter a Lear. While the paparazzi mill around at Heathrow, the glitterati can slip into Biggin Hill and be on their way to the Dorchester without anyone but the staff at Biggin's tiny Customs post being the wiser.

The red crust of the Colorado Plateau slid beneath us. Ninety minutes later we had crossed half the USA and were already starting our descent on the Midwest.

The farm town of Wichita, Kansas is surrounded by a million square miles of table-flat farmland, yet is the home to Learjet's main factories and a big chunk of the American aviation industry. 'They say it's because Wichita's close to the geographic centre of the US,' said Will acerbically, 'but I think it's because Wichita is America's most boring city. Plane building developed here so that people could get away as quickly as possible.'

We were to spend the night in Wichita. The next day the Lear would say its last goodbye to its makers and fly across the Atlantic to its new home in London. Over dinner, Will told stories of his days as a charter pilot. These included an escape from a Central African airport with an ailing dictator aboard, only achieved by handing the army officer controlling the airport a suitcase containing the plane's 'contingency fund' and taking off without waiting for a receipt. Will the Company chairman may have gained the ascendency over Will the adventurer; but his hobby is display aerobatics, in a shiny red Pitts S2C.

The next morning I visited the Lear 45 production line. Down in a great shed, the fuselage sections progress, slowly being married with nose sections and tails, engines, wings. The factory roof is hung with the flags of many nations, because the components of a Lear are manufactured all over the world. T-shirted, baseball-hatted workers wander around with the air more of enthusiastic hobbyists than disciplined employees.

While I toured the factory, Will and Tom Burke slept, in preparation for the long flight ahead. When they returned from the hotel, the 45 had been refuelled and vital human fuel—a range of expensive-looking sandwiches—was stowed in the chiller. But tense conversations were being had: a great mass of snow was paralysing the entire eastern seaboard, threatening our transatlantic flight. It was dark when we took off and flew east, the sodium dots of cities and highways interrupted by the black holes of the Great Lakes. I looked down on Lake Ontario and realised that this was where I had learned to fly, less than a year ago.

Our last fuel stop needed to be as far east as possible, since the Lear 45 is not designed for inter-continental flights—it carries just enough fuel to get across the Atlantic with an acceptable safety margin. As we sped east, printouts showing fast-moving blizzards peeled out of the cockpit computer, keeping us in a state of uncertainty. As unadvantageous easterly winds blustered out in the Atlantic, we were threatened with diversions to Greenland or Iceland. We approached Newfoundland with three potential refuelling stops, the pilots peering at the weather updates flickering on their screens. Airports in Nova Scotia closed, opened, closed again. At the last minute the decision was made to abandon Gander and opt for Stephenville, where we touched down in driving snow at 3 a.m. local time. We had around thirty minutes before the engines iced up and probably the same amount of time as our 'weather window'. Another tiny corporate jet emerged magically from the swirling snow and parked beside us. I walked past snowploughs to the shack where coffee and stacks of the ubiquitous doughnut waited to reinforce passing aviators. A glass-fronted cabinet in the corner of the room contained bottles of duty-free rum and whisky. It didn't look as though duty-free played a big rôle in the Stephenville economy: the cabinet was secured with locks and chains wound round it.

By dawn we were almost halfway across the Atlantic. The on-board computers crunched fuel figures. The weather had not been bad enough to force a diversion to Greenland or Iceland, but the headwinds were strong and it looked as though we'd have to refuel in Ireland.

Then, mid-Atlantic, the wind swung round behind us and the read-outs indicated we had enough fuel to reach Biggin Hill.

Lear pilots sit before three capacious TV screens, which represent and integrate the scores of rotary dials on a conventional instrument panel. The possible configurations are almost endless; the overall effect is clear, soothing on the eye and immensely reassuring. Three tiny rotaries, conventional instruments, are tucked high in the panel, for use in the event of a total electrical failure. High-tech the Lear may be, but there are real rods and wires connecting the pilot with the control surfaces. Even the undercarriage can be cranked down, in an emergency, by hand.

I took the co-pilot's seat beside Will Curtis (an invisible, automatic pilot was flying us). The cockpit was eerily still and even more silent than the cabin. The sky straight ahead of us, due east, was steadily growing pink. Then a gash of red rent the cloud. The new sun appeared and began to rise—rather faster than usual. I am sure I'll never forget that still and silent sunrise over the Atlantic, and later, the sky's indigo blue—far darker than at lower altitudes—and the so-visible curvature of the earth.

Will pointed down. 'I used to be down there, you know. I was a yacht delivery captain. There was this one transatlantic crossing that was particularly nasty—I mean, *really* wet. I got to the airport in New York to come back home and as they were weighing my luggage there was sea water literally dribbling out of my suitcase onto the scales! I climbed on to the plane and I thought, "Whoever flies this thing gets across the Atlantic in hours rather than weeks and never gets wet. And he probably sees his family more than I do.' I got back and told my wife I wanted to train to be a pilot. Six months later I had my licence.'

In the last decade he has gone from being an impecunious yacht captain to managing director of Gold Air International, taking delivery of five Learjets at a cost of $50 million.

Charter companies usually fly older aircraft—I have seen some that belong in museums. It's argued that the touch-and-go economics of charter flight make a new fleet of glamorous Learjets unaffordable. But Will, with his investment of $50 million, was hoping—and needed—to prove them wrong. Most of Gold Air's work comes from business people who can hire a Lear and do four European cities in a day, which would probably take two days by commercial flights. 'The 45 is a time machine,' Will argued, 'very fast, and its fuel cost per passenger approaches that of some cars. I believe it's going to change the face of small-scale commercial aviation. Well, that's the risk I'm taking.'

His instincts were to prove extraordinarily sound. In the weeks after the 11 September attacks on New York and Washington, the demand for private jets soared. It has stayed high.

CHAPTER XXV
Getting High

THERE IS A VISUAL gag in the film *Airplane* that I have never forgotten. The in-flight movie, contentedly watched by post-prandial passengers, is an air crash, filmed in slow motion, the silver machine blossoming into orange flame. The cinema audience's laughter seemed to have a tinny, faintly hysterical note—a taboo was being flamboyantly transgressed. Air crashes are not supposed to be funny, the joke was stirring some of the audience's most assiduously buried fears.

Consider the morbid press ecstasies whenever one of those vulnerable aluminium tubes plunges into ocean, mountain or municipal housing unit. We are happy to drive along a wet motorway at 90 mph with spouse and newborn sleeping beside us—that's acceptable risk; but when an aeroplane crashes, we are irrationally disturbed. Why? What fool believes that aeroplanes are safe? When the 747 'Jumbo Jet' was introduced, pilots disliked its long take-off runs, the immense time it took to lumber to cruising height. The captain of the Air New Zealand 747 told me over the Pacific, 'The fuselage fuel tank on this thing is the size of a swimming pool.' The 747 carries more weight in fuel than the empty weight of the first airliner I ever flew in, a 707. Jumbos have proved to have a good safety record but, like all aircraft, they're flying bombs. The world's worst aviation accident: in 1977 two jumbos collided on the ground at Tenerife. 583 deaths.

Rationally we know all this, but we kid ourselves about the risks, because we want the convenience. We fly in denial. Hence our profound unease when we hear of air accidents.

For most of us, aeroplanes belong to the realm of magic. We all made paper planes at school, but the spectacle of a 365-ton jumbo ponderously mounting the thin air over our heads fills us with a superstitious sense of nature violated. Magic claims to control the gods (unlike religion, which seeks to appease them). But airline passengers know they've propitiated no one, signed no Faustian pact—they are mortally exposed. Just two trembling wings and a clutch of fallible engines to keep them airborne. And what about human error? All this rocket science depends on the two gold-braided fly-boys (they usually are males) sitting up front; events (remember the Russian pilot who let his knee-dandled son plough an airliner into the ground, the British Airways pilots who ended a drinking binge only hours before a flight) have taught us that they are not angels.

Aeroplanes could have observation platforms, like 1950s American locomotives, but they don't. They are introspective, dingy. There are cabin dividers, partly to hide the hedonisms of First Class from the unwashed masses in Economy, but partly to mask the cabin's visible flexing. The waxen grins of the cabin staff, the in-flight videos and soporific Muzak, the bland unreality of the safety demonstrations (*Inflatable rafts*? Who are they kidding? If this thing crashes, we're toast!)—all conspire to distract us from the terrible and awesome reality of flight.

In the mid-1960s, my father took a job with the United Nations and we flew *en famille* to Turkey, via Rome, in a Boeing 707. Flight was still romantic then and Pan American had yet to become a victim of deregulated airways and go bust. Our Boeing was an aluminium incarnation of modernity. The hostesses (wearing crisp, virtually seamless minidresses like Hardy Amies's creations for Stanley Kubrick's *2001: A Space Odyssey*) gave us children crayons and colouring books. The outline drawings showed airliners and airports and trilbied drip-dry-suited emissaries of capitalism grinning as they passed through sleek and streamlined terminals that were Utopian symbols of modernity.

What happened to it all? When did the giddy romance of flight implode into mass tourism, polyester seat covers and thrombosis-inducing foot wells, stuttering baggage carousels and hectares of industrial carpeting?

It was the Boeing 707 which inaugurated a billion package holidays, the final banalization of Icarus's dream. William Boeing was the most successful of the men who struggled to turn the potential of the aeroplane into commercial transportation. Today, Boeing is the largest manufacturer of airliners in the world, the jewel in the crown of an industry so vital to the US economy (its second-largest export earner) that in the aftermath of '9–11' a conservative President with a declared credo of cutting public expenditure decreed a $26 billion 'aid package' and exhorted Americans to 'return to the skies'.

Convenience, cheapness, speed. These things we citizens of industrial societies worship. Has the airliner done much to improve the human condition? Of course not. George Cayley's invention would one day strike a blow to his own town, when charter flights encouraged Scarborough holidaymakers to desert this brisk English seaside resort for the balmier shores of Spain.

Our Pan Am Boeing 707 was an aluminium incarnation of modernity . . .

Every technological breakthrough is the death of something that went before. One of my favourite films, Arthur Miller's and John Huston's elegiac *The Misfits*, has a scene in which an aeroplane is used to round up wild mustangs in the desert, which will be sold to the slaughterers. For the character played by Marilyn Monroe this is a perversion, an ultimate wickedness. We are still barbaric creatures, who use our marvellous imaginations to excavate every idea for its most sinister potential.

The twentieth century was mankind's century of aviation; the Wrights' historic flight at Kitty Hawk and the assault on the Twin Towers were separated by ninety-seven years, ninety-nine days and

500 statute miles of the United States' eastern seaboard. The Wright Flyer was a cumbersome machine, but at Le Mans in 1908 it showed that the world had changed for ever—possibly for the worse. In Baden-Powell's words, 'Wilbur Wright is in possession of a power which controls the fate of nations.'

It is rare for aviation's twin uses, for transport and for war, to become one. But on 11 September 2001 airliners became flying bombs. Many pilots, if they're honest, had been grimly anticipating such an outrage. I remember the prediction of a fellow student at Linvic. It was September 2000 and a few of us were lying on the lawn among the tied-down Cessnas, enjoying the autumn sunshine, discussing the dangers inherent in a pilot's life. I'd no ambition to fly for a living, but the men around me were likely to notch up 30–40,000 hours each in the careers ahead of them. Asked about the dangers of an accident, they would shrug fatalistically. And hijack? 'Well, if they want to, they will, won't they?' said someone. 'Let's face it, a cockpit is not exactly a strongroom. Anyone who's really serious about getting in, can. When you think about it, it's amazing there aren't more hijackings. A plane's a flying fuel tank. What's to stop some nutter hijacking a jumbo jet and flying it into the Empire State Building?'

As I wrote the last pages of this book, a few days after 11 September 2002, it seemed to me unlikely that any other flying vagabond would be given the welcome and access I had. But pilots love most of all to fly, and next, they love to be with others who love flying; '9–11' will come to be seen as an outlandish deviation, but flying will be something we still do and, when we're not doing it, gather in knots of the faithful to murmur about like carefree schoolboys.

After a century of aviation, factories and workshops around the world have turned out around two million aeroplanes. Hardly an impressive number in an age of mass production (it pales beside the figures for car production: two billion) and well over half of those two million were warplanes. Aeroplanes have remained complex, expensive and beyond the means of most people. Automation and mass production could change all that. But for the time being, it is a specialized skill, requiring an initiation.

Initiation: it brings us back to the mystery of flight. It is sometimes said that the desire to fly is natural to humans of all ages, because we do it in our dreams. An ancient memory, some say, of our simian ancestry, swinging through the jungles. Then there are the shrinks who tell us these dreams are about 'individuation', the growing into a sense of one's self—the chick leaving the nest.

Everyone who flies small planes, who hang-glides or goes ballooning, does so in part because it is a spiritual experience, perhaps even a transcendent one. All those old myths, Mercury and Pegasus, King Ram and Saint Joseph, angels and archangels, the metaphysical made not flesh, but motion. However banal or wicked the uses to which aircraft are put, there will still be those who, having watched a bird or a sycamore leaf, dream of flying themselves. When they learn to do so, they become communicants.

In the 1970s the microlight introduced a form of flying as visceral and cheap as owning a motorbike. Most recently and even more simply, motorized paragliders—gliding parachutes with a tiny motor that turns them into powered aircraft—have allowed people to take off and fly from any field or hillside. These are not luxurious machines and they have to be flown in mild weather and low winds. But a simple flying machine for the Common Man is finally with us.

I am walking across the great mount that looms 1500 feet over Abergavenny, in south-east Wales. I have finished writing *Absolute Altitude*, but something remains. I want to try for myself one of these new types of flying machine.

The paraglider takes us back to the parachute, the first device ever to 'fly' with a human passenger, demonstrated by those magicians and fakirs of the Far East centuries before the birth of Christ. Yet a modern paraglider is also the highest of technologies, designed by computer programme and woven from strong yet unbelievably light man-made fibres.

I went through small ads on the Internet and found someone selling a second-hand kit for under £2000. Chris White, a Welshman, turned out to be the last of the flying fanatics I would meet in the course of this story. It takes around a week to learn to paraglide, but Chris has a 'tandem' version—one that lets him carry a passenger. As an evangelist, he was eager to take me up.

It happened that the next day was forecast to be dry and sunny; Chris was planning to go flying. So it was that a little after 9 a.m. the following morning, we were striding through the scrub on Blorenge, a bleak Welsh tor.

'Our flying club actually owns this mountain,' Chris told me.

'Wow. I've never met anyone who owns a mountain before.'

'We already used to fly up here, you see. Then the Coal Board put the mountain up for sale and we were worried that the new owner might not let us use it for flying. So we had a whip-round and bought it. Cost us just over £50,000.'

'Not a bad price, for a mountain.'

We reached the point where the flattish crest of Blorenge tips into a steep slope. To the north and west were Sugar Loaf and Skirid-Fawr mountains. Below us, Abergavenny lay like an illustration from a children's book, a little town nestled in green hills, with neat rows of houses, a church spire, a river, filaments of smoke rising from chimneys.

Chris spread out the fabric rectangle on the ground and enlisted my aid in ensuring that none of the lines were tangled. He demonstrated the structure of the paraglider. Unlike a parachute, which is essentially designed to produce resistance, a paraglider is a wing. It has two layers, with lines of stitching running fore-and-aft to produce 'cells'. When the 'chute is tugged into the air wind fills the cells and gives the structure rigidity. It is now a wing, capable of generating lift.

We clambered into our harnesses, then I stood in front of Chris and he clipped us together with, reassuringly, mountaineering karabiners.

'Now basically,' Chris told me, 'we both have to run. I'll say, "three, two, one"—then just go like the clappers. Try to keep your legs fairly close together, 'cause I'll have mine out on either side of you.'

'Right. So, just run down the hill?'

'Straight down the hill. Are you nervous?'

'No; should I be?'

Chris uttered his countdown and we scuttled down the slope. There was an immediate resistance from the wing behind us. The hillside was uneven and I stumbled, found my feet again and kept running. I couldn't see the great yellow 'chute that was presumably rising above us, but I knew that Chris would have his eye on it. Suddenly the straps bit into my shoulders and we were off. My weight against the earth fell away. We swung forward, the hill we had so recently been scampering down dropped out of sight, and we were in the air. Flying like a bird—I mean that. No other experience in any of the planes I'd piloted had given me such a direct, immediate experience of flight. There was nothing between my body and the air; I could not even see any of the apparatus that was supporting my weight and bearing me forward. A rush of euphoria overwhelmed me. I felt like an angel, just as I had, half a dozen years earlier, above the bosomy Cotswolds. And at once I was struck by the silence. There was none of the wind rush you hear even in a conventional glider. We drifted and the sound of church bells—it was Sunday morning—wafted up to us.

Chris gave me the controls—two stirrup-like handles that hang on either side of you—and I made gentle zigzags in the air. Slowly we descended, over the Monmouth to Brecon Canal that was cut, with Victorian chutzpah, into the hillside below, over houses and trees, and across the winding River Usk, a half-mile journey to land in broad flood meadows.

I was won over.

Later that day Chris brought out his paramotor. The wing and

harness were the same, but Chris strapped on his back a circular metal frame, with a small 200 cc motor and a slender propeller. It's a new sport, which few have yet discovered. You don't even need a licence to do it—though paramotoring instructors take a fussy line. 'If some nutter uses one of these to try and have tea with the Queen, or something,' said Chris, 'the aviation authorities'll be down on us like a ton of bricks.'

Paul Williams, Chris's friend, sells these machines in South Wales.

He had just taken delivery of the latest model, adorned with new sound baffles and a glossy wooden propeller. With evident glee he strapped it on, took off before us and with a purposeful hum disappeared in the east. While the winds were right, he wanted to fly the few miles to his home and telephone his little girl on his mobile to tell her to come into the garden and see Daddy in the sky.

With the thrust of a motor behind us, Chris and I were able to take off on the flat. And, unlike a paraglider, which must find thermals and updraughts to stay in the air, we began at once to climb. We crossed a fenced area marking the site where a Lancaster and its Canadian crew crashed into the hillside during World War II. Then we were circling over Blorenge mountain, from where we'd glided that morning.

It is a rugged landscape, around Abergavenny. The hills, riddled with mining tunnels, have few trees. Indeed, much of the landscape is coal slag on which, since mining ended, a rough moorland scrub has begun to get a purchase. But the hills have a sinuous beauty and around them rise bolder tors, Llanwaelie and Sugar Loaf, and in the distance the profiles of the Black Hills and the Brecon Beacons.

At 3000 feet we cut the motor and drifted in silence. Here, I thought, is the dream of ages realized. The vision of those ancient bird-men is with us at last. Affordable, simple flying for the masses. And who's to stop us?

I looked down. My feet were swinging in space. We began to cross farms and I looked at cottages and tractors, an abandoned cultivator covered with weeds. A horse cantered alone in a green rectangle. But I was free, and around me were infinite expanses of blue.